Gender Shrapnel in the Academic Workplace

Ellen Mayock

Gender Shrapnel in the Academic Workplace

palgrave
macmillan

Ellen Mayock
Washington and Lee University
Lexington, Virginia, USA

ISBN 978-1-137-51462-2   ISBN 978-1-137-50830-0   (eBook)
DOI 10.1057/978-1-137-50830-0

Library of Congress Control Number: 2016941503

Printed on acid-free paper

This Palgrave Macmillan imprint is published by Springer Nature
The registered company is Nature America Inc. New York

For Patrick,
who helped to clear the shrapnel,
and for Susanne and Charlie,
who laughed and played away the bad gender days

WHAT HE TOLD ME WHEN I COMPLAINED
ABOUT THE BOYS' CLUB

There is no Boys' Club.
Pay no attention to the men who are in charge.
They are not "bound by gender."
They care about who is most qualified, not about men and women.
See, that's how we know that there is no Boys' Club, 'cause the men in
    charge
Are the most qualified.
Like, Obviously! They aren't types who choose people by sex
Or skin color.
Like, Obviously! Or they wouldn't have the big jobs.
It's just such a shame the women can't get off the "gender thing,"
Like, Duh. There's obviously no discrimination.
For one thing, and for another thing,
There's the issue of fit. Like, we want to include all qualified people
But they have to be the right ones for the job,
Like, Obviously! There's a lot more to these jobs than just
Paper qualifications. There's fit, too.
And just that ability to *deal with people*. Some of these women
Are so angry they can't *deal with people*, they can't be a
Neutral Presence. Which is like, Obviously, why they weren't chosen.
You Know, they're just so high maintenance, some of them.
I mean, it's a shame, really, because if they wouldn't go on and on so much
People would listen to them.
Especially if they didn't sound so angry all the time.
Like, Obviously—no one wants to hear all that anger all the time.

So, you know what I mean, they are just so Bogged Down.
And they aren't doing themselves a service, either.
If they could just Shake It Off and get back to work, like, there
Wouldn't be a problem.
'Cause, like, Obviously, there isn't any Boys' Club.
As If!
As if, when we are all standing around in the gym showers together
We would actually bother to talk about this stuff.
Give me a break.
Like we would really waste time plotting to do in our female colleagues.
There is no Boys' Club.
We don't even notice them.

Robin LeBlanc

ACKNOWLEDGMENTS

This text that weaves together research and narratives owes many debts to the kind people who have supported the scholarship and the stories. I wish to extend sincere thanks to the Palgrave Macmillan editors for their support of the project and to the anonymous reviewers who made key suggestions for the work. Edurne Portela enriched the text with her keen reading of it and consistent support, while Robin LeBlanc has generously allowed me to use her poem, "What He Told Me When I Complained About the Boys' Club," at the beginning of *Gender Shrapnel*. In addition, I thank Sally Burns, whose outstanding suggestions for the gender equity plan (Chapter 14) are much appreciated. Editorial Fundamentos gave generous permission to reprint parts of my book chapter, "Gender Shrapnel and Institutional Language in the Academic Workplace" (*Estudios de Mujeres. Volumen VII. Diferencia, (des)igualdad y justicia*. Eds. Antón-Pachecho Bravo, Ana, Isabel Durán Giménez-Rico, Carmen Méndez García, Joanne Neff Van Aertselaer, and Ana Laura Rodríguez Redondo. Madrid: Fundamentos, 2010. 149–15) for Chapter 5 of *Gender Shrapnel*.

Washington and Lee University has supported this work through the Lenfest Summer Research Fund and a sabbatical leave, for which I am very grateful. I appreciate Suzanne Keen's support of the *Gender Shrapnel* enterprise. Shirley Richardson has aided my work in too many ways to detail here, but I extend profound thanks to her. Thanks go as well to Karen Lyle for her help in the late-going. I also thank Elizabeth Polanco (W&L, '09) and Jean Turlington (W&L, '16) for their research assistance. Several Washington and Lee colleagues and dear friends read and commented upon early drafts of the work: Thank you to Laura Brodie,

Chris Gavaler, Mohamed Kamara, Julie Knudson, Robin LeBlanc, David Millon, Deborah Miranda, Domnica Radulescu, and Lesley Wheeler—for reading, understanding, and supporting. In addition, Melina Bell, Beth Belmont, Theresa Braunschneider, and Katherine Crowley know what it is to be in the "gender trenches," and I thank them all for their keen eye and collaborations. Paul Hanstedt and Amy Balfour, thanks to you for your careful comments on parts of the manuscript. To these stellar colleagues, and to Jeff Barnett, Kathleen Bulger-Barnett, Jan Hathorn, Jeff Knudson, Julie Knudson, and Matt Tuchler, *amig@s de pecho*, thank you.

Palmar Álvarez-Blanco, Dinora Cardoso, Ana Corbalán, Mary Ann Dellinger, Teresa Herrera, Beatriz Trigo, and Karla Zepeda have all supported this project through thick and thin and have been generous enough to collaborate with me on other projects at the same time. Judith Levine kindly read through several parts of the manuscript and "got" the funny bits. Jane Gilbert Hancock was there the whole way through as a friend indeed. Nancy Johnston's counsel for life and for writing has been a sustained influence for many years now, and for that I am most thankful.

Jeanine Silveira Stewart's smart, disciplined, and brave administrative style deserve great respect, and *Gender Shrapnel* owes much to her keen analyses of inequities of gender, race, and ability in the workplace. I extend the warmest of thanks to Stacey Vargas, whose daily observations, poems, and collaborations have sustained me, this work, and our shared work on gender for years now. To Ellen Satrom goes deep gratitude for her keenly perceptive understanding of gender shrapnel and her generous readings of *Gender Shrapnel* materials. Robin Alperstein stepped in at one of the most acutely difficult of moments and cleared the path in a no-nonsense and utterly big-hearted way. Thank you.

Gender Shrapnel in the Academic Workplace, despite its evocation of battles, war, and destruction, is borne very much of the thoughtfulness, humor, and love of many people around me (many of whom are mentioned above). Patrick Bradley understands gender shrapnel at its core and has spent countless hours listening to and analyzing instances of gender imbalance and gender inequity at work. I thank Pat for decades of love and companionship. Charlie Mayock-Bradley and Susanne Mayock-Bradley are the lights of my life. I am profoundly grateful to Susanne Trainer Mayock and Molly Mayock for being such strong women and formidable role models for me and many others. They found their own way in the workforce and made it happen. Mike Mayock, Sr., whether he knows it or not, was a very positive influence on my understanding of equity. I owe my wonderful parents an enormous debt of gratitude. Besides getting to spend formative years with Molly Mayock, I was so very fortunate to grow up with Mike Mayock, Mark Mayock, Dan Mayock, Peter Mayock, and Matt Mayock, each of whom in his own way embodies the thoughtfulness, humor, and love that we need more of in our world. I want to include in this group as well my sisters-in-law, Alix Mayock, Jen Mayock, and Kristen Kirk Mayock, and the Bradleys all of whom are dear and unfailingly generous family.

CONTENTS

PART I

Gender Shrapnel

CHAPTER 1

Gendered Stories, Hybrid Methods

As an employee in her 15th year at her institution, a professor goes to her annual performance evaluation meeting with a supervisor. He looks over the paperwork in front of him and remarks, "You have been really busy—new publications, plenty of students, long hours of service." The employee is thinking, "Yep, you got that right. It has been a busy and productive year," but then she is completely taken off guard when the very next thing out of the supervisor's mouth is, "How does your husband deal with this?" "Ouch," she thinks extremely loudly inside her head, "did he really just say that? What is my husband doing at my performance evaluation meeting?" She wonders what her face must look like at that moment, because it feels as if the skin is peeling off in chunks. One part of her brain tells her to maintain composure and to carry on with the meeting, while another, distant part of the brain is screaming inside her head, "What the hell? Isn't it *good* that I've taught new classes, published new works, done the necessary service?" As she hears herself say, "My husband is busy, too," the other part of her brain is pissed off and screaming, "Don't continue this unfair line of conversation. Get to the performance review. This person is too busy thinking about your role at home and not your role at work." The performance review continues for another 40 minutes, but it doesn't go well. The employee keeps wondering why her home arrangement came up, and the boss keeps assuming that his employee doesn't spend much time with her kids. He feels sorry for the husband, who seems lamely to have to put up with this gender role reversal.

© The Editor(s) (if applicable) and The Author(s) 2016
E. Mayock, *Gender Shrapnel in the Academic Workplace*,
DOI 10.1057/978-1-137-50830-0_1

The meeting ends. The evaluation was strong enough, but the professor is left wondering how she can ever be treated as just another employee, and not the workplace wife and mommy. She is sputteringly aghast, still only in her head, until she reaches a co-worker's office and vents to him. "Jeez," he sympathizes sincerely, "that sucks." "But what can you do?" What can you do, indeed?

When you're evaluated on your performance at work *and* on your perceived performance in the home, you've been hit by a form of gender shrapnel. The first time you're hit by it, you have no idea what it is, where it came from, or why. You just know that something went wrong, that something's not fair, and that you probably can't do much about it. When it happens again—maybe you're asked at a meeting why there are no cookies, as if you and Betty Crocker had better get busy taking care of the workplace troops—you start to figure out all too clearly that the unsettled events are indeed largely about gender. If you ever try to confront the events, you feel half-crazy and afraid, mainly because we just don't go around the workplace pointing out all the shrapnel. We keep it quiet and get the work done. It's only after an accumulation of gender shrapnel that you reach that "last straw" moment of confrontation. You name the behavior and ask for a change, and that's when you've really done it, you've called the organization out on its inequities. People start to tell you to calm down, to pick your battles more carefully, and to be grateful for what you've got—in essence, to just *be quiet*. As you obey and shut yourself up, you start to notice more of what is happening to other women around you. The shrapnel itself and the silence surrounding it start to seem more and more absurd. You start coming up with nine-block cartoons and lyrics for a sexual harassment musical. You wonder who's crazier now, the employee who's writing cartoons and lyrics, or the employers who don't understand why you just can't say some things. The more you look around you and the more you read, the more you realize that gender shrapnel is all around us.

If Clarence Thomas, Bill Clinton, John Edwards, the Catholic Church, and the alarming sexual assault statistics on our college campuses aren't enough to convince the US public of the enduring issues of sexual abuse and harassment in the workplace, then perhaps the spate of 2011 news stories is. Penn State's Jerry Sandusky and Republican presidential hopeful Herman Cain revealed to the US public the prevalence of sexual abuse and harassment in the contemporary workplace, the cultural, political, and social depth of the issues, and the importance of gender as a tool of analysis to understand the workplace problems and offer viable solutions for improvement. In 2014–2015, national news focused on sexual violence on campuses and the reach of Title IX in adjudication of these cases. The topic of sexual discrimination and harassment comes alive or goes dormant in cycles, depending on the ebb and flow of political news. In the world of the workplace (education, and also business, law, medicine, politics, etc.), no matter the sexiness or dormancy of the topic in the national news, understanding and prevention of sexual harassment remains vastly important—for the well-being of students and employees, for the legal implications of Title VII and Title IX, and for the coherence of mission and practice. *Gender Shrapnel in the Academic Workplace* aims to keep the understanding and prevention of sexual discrimination, harassment, and retaliation on the front burner of educational institutions and of the individuals who are a part of them. In addition, *Gender Shrapnel* sees sexual violence as part of the discrimination, harassment, and retaliation continuum and therefore contributes to the conversation about how to reduce all of these phenomena in the education workplace.

The twenty-first-century workplace, with its dizzying need to keep up with technological innovations, media messages, and proven output, looks very different from the workplace of old except, unfortunately, for the prevalence of sexual discrimination. The Clarence Thomas case of the early 1990s, with its utterly bizarre resurgence through Ginny Thomas' 2011 early-morning phone call to Anita Hill, reveals to us that male power runs deep, that female employees who have experienced sexual harassment are often silenced, that many of us are afraid to question privilege (gender privilege, White privilege, etc.) and its functions, and that we are particularly afraid to correct the ways in which men treat other men in public, no matter their actions in private.

Gender Shrapnel in the Academic Workplace argues that experts in law, organizational management, and education have not gone far enough in their examinations of gender operations in the workplace and that a broad, interdisciplinary approach that provides a bigger-picture view is warranted in this changing twenty-first-century workplace. *Gender Shrapnel* posits that women's more ample presence in the workforce foments a certain Betty Friedan-esque "problem with no name," or a "professional mystique," which is still unresolved in both the home and office workplaces. We still do not value "women's work" in the home and are therefore unsure about how to value the work that women do in the away-from-home workplace. The women—wives, lovers, mistresses, mothers, ball-and-chains—who are mislabeled at home come to the workplace and are labeled and mislabeled there as well. In *Gender Shrapnel*, I use this metaphor of shrapnel to suggest that oftentimes no one person or organization is purposefully discriminating against women based on sex, but that the gender norms of our homes and of our public interactions that consistently follow a patriarchal flow are replicated and entrenched in the workplace. These interactions become the fabric of a pattern of sexual discrimination that is usually not consonant with the organization's professed values and that is often in direct opposition to Title VII and Title IX law. And so, many women are surprised to find themselves hit with shrapnel, crying out, "Ow, what the hell was that?"

Gender shrapnel is a series of small explosions in the workplace that affect women and men and reveal an uneven gender dynamic at all levels of the organization. Gender shrapnel is damaging, even if the principal actors never intend or understand that the actions they take place at least one woman at a disadvantage and send the message to all male and female laborers that this type of disadvantage is the way of the workplace. How do you describe a phenomenon that you have to experience to understand? This book is an attempt to give texture to the concept of gender shrapnel by defining concomitant terms, reviewing and analyzing current literature on women in the workforce, and telling real stories from a variety of sources so that readers can grasp more clearly how gender shrapnel plays out, step by step.

My own story, in brief, is that my administrative mettle was proven at one point and then severely tested afterward. I served in an administrative post, and my aim was to work with and welcome all new colleagues—with respect, knowledge, and a spirit of collaboration. My approach was complicated by two factors: questions about retention of women faculty and administrators and the launch of an initiative to commemorate the 20th anniversary of co-education on the undergraduate side and the 30th anniversary of the first graduating class of women on the law side of our campus. A series of gender incidents piled up, whether intentionally or not, and this amounted to gender shrapnel and translated into negative consequences for individuals and groups involved, as well as for the organization as a whole.

The two factors—being the only woman in academic administration and being the "voice" of women at my institution by chairing the year-long series of events about co-education—shaped the rest of that year and allowed me to understand fully the concept of gender shrapnel and to begin to name and describe the phenomena involved. That academic year was by far the most visibly challenging of my life. I continued my "regular" job of training new faculty, allocating space, preparing the capital budget, overseeing faculty development and speakers funds, completing performance reviews for non-faculty staff, participating in strategic planning efforts, and advising students. The additional jobs given to me included the co-education programming and serving as the institution's head designated officer, who oversees processes of formal and informal complaints of violations of university policy. During my time in that post, every complaint I handled had to do with gender discrimination, thus adding significantly to my visibility as the "point man" on gender issues. An extra bit of irony was that I was completing a two-year round of teaching our introductory course for the Women's and Gender Studies Program. In a nutshell, my work was defined by gender, and the reaction to me and my work was characterized by gender shrapnel.

As the only woman in academic administration, I became the token female on academic issues, and thus found myself more in the spotlight among all university constituencies—students, staff, faculty, communications officers, admissions and development officers, administration, and, especially, alumni. In addition, my work as an academic in gender, coupled with my assigned administrative work having to do with gender, brought me into the public view in ways that I neither sought nor relished. It started to feel like it was feeding time at the gender zoo. The visibility was not necessarily a result of appreciation for jobs well done, but rather for a discomfort with a (then) not-so-radical feminist doing her job—a job increasingly defined by gender chores—in a way that was authentic to her. I think the discomfort stemmed from a sense that I was somewhere I didn't belong—that a younger woman didn't belong in administration, that a new mother should be at home tending to the new child, and that the question of gender in and of itself was being addressed too directly, which felt somehow "uncivil" to more traditional sensibilities.

Without the eagle eye of my partner and his homegrown feminist legal expertise, I might have surrendered. He propped me up again and again throughout the "shrapnel years." Just recently, my partner and I watched Meryl Streep in *Julie* & *Julia*. Two features of the movie struck me as highly relevant to gender shrapnel. The first was Julia's and her sister's physical stature and the ways in which it did and did not define them. Julia's sister says somewhat merrily at Julia's wedding, "You're different, and others see you as different, and then you are that—different."

This ended up being the way I felt in my workplace—kind of merrily different, but necessarily so. (And I've learned to be *in*different at times, which has protected me when I haven't had the strength to speak out or to protest.) The second scene from the movie that stayed with me was the one in which Julia's attempts to get her first cookbook published have been foiled again. She comes home to her husband, Paul, played so well by Stanley Tucci, explains the situation, and cries in frustration on the couch. Paul comforts her, assuring her that her cookbook will get published, maybe by someone else, but it will get published. He hugs Julia and kisses her and generally makes her feel better. When her sobbing subsides, Paul adds, "And fuck them. Fuck them!" This combination of gentleness and well-placed outrage, along with some understanding of feminist legal scholarship, is part of how we can work through the worst of the gender shrapnel years.

The major American Association of University Women (AAUW) study of the 1990s regarding gender in schools, *Schoolgirls. Young Women, Self-Esteem, and the Confidence Gap*, authored by Peggy Orenstein, documented case after case of neglect and/or harassment of girls in primary and secondary schools. The AAUW followed up 18 years later with an additional study titled *Crossing the Line. Sexual Harassment at School.* The findings demonstrate that sexual harassment is more, not less, prevalent, even after two decades of academic studies, articles, books, and increased education for prevention.[1] Could it be that our leaders in higher education, politics, and business are sending a stronger message—a message that gendered behaviors are fine, that boys will be boys, that concealment can work for a long time to the detriment of many—than any number of careful, data-filled, thought-provoking, sensitively wrought studies have? I believe so. Media are a powerful force, as Betty Friedan stated 50 years ago in her work to understand women's disenfranchisement in the home and the traditional workplace.

A colleague (professor and novelist Domnica Radulescu) and I co-edited a volume in 2010 that treated feminist issues and activism in the academic workplace. Our experience in the time since the publication of the academic volume is that (1) the volume keeps selling, telling us that the issues addressed are of interest to a broader reading public than just the few professed feminists in the academic world, (2) when we speak to audiences about the collection, we gather more and more stories from the women in the audience, which reinforces for us the degree to which our stories about gender problems really matter, and (3) it is important in these times to retain the aspirational aspects of activism. Why be activist if you don't believe change is possible? The scholarly heft of the volume, the ways in which the volume has elicited more and more stories, and the hope embedded in the concept of activism clearly signal that more needs to be done and can be done. By gathering and telling stories in an intelligent, informed way, we can understand common gender problems in the workplace, get to the root of the problems, and start to suggest viable solutions for employers and employees.[2]

As the world of publication changes and adapts to the many new platforms for writing, it must take into account the ways in which blogs and tweets have re-emphasized the fundamental importance of storytelling, of day-to-day details that, when accumulated, can speak to the evolution of broader cultural phenomena. To this end, *Gender Shrapnel in the Academic Workplace* incorporates several narratives in order to give voice to the often-silenced problems of sexual discrimination, harassment, and retaliation. The inclusion of additional national news stories also avoids the perennial problem of lumping together "certain groups of women" as if we all had exactly the same thoughts and platforms. In addition, it gives more space to questions of gender's intersectionality—the ways in which other "protected categories," such as class, race, religion, sexual orientation, age, and ability, crisscross with gender and reinforce and complicate notions of male and White privilege.

Derald Wing Sue's excellent *Microaggressions in Everyday Life* examines everyday occurrences of discrimination based on race, gender, and sexual orientation. His eighth chapter focuses on "gender microaggressions and sexism." Sue states:

> Similar to racial microaggressions, gender microaggressions are brief and commonplace daily verbal or behavioral indignities, whether intentional or unintentional, that communicate hostile, derogatory, or negative gender slights that potentially have a harmful impact on women. [...] Likewise, gender microaggressions are often delivered through educational texts, mass media, institutional norms, and cultural scripts that are not necessarily overtly sexist, but communicate hidden messages that may be internalized by both perpetrator and victim. (164)

A term originally coined by Chester Pierce (Sue 5), "microaggressions" is a term I now hear frequently among colleagues in higher education because it is such a useful way to sum up this daily, frustrating, energy-sucking phenomenon of dealing with (and/or repressing) repeated occurrences of discrimination. This concept of gender microagressions is intimately linked to gender shrapnel, but I also want to emphasize that the impact is harmful not only for women but also for all employees in the work environment. It foments a limited way for individuals and collectives to exist in the workplace and stifles creativity.

In addition to Pierce's and Sue's conceptualizations of microaggressions based on race, gender, and sexual orientation, Kimberlé Crenshaw in 1989 published her groundbreaking work on the need for increased critical attention to intersectionality, and two years later she published an article linking intersectionality to identity politics and violence against women of Color:

> With identity thus reconceptualized, it may be easier to understand the need for and to summon the courage to challenge groups that are after all, in one sense, "home" to us, in the name of the parts of us that are not made at home. This takes a great deal of energy and arouses intense anxiety. The most one could expect is that we will dare to speak against internal exclusions and marginalizations, that we might call attention to how the identity of the "group" has been centered on the intersectional identities of a few. Recognizing that identity politics takes place at the site where categories intersect thus seems more fruitful than challenging the possibility of talking about categories at all. Through an awareness of intersectionality, we can better acknowledge and ground the differences among us and negotiate the means by which these differences will find expression in constructing group politics. (1299)

Since my story is a part of this work, I would like to make clear that my own intersectional experiences in real life include primarily those of gender and class. I am a White woman from a working-class background, and I have had the good fortune of access to education and then access to a tenure-track job at a liberal arts college. I recognize this privilege with each word that I write. If a White woman of relative privilege is experiencing sexual discrimination, harassment, and retaliation in the workplace, then significant additional attention must be paid to those who are experiencing the intersections of their gender with race, sexual orientation, age, and others of the so-called "protected categories." At many points in the text, I extrapolate from my own position to attempt to understand the additional obstacles for others. Two excellent volumes that offer multiple voices of women of Color are *Presumed Incompetent. The Intersections of Race and Class for Women in Academia* (eds. Gabriella Gutiérrez y Muhs,

Yolanda Flores Niemann, Carmen G. González, and Angela P. Harris; 2012) and *Mothers in Academia* (eds. Mari Castañeda and Kirsten Isgro; 2013). While my lived experience speaks to a position of White privilege, my scholarly work of the past 20-plus years has focused on examining, analyzing, and advocating for change at the intersections of gender, race, class, and national origin.

For *Gender Shrapnel*, the stories I have gathered and deconstructed come from friends and colleagues, both of Color and White, primarily from the education field, but also from business, law, medicine, and politics. While I have few accounts from the military workplace, several major scandals speak very persuasively to the fact of male privilege and sexual harassment in the armed forces.[3] The firing of high-level Marine trainer Kate Germano in the summer of 2015 (Phillips) speaks to the continued need for negotiation and improvement in the military gender arena. The stories I tell here also come from scholarly research and the popular press. In the end, I hope that this combination of narratives will gather steam and context to allow me to provide vivid texture surrounding sexual discrimination, harassment, and retaliation, to describe coherently gender problems in the workplace by offering concrete, recognizable terms, and to knowledgeably suggest remedies to make the workplace more equitable for all.

Title IX has been much more in the national spotlight of late, as colleges and universities have been subject to increased legal and media attention, no longer quite as focused on the question of equity in athletics at institutions of higher learning, but much more centered on sexual assault of female students. Increased knowledge about Title IX among all higher education constituencies is very welcomed, but the more visible hiring and "deployment" of Title IX officers on college campuses bring with them the problem of administrative stagnation on these questions. Most Title IX officers hired are lawyers, and they work closely with the general counsel of their institutions. I anticipate that this relationship will be complicated by the need to evaluate institutional risk of counter-complaints by alleged perpetrators (the tendency to cover up how bad these situations can be) and possibly to the detriment of students who are discriminated against or sexually assaulted (gender shrapnel in the risk evaluation game). This question of the use and abuse of Title IX is woven throughout *Gender Shrapnel*.

Just as some documentaries examine journeys and trajectories of an object or an idea (e.g. National Geographic's tracing the production, transportation, and sale of a Nike sneaker from the plant in China to the port in Los Angeles to the marketplace ["America's Port: The Port of Los Angeles"]), this book examines how one small comment or one minor deed that relays gender inequity takes a series of zigzag paths—the route(s) of gender shrapnel—to arrive at bigger organizational mishap and entrenched labor and cultural problems in the workplace. The examination of these paths is part of the storytelling component of *Gender Shrapnel*, through which readers will hear my voice, understand the commonalities of the issues at play, and capture the constructive thrust of offering solutions to these problems. *Gender Shrapnel* may read for some as a practical guide for individuals who have been harassed based on their sex, for others as a practical guide for administrators and Title IX officers to get at the root of sexual discrimination, harassment, and retaliation, and for yet others as simply a series of compelling stories with a few lessons along the way. Perhaps what I have come to call "bad gender days" can be alleviated or eradicated with more knowledge and more deliberate thought, analysis, and action.

The *Chronicle of Higher Education* runs several advice columns for workers in academe, including the popular "Ms. Mentor" column. The Academy, dripping in privilege and hierarchy, invites the mentor/mentee relationship so that those with lesser status in the hierarchy can navigate the landmines of the academic workplace.[4] The column's existence is testimony to the need to level the organizational playing field. In addition to defining gender problems in the workplace with new terms that are broadly applicable to the academic workplace and offering concrete remedies, *Gender Shrapnel* illustrates the solutions by outlining training principles and employing case studies on gender in the workplace. As Maher and Thompson Tetreault did in their excellent book titled *Privilege and Diversity in the Academy*, I am employing a type of institutional ethnography in order "'to explicate the actual social relations in which people's lives are embedded to make...the ruling relations themselves, including the social organization of knowledge,' that shape everyday university life visible for investigation" (5).

This work examines national rhetoric surrounding gender, organizational management, legal issues, and higher education and tensions and dynamics at educational institutions to uncover underlying phenomena that contribute to discourse on privilege and gender in the workplace. I am focused in part on the inner workings of academic institutions, which allow me to give name and shape to problems based in gender and to suggest possible solutions, and in part on gender issues in the national media. As do most researchers who treat issues of harassment in the workplace (e.g. Chamberlain, Mitchell, Oppedisano), I take series of examples that I have observed in the workplace or that have been recounted to me and, through careful analysis and use of pertinent secondary literature, pull from them the common elements of gender shrapnel. An article from the November 1, 2014, of *The New York Times* titled "Handling of Sexual Harassment Case Poses Larger Questions at Yale" presents yet another classic, "textbook" case of sexual harassment at higher education institutions. My point here is that these cases follow similar trajectories and can therefore teach us a lot about our gendered expectations and norms in the workplace. We have to be willing to learn from the similarities among the cases and from the proliferation of these cases. In her article titled "Academics' shame: our failure to confront sexual harassment," Jeannette Oppedisano cites 27 examples of sexual harassment at academic institutions. All 27 connect in one way or another to the incidents I recount in *Gender Shrapnel*. I combine these elements with the literature on higher education at the national level and on gender issues in the workplace, conversations, interviews, and experiences in order to extrapolate meaning for other institutions.

I am a humanist who works in language, cultures, and literatures. My work on gender studies, and specifically on gender in the workplace, stems largely from my training in the humanities. Nevertheless, this book draws heavily upon and owes a debt of gratitude to scholars who have worked in communication theory, the sociology of organizations, organizational management, social psychology, higher education history, and the law. My work underscores that Western feminism and, in particular, Western academic feminist theories, have not overcome patriarchy by any stretch. In fact, capitalism and organizational management's emphasis on hierarchy continue to encourage all-too-familiar separate spheres prescriptions and to plant the false idea that feminism has done its work and that all the feminists are now free to just go home.[5] In this sense, I have appreciated Meyerson's and Kolb's "dual agenda" ("Moving out of the 'Armchair'" 555) for their research, which combines an emphasis on keeping the gender question front and center with a secondary, and very intertwined, goal of increasing organizational effectiveness. This dual agenda admits or accepts the existence of capitalist financial structures and works within the structure (for better or for worse) to attempt to signal and correct labor inequities, while all the time offering improvement in how work is managed.

The methodological approach of *Gender Shrapnel*—the combination of current, varied stories with close readings of workplace "texts"—allows for a display of the characteristics of the "tempered radical," defined by Meyerson and Scully in the following way:

> The tempered radical represents a special case in which the values and beliefs associated with a professional or organizational identity violate values and beliefs associated with personal, extra-organizational, and political sources of identity. In the tempered radical, both the professional and personal identities are strong and salient; they do not appear alternately for special situations. In most situations, the pull of each identity only makes the opposite identity all the more apparent, threatened, and painful. ("Tempered Radicalism" 587)

Gender Shrapnel contains five parts. The three chapters that comprise Part I provide a methodological framework, offer definitions of *gender shrapnel* and the *professional mystique*, trace a trajectory of consciousness about the issues, and recount stories of gender shrapnel. This part introduces the principal concepts surrounding gender shrapnel, places them into a twenty-first-century context, and offers gender shrapnel narratives to give texture to the concepts. Part II ("Problems") examines underlying cultural trends that contribute to gender divisions in the workplace. Chapter 4 explicates Friedan's *The Feminine Mystique* in order to highlight problems that were brought to the forefront over 50 years ago and to summarize how the seminal text has influenced current conversations about women in the workplace. In Chapter 5, I look at institutional language (rhetoric) and its enactment (practice) through the lens of communication theory. Sexual harassment and discrimination are the problems outlined in Chapter 6, which uses legal scholarship, management studies, and domestic violence literature to examine the cycle of harassment in the academic workplace. Chapter 7 is an investigation of the place of emotions in the workplace and the dangers of silencing and "shutting up," while Chapter 8 underscores issues of gender in hiring, training, promotion, and the proverbial glass ceiling.

Part III offers a series of solutions to the problems outlined in Part II. Chapter 9 responds to the issues of institutional language outlined in Chapter 5 by looking at the question of "political correctness." Chapter 10 offers several innovative ways to craft institutional language so that it is more inclusive, flexible, and sustainable. In Chapter 11, I look for common denominators in academic communities that allow for sites of potential union and collaboration. Chapter 12 picks up the theme of tempered radicalism and places it in the context of the academic workplace by offering suggestions for how upper-level administrators can hold themselves accountable and be held accountable. "Small wins" (Weick) is the subject of Chapter 13, which makes recommendations for dependable but flexible institutional structures. Finally, Chapter 14 offers basic training principles to avoid gender shrapnel and to ensure the creation and maintenance of a more equitable workplace.

In Part IV, readers can map problems and solutions through eight case studies that demonstrate how gender shrapnel occurs in a variety of settings and how it can be prevented. The Appendix serves as an instructor's guide to the case studies. Part V offers final remarks.

Gender Shrapnel in the Academic Workplace addresses the following specific questions:

- What is "gender shrapnel," and how can we use it to conceptualize a more equitable workplace?
- How does the popular press influence our view of gender at work?
- What is the significance of personal stories? How do they reflect, complement, or negate the sustained images we get from the popular press?
- What are the stages of confronting sexual discrimination, harassment, and retaliation?
- How has Betty Friedan's *The Feminine Mystique* affected the ways in which we talk about gender in the workplace? What is the "professional mystique?"
- How does gender intersect with other protected categories, such as race, class, sexual orientation, national origin, and age?
- How do Title VII and Title IX interact with questions of internal investigations and employer liability?
- What are the components of language use in the workplace, and how do they contribute to gender shrapnel? What is the relationship between and among language, silence, and power in the workplace?
- What is the cycle of sexual harassment?
- What are the current data on hiring, training, and promotion of women? What are the effects of gender shrapnel on potential improvement in gender equity in these areas?

- What is "tempered radicalism," and how can it help individuals and groups in the workplace to understand different motivations for change?
- How can "small wins" approaches effect positive change and diminish the occurrence of gender shrapnel?
- What are solid training principles for employers and employees who understand the benefits of gender equity in the workplace?

NOTES

1. See Bibliography for a long list of resources published over the last five decades, and especially since the early 1990s.
2. In their 2000 article titled "Advancing Gender Equity in Organizations: The Challenge and Importance of Maintaining a Gender Narrative," Ely and Meyerson emphasize the importance of keeping conversation about gender consistently on the table in organizations and promote narrative as "a central component of organizational change": "The notion of narrative as a central component of organizational change is based in our understanding of reality as socially constructed, maintained, and modified in large measure through the stories organization members tell about particular persons or events, the sense they make of their own and others' organizational experiences (Ewick and Silbey, 1995; Ford and Ford, 1995). Narratives, therefore, are not just stories told *within* social contexts; they are social practices that are *constitutive of* social contexts. They reproduce, without exposing, the connections of the specific story and persons to the structure of relations and institutions that make the story plausible. As such, they are as likely to bear the imprint of dominant cultural meanings and relations of power as any other social practice." (603–04)

Significant problems in the military are revealed in a 2012 article in *The New York Times* titled "Men Struggle for Rape Awareness": "In one study of 3,337 military veterans applying for disability benefits for post-traumatic stress disorder, 6.5 percent of male combat veterans and 16.5 percent of noncombat veterans reported either in-service or post-service sexual assault. (The rates were far higher for female veterans, 69.0 percent and 86.6 percent respectively.) A Pentagon report released on Thursday found a 64 percent increase in sexual crimes in the Army since 2006, with rape, sexual assault and forcible sodomy the most frequent violent sex crimes committed last year; 95 percent of all victims were women." These data reveal profound problems with sexual assault and abuse in the military, which of course are intimately linked in cause and effect to a culture of sexual harassment.

3. See Justin Simien's 2014 film "Dear White People" for a satirical examination of White privilege in the Academy.
4. See Clare Hemmings' *Why Stories Matter. The Political Grammar of Feminist Theory* for a useful critique of many of the false dominant narratives embedded in Western feminism.

REFERENCES

Castañeda, Mari, and Kirsten Isgro (eds.). 2013. *Mothers in Academia.* New York: Columbia University Press. Print.

Crenshaw, Kimberlé. 1989. Demarginalizing the intersection of race and sex: A black feminist critique of antidiscrimination doctrine, feminist theory, and antiracist politics. *University of Chicago Legal Forum* (1989):138–167. Print.

Dear White People. 2014. Dir. Justin Simien, Perf. Tessa Thompson, Tyler James Williams, Teyonah Parris, Dennis Haysbert, Brandon Bell. Code Red, Film.

Ely, Robin J., and Debra E. Meyerson. 2000. Advancing gender equity in organizations: The challenge and importance of maintaining a gender narrative. *Organization. The Interdisciplinary Journal of Organization, Theory, and Society* 7(4): 589–608. Print.

Gutiérrez y Muhs, Gabriella, Yolanda Flores Niemann, Carmen G. González, and Angela P. Harris (eds.). 2012. *Presumed incompetent. The intersections of race and class for women in academia.* Boulder, CO: Utah State University Press. Print.

Rabin, Roni Caryn. 2012. Men struggle for rape awareness. *The New York Times*, 23 Jan 2012. Accessed 25 Jan 2012. Web.

CHAPTER 2

Back When I Wasn't a Feminist

When I was a graduate student in 1994, I was training myself as a women's studies scholar in order to write a dissertation on Spanish women writers. At that point, I was just learning how to use gender as a tool of scholarly analysis and was not yet in the habit of applying theory to the practice of gender relations in the workplace. I had always found it equally easy to work with women and men and to have them as colleagues and friends. I saw no reason to think that this would not carry over into the workplace when I started my first job after graduation. The two main elements I was ignoring were privilege and hierarchy and how they affect the jobs we do. I would come to learn that, while privilege is invisible and protects those who enjoy it in a host of unspoken ways, hierarchy is highly visible and reinforces the power of privilege and authority. I came to understand that organizations that remained unaware of these two phenomena and their impact on workers would never progress.

Back in 1994, on a road trip, I saw bumper stickers in South Carolina that said, "Save the Males." I was well aware of the Citadel's clumsy attempts to co-educate but, somehow, I actually believed that the stickers meant something like "Save the Males from Themselves." In other words, I thought the message was "get over the gender thing, this is no big deal, we've got this co-education thing covered." When my partner pointed out my completely erroneous take on the matter, I laughed at myself. Now I'm nostalgic about the younger woman who believed that "not everything is about gender." Of course, most social issues treat in some way power and authority in a hierarchy, which means that men and

© The Editor(s) (if applicable) and The Author(s) 2016   19
E. Mayock, *Gender Shrapnel in the Academic Workplace*,
DOI 10.1057/978-1-137-50830-0_2

women without privilege are vulnerable to inequities in the workplace. It is essential to keep in mind, however, that far more men enjoy positions of authority in the workplace than do women. Furthermore, many men in positions of authority gravitate toward other men, whether in positions of authority or not, thus reinforcing the pattern of male (and, often, White) privilege. Of course, gender, then, is a major factor for the examination of the shrapnel of inequity.

Two years later, I heard a good friend and my mother talking about gender relations in the workplace. My mother was saying that she could cut older men a break for their sexist attitudes and behaviors because they had not grown up in a society that demanded them to be otherwise. My friend replied, "Well, they've had about 20 years to get up to speed. I don't think managers or employees would be cutting them a break in other areas of their work." I have come back to this often and have remembered a New York banker's statement: "Sexual discrimination and harassment prevention training is like office furniture: it's the first thing you get for your office and something you always keep up-to-date." I would take that a step further—the key is not just the prevention of sexual discrimination and harassment, but rather the promotion of a work environment that allows all individuals access to the hiring process, fair evaluation and announcement of successes, promotion, and respect. This is no easy task. Rhetoric is usually leap years ahead of practice, especially when we consider the lofty goals of the mission statements of many higher education institutions.

At my university, I have witnessed the difficulties of maintaining administrative equilibrium as different constituencies vie for the articulation of core institutional messages. The Board of Trustees and some alumni are still adjusting to a co-educational model, one that not only accepts women as students and employees but also works assiduously to ensure equal access to opportunity and success. Some faculty, many of whom are also alumni, find themselves in this group. Other faculty are interested in a progressive model that pays attention mostly to faculty perquisites and emphasis on research, but they keep their heads low when oppositional politics arise. Still other faculty members are concerned about the lack of promotion of women to department chair, endowed professor, and dean, but they recognize that the number of times they can be political in the face of retrenchment of the status quo is limited. Many of the Women's and Gender Studies faculty, obviously trained in parsing gender issues, recognize problems of rhetoric, implementation, and general practice.

Nevertheless, these faculty members often are not selected to be on standing or ad hoc committees that have actual power to move toward institutional change. Many of the concerns that faculty members have about employment equity are shared by staff members in mid- and lower-level administrative posts. Women in facilities and administrative staff positions cite the following as manifestations of gender inequity: inequitable distribution of work space, uneven performance evaluation practices, work assignments across multiple departments, unclear job descriptions, and "job creep," the increase in responsibilities that goes unrecognized in job descriptions and performance evaluations.

At some point, I went from the idea that this gender thing is not my problem to a consciousness about how institutions operate around gender and how those operations affect individual employees and the overall quality of work produced. I started to call myself a feminist, loudly and proudly. I realized that I needed an official, activist term to set the tone for living a life outside the gender bubble. In an interview with *Women's Review of Books*, Katha Pollitt states that feminists need to "come out": "Coming out is a very good analogy. Far more than any rational argument, by simply revealing their existence to their friends and their families, gay men and women changed dramatically the way they were perceived in America, and lowered the level of homophobia. Simply living their lives as openly gay. Feminists need to do the same thing. If you're a secret feminist, you're missing a big opportunity to educate people" (15). The year 2015 so far has brought greatly increased national attention to the questions of both gender and race, very much out of necessity, and this trend must continue. We must acknowledge, however, that "educating people" is an uphill journey. Notwithstanding people's and institutions' willingness to be educated, gender shrapnel is everybody's problem because institutions cannot function well within a culture of fear and defensiveness about gender inequities and with the repetition of random, often ineffective, attempts to contain the shrapnel. Gender shrapnel affects most profoundly women with the least amount of power in the organizational hierarchy, but it also has its glass-ceiling influence on women who are ostensibly more powerful in the hierarchy (e.g. associate and full professors and women in administration, associates and partners in law firms, doctors, and politicians).

I have observed at some universities that non-tenured women who express non-traditional or even anti-establishment opinions are often viewed as "cute," "impetuous," "interesting," even sometimes "compelling and on point." Nevertheless, those same women who "grow up" by getting tenure and promotion are expected to have grown up in one of two ways—either they express fundamentally traditionalist views or they grow up by shutting up.[1] Therefore, in certain ways, the glass ceiling is intimately linked to the questions of institutional tradition, mission, and academic freedom. Essentially, the women who are able to accede to and maintain power at my institution understand the roles available to them and adhere to them. The women who behave as they had before tenure—who express opinions openly, perhaps much as they had as graduate students and/or professionals in other fields—become outliers. The way for women to accede to and retain power, then, is to behave, to speak the speech of their male colleagues and, in some cases, to perform a traditional, abnegating femininity that does not challenge old-time gender assumptions. Unfortunately, tenure-track and adjunct women faculty no longer have even the luxury of speaking their mind until the "maturity" of tenure is upon them. In a way that I never was before tenure and in a much more precarious university job market, these women are very reasonably afraid of losing their jobs.

This limited set of choices—be yourself, speak your mind, be hard-working and ambitious in the workplace, or be as you're expected to be, speak only the mind of the institution, be hardworking, and seek no gain—is not only disheartening but also contributes to the broad gender gap in workplace earnings and in work satisfaction.[2] This Manichean set of choices alienates some women from the institution and its status quo, an alienation which, when combined with women's desire to speak and be heard, cements some women's place in an oppositional culture. I believe that those of us who find ourselves in this position are surprised to find ourselves there. We always had the good of the institution at heart (and mind), so how is it possible to be viewed as anything but engaged in a lively debate about the most positive advancements for the institution? Ultimately, there is no need for the dichotomy of mainstream versus oppositional culture, because each offers visions of the institution that are potentially beneficial. Welcoming varying viewpoints only strengthens organizational culture.

Organizations need to undo the binary and value their variety of voices. Mumby and Putnam assert that, "Tolerance of ambiguity would facilitate the formation of organizational structures that recognize divergent and even contradictory positions among organizational members" (475). They believe that this type of tolerance leads to the promotion of heterarchy, rather than hierarchy (475). Cameron offers the idea that, "Rather than being treated unequally because they are different, men and women may become different because they are treated unequally" (12). I believe this to be a fundamental point in the consideration of gender shrapnel *and* of intersectionality. Do essentially similar employees become different (or at least consistently perceived as different) through their unequal treatment in the workplace?

In my case, I always feel a pull to obey—that is, to be the type of professor valued by my institution (and by me), to read and know documents and policies, generally to do what the upper administration asks of me. In addition, it becomes clear that those who obey the mandates and the unspoken cultural norms of the environment are rewarded more readily. This reality is at odds with my institution's desire to promote critical thinking and its endeavors to train the students in advanced critical thinking. "Behaving," toeing the line, holding up the status quo, then, contradict the rhetoric of serious examination and introspection, critical thinking, and academic freedom. It is incumbent upon institutions and organizations to bridge this divide, and the first step is to assess the consonance between institutional rhetoric and practices, beginning with the institution's mission statement.

The mission statement of my institution used to state the following:

[The institution] has two preeminent objectives: to dedicate all its resources to developing in its students the capacity and desire to learn, to understand, and to share the fruits of their intellectual growth, and to pursue its educational mission in a climate of learning that stresses the importance of the individual, personal honor and integrity, harmonious relationships with others, and the responsibility to serve society through the productive use of talent and training. Independent, non-sectarian, and privately endowed, it comprises three divisions, one graduate—the School of Law—and two undergraduate—the College and the School of Commerce, Economics, and Politics. With a rich heritage from the past and a history spanning more than two centuries the University has a profound sense of tradition, but it likewise has a firm commitment to the ideal embodied in its motto, *non incautus futuri*, and therefore remains responsive to changes and innovations that contribute to the realization of its aims.

While this version of the mission statement does address acquisition and application of knowledge and service to a community, it neglects to address the questions of creative inquiry, critical thought, and international initiatives. The current version incorporates these elements very well. Most institutions of higher learning in this day and age are at least making the nod to these concepts. The specific mention of honor in my institution's previous and current mission statements is extremely fraught, given that it is borne of the masculinist traditions of promotion of the privileged, protection of the "weak," and silencing of the marginalized (through a widely touted code of "civility"). Maher and Thompson Tetreault frame this dynamic as the "sense of faculty cultures talking past one another: an older generation ignoring a younger one, White men talking past men of color, the tradition of great books talking past feminist interpretations, the discourse of a common culture deaf to the diversity of the American experience" (74). Intelligent discourse surrounding *what we really wish for ourselves and our employees and/or students* and *what our practices really are* will allow us to bridge the divide between rhetoric and application and between the privileged and the marginalized.

Twenty years after the "Save the Males" bumper stickers, I realize that my training in gender analysis has come first through experience and then through traditional research and inquiry. My coming to consciousness accelerated when I found myself confronting the tension between obedience and authentic voice.

I know why I am engaged in questions of gender in the workplace. Why should those who are not invested in equity or those who do not seek to lose privilege get on board with a move toward collective consciousness about gender dynamics and social justice? Even if institutional groups have no personal stake in redressing gender problems in the Academy, they can recognize the following: (1) The demographics of the labor force have changed significantly. Female students now outnumber male students in colleges and universities, and 59% of working-aged women are employed outside the home (Bureau of Labor Statistics Spotlight on Women at Work). By 2050, women are expected to comprise 48% of the labor force (Toossi). In addition, the increase in the numbers of women of Color in the workforce has made more acutely necessary the recognition of intersections between gender and race (see Table 3 of Toossi report). Simply put, the workforce is no longer a protected, male-only and White-only space, and the workplace has to respond to that reality; (2) The nature of work has changed with its increased emphasis on technology, mass communications, international trade, and open-ended workdays; (3) Economies have changed, and so have societal norms. Most traditional and non-traditional families need two working adults to survive, and many women have more sustained tenures in the labor force than they did even just 20 years ago. Women are no longer "aliens" in the workplace; (4) Friedan's 1983 conceptualization of the need for an increased "attunement to life" (xxvii) in the workplace has been justified and exemplified through the coining of the phrase "emotional intelligence." The contemporary workplace purportedly values this talent more than it ever had, as employees in general need to have or to learn an increased awareness about the needs, desires, and modes of expression of those around them (either physically or virtually). For the first time in the history of labor, a stereotypically "feminine" quality has been accepted as a vital need in the profile of the workforce.[3] As Deborah Cameron has said: "But this is the age of Venus: we are constantly told that the modern way to get things done is through cooperation, negotiation, motivation, and teamwork. These are buzzwords in business as well as in politics. [...] Ours may be the first time and place in history to hold such unequivocally positive beliefs about women's ways of speaking" (38). Cameron makes sure to contextualize her use of "Venus" through popular culture's fascination with the separate linguistic spheres notions (despite the fact that data repeatedly prove it wrong); (5) Rapidly changing economies, administrations, personnel, societal norms, and international relationships require an agility surrounding change. Again, this type of characteristic is associated with the traditionally "feminine"—anticipation of others' needs; understanding of the extended workplace; ability to multitask; ability to adapt to new or changed surroundings.

Now it is time for workers—administrative staff, mid-level employees, facilities management, upper administration—to consider collectively how to hear competing voices, legitimately pay attention to them all, and incorporate them into the overall vision and day-to-day practices of the organization. Gender shrapnel is everyone's problem and is inextricably connected to questions of race, class, ethnicity, religion, age, sexual orientation, national origin, and ability.

NOTES

1. This phenomenon relates to Deborah Cameron's assertions about preadolescents who begin to participate in the "heterosexual market": "Although they are still pre-adolescent, and in most cases not yet interested in sex as such, their interest in the trappings of adult heterosexuality is driven

by what Eckert points out is an overriding social imperative among children: the need to demonstrate maturity by moving away from the 'babyish' behaviour of the past. For pre-adolescents, this entails cultivating more 'adult' forms of masculinity and femininity that obey the heterosexual principle 'opposites attract'. Though both sexes engage in this project, it changes the girls' lives more profoundly. Boys cultivate a more adult masculinity through the same activities that were important to them before—for instance, sporting activities that show off their physical strength and athletic skill. For girls, on the other hand, cultivating a more adult femininity means replacing the activities and accomplishments of childhood with a different set of preoccupations" (70). The parallel in the academic workplace is that the qualities that get men and women to successful positions in the workplace continue to be recognized and admired in men, but, at the time at which women achieve tenure, are undervalued or not at all appreciated in women. Women are overtly or subtly encouraged to mute these qualities.

In many cases, tenure provides the luxury of unfettered speech and of feminist activism, but at a cost. I always have in mind that I am in a luxurious position in which I can continue to work in a job, most parts of which I like, and can speak out as I do. Chapter 3 of Judith A. Levine's *Ain't No Trust. How Bosses, Boyfriends, and Bureaucrats Fail Low-Income Mothers and Why It Matters* provides narratives and data of cases in which women share few or none of these advantages.

2. In her February 15, 2007, *New York Times* op-ed piece, Judith Warner addresses the value of emotional intelligence within the context of the ousted President Larry Summers and the new President Drew Gilpin Faust at Harvard: "The selection of Faust seems to be about much more than the replacement of a man by a woman. It appears rather to be about the promotion of a certain kind of person: a person who can, at least minimally, show respect for other people's feelings. Who can do the little dance of ego-flattery and mirroring it takes to make other people feel acknowledged, recognized and appreciated. This ability is very often considered the specialty of women. But in today's world, it isn't a gender thing. It's a human thing. To insist otherwise is to cut Faust off at the knees just as she's poised to spring into history."

REFERENCES

Friedan, Betty. 1983. *The Feminine Mystique*. New York: Dell/Laurel. Print.
Warner, Judith. 2007. Compassion gets a promotion. *The New York Times*, 15 Feb 2007. Accessed 16 Feb 2007. Web.

CHAPTER 3

Narratives of Gender Shrapnel

Narratives of gender shrapnel allow "for a reflection on how experience fits into a labor system in academia with masculine norms, a model of domesticity, and poor enforcement of federal law."[1] In addition, much as we might like to believe that "old school" sex- and gender-based discrimination no longer occurs, these accounts remind us that it is both recent history and current story. The stories presented here, all of which have occurred over the last decade, serve to provide texture and rhythm to occurrences of gender shrapnel.

WOMEN IN ADMINISTRATION

Not long after she was awarded tenure, Jessica was energized by being back in the classroom and accomplishing steady research, and had no thoughts about working in administration. She was then offered a position to concentrate on faculty needs—space, technology, equipment, training, information, development, and speakers funds—so that others could focus on major projects, such as increased hiring needs, building a fundraising infrastructure, capital projects, and strategic planning. She thrived on work, organization, and challenge, but somehow was still surprised when the administrative post allowed her to explore a different type of work environment. One of her supervisors seemed to lack ego and to flourish individually through the overall success of the office. This supervisor carved out authority-endowed chunks of the job to share with others and

© The Editor(s) (if applicable) and The Author(s) 2016
E. Mayock, *Gender Shrapnel in the Academic Workplace*,
DOI 10.1057/978-1-137-50830-0_3

anticipated when Jessica needed advice and guidance and when she was managing fine on her own.

Before she officially occupied the post, she discovered that she and her partner were expecting a child. Jessica called a supervisor to sort through how this might change the look of the upcoming academic year. The supervisor was characteristically congratulatory, encouraging, and accommodating. Everything was possible, and this news seemed to change nothing. As a result, Jessica felt confident that having a baby while adjusting to the new job was not only possible, but very feasible.

Jessica became the first administrator at her institution to give birth during her time in an administrative post. As her pregnancy became more apparent, she watched many others think of her less as an administrator and more as a "mommy." Oftentimes individuals would enter the office and politely ask her if Dean Johnson was in. "You're talkin' to her," she'd say. She was amused and not at all frustrated at that point. She didn't yet know what gender shrapnel was.

During that year, Jessica learned a lot about academic administrations, politics, and work modes. She watched one of her supervisors toil daily in a creative way to have faculty and staff sense direction and feel engaged. She also watched this person negotiate difficult institutional politics and decisions. She didn't know what to call it when she saw her supervisor being yelled at or simply being ignored at meetings, when she observed her being asked to do work typically requested of administrative assistants, or when she saw administrators seeking counsel on the office operations from people in more junior positions. What she learned is that you don't always come up with apt terms for new phenomena until they happen to you. It wasn't until the following academic year that she came to understand fully that what that supervisor had experienced, and what she was experiencing head on, was gender shrapnel. Maybe you just can't know what it is until you yourself yell, "Ow, it got me!"

The workplace's gendered circumstances in and of themselves might have just caused a few problems. Jessica felt that one of the supervisors had a physical presence that began to affect the sanctity and security of her workspace. She believed this person to be someone who likes to be seen as informal, and she observed that he was very at ease opening closed doors, interrupting his colleagues' meetings, taking phone calls during his own meetings with others, and touching shoulders and patting legs. Jessica is a pretty casual person, too, but she has realized that her casual ways with people in the workplace come only after having formally addressed them, gotten to know them, and understood their levels of comfort with a casual approach. In other words, for her, there is still a decorum that needs to be maintained in the workplace because it protects people's selves, their physical workspace, and their own approach to meetings and office communications. Within a few weeks, a higher-level administrator had closed Jessica's office door behind her and backed her against it, touched her shoulders from behind while she was seated and working at her computer, complimented her for being "nurturing," and threatened to undo the terms of the contract she had agreed upon with other supervisors. On the other hand, he had also had the whole office and their significant people over for a barbeque and seemed sincere about making things work. At that point, Jessica was still optimistic that the kinks in the work environment, for others and for her, could somehow smooth themselves out.

Not long thereafter, there were daily threats to change the terms of Jessica's original contract. Several people seemed intent upon changing the agreement that she would maintain an administrative salary upon return to a regular faculty post. She learned much later that these agreements were usually worked out for people in that kind of administrative post, but that they were not put in writing. Those who returned to the faculty were just to be given larger incremental raises in the one to three years beyond the time of service. After a long battle (that, in the end, Jessica lost), she did keep her administrative salary, only to learn later that the salary was exactly where it should be, or maybe a little behind, in comparison to others at her rank and time of service.

Gender Politics in the Academy

Maria, an administrator charged with coordinating visiting speakers, was collaborating with a student-sponsored organization to bring a high-profile woman speaker to campus, something that would be in tune with the theme of recognizing the short history of women's presence on campus. When Maria expressed a preference for inviting Hillary Rodham Clinton over Laura Bush (making clear that she wanted to invite an individual who was very active in politics), one of the student newspapers published a lead article about Maria's suggestion and delayed the normal Tuesday release of the paper for a special, Friday release for Parents' Weekend. In that and subsequent issues of the paper, students gave clear misinformation about the conversations and used the term "feminazi" in reference to Maria. Later in the year, another publication picked up the term "feminazi" and then criticized Maria's introductory women's studies course for having too liberal an agenda and for omitting Susan B. Anthony from the syllabus. The syllabus was a standard intro syllabus and did, in fact, include Susan B. Anthony as one of the "foremothers" of the nation. The only creative, more unusual elements of the syllabus were invited speakers from different community organizations, such as the local women's shelter, a service-learning component that had students working with women in the community, and a requirement that students attend two events related to gender studies.

To find herself in the maelstrom of "malestroms" was stressful, to say the least. Maria was asked to occupy an administrative post due to others' appreciation for her teaching, research, committee work, organizational abilities, and fair and just practices. She had a tough time in the post for exactly the same reasons. She started to characterize days as good or bad "gender days," and her partner replaced the "How was your day, honey?" with "What did they do to you today, sweetie?"

One day in late November, not long after the Parents' Weekend release of the newspaper issue, a university official called Maria to his office. He let her know that an alumnus from Texas had called him and was quite undone by the student newspaper article and wanted to talk to her about her comment about Laura Bush. The official said that "all she needed to do was to call the gentleman so that he could get a sense of Maria as a person and to reassure him that his alma mater was still his alma mater." This conversation frustrated Maria, and, ultimately, made uncomfortably clear where the institution was placing its priorities. What was the official really requesting? He was asking Maria to calm down an alum by reassuring him that *she was the bad guy* and that there was no need to worry, that this kind of bad guy (i.e. bad girl) doesn't really have any power at the university. Maria told the official that she would sleep on the request and let him know in the morning what she had decided.

By the morning, Maria was more convinced that calling the alumnus would be selling her soul. At an early-morning meeting with two university officials on a different matter, Maria described the situation and asked them to take care of it, that is, to make sure that her good name was reaffirmed and that she would have no contact with the alumnus in question. They assured her that they understood, sympathized, and would make sure Maria heard nothing more about it. Two days later was a particularly snowy day when most people were headed home to avoid bad roads. An upper-level administrator entered Maria's office to tell her that he had tried to "reason" with the alumnus in question, but that he wasn't sure that he had been effective. When Maria's office phone rang several hours later, she thought that it must be her partner advising her to drive home before it was too late. Instead, it was the angry alumnus calling to yell at Maria, to ask her to list her credentials, and to inquire as to her understanding of the culture of the university. In the end, the university had washed its hands of the problem, thus revealing to this alumnus, to Maria, and to numerous bystanders that it's okay to offer up the girl as the sacrifice, as long as the institution's masculinist culture prevails. The phone call was another hit of gender shrapnel. Maria hasn't yet figured out what it's called when you're hit repeatedly by different scraps of this type of shrapnel, but she knows that it has to do with being fired, both literally and figuratively.

GENDER SHRAPNEL AND HIRING PROCESSES

Paula was participating on a search team for a Latin Americanist in another department. The lead Latin Americanist from her home department was on leave, so she was asked to step in. She was pleased that they were making this key hire and was willing to participate as requested. At that time, the hiring department was comprised of all men except for one woman. At most of the meetings scheduled for the Latin American search, Paula was the only woman present. This would not have bothered her in the least if it had not bothered her other colleagues. At one meeting, there was a plate of cookies in the middle of the table. One of the professors thanked Paula for bringing them. When she replied that she hadn't brought them but would love to try one, another professor replied, "Excuse his mistake. It's just that you were the only maternal presence here." The final deliberations for the search were tense, as yet another of the professors scolded Paula for "pushing a female hire down their throats" and then said that he would like to come over to the French Department to "tell them to hire a man."

Many fragments of gender shrapnel were flying through the air: Paula was viewed as a woman trying to push a female hire, rather than as an outside expert lending her expertise; she was credited with teaching French (a "chick" language?), instead of Spanish, which further debunked the notion that she was there for her expertise; the professor assumed that the French department had more women than men in its ranks, which was not the case. In addition, an upper-level supervisor was present at those deliberations and used none of his authority to attempt to correct the biased language and to put the conversation back on track. His lack of action seemed to signal to his colleagues that their actions were fine. In effect, it silenced Paula so that she would not be able to offer further comments—in that context or any other with those same colleagues.

GENDER SYMBOLISM IN PUBLIC SPACES AND EVENTS

Lauren, an associate professor of English, was asked to meet with a university official. He wanted her to lead a committee that was working to recognize contributions of women students, past and present, to life at the university. Lauren agreed to take on the work and quickly started to organize the large committee. The committee members agreed to distribute bookmarks to publicize the focus week they were planning. The bookmark was to have a commissioned poem by one of the university's professors, as well as a poem written by a student minoring in women's and gender studies. The university official soon let Lauren know that the commissioned poem was fine, but that the student's poem wasn't "appropriate" for a publication sponsored by the school. When Lauren asked the person to explain what wasn't appropriate about the poem, he got flustered and had difficulty explaining his stance. She found herself going into literature professor mode and attempting a close reading of the poem. She said, "If you read this line and this one, you'll see that this is how the poetic voice feels as she senses the power of her own womanhood. If you read this one and this one, you'll see that part of the maturity she is feeling is an understanding that she is swimming against the current. In this line and this one, she is expressing pride in being Black and in being a woman." The poem really was a coming-of-age poem for a Black woman in a primarily White environment. It revealed the intersections and interstices of race and gender for a person who is growing up. The official appeared uncomfortable with this portrait and forbade the use of the poem. Lauren felt deflated and defeated. What she had most wanted was the transmission of current students' voices through the committee's events, but one of its most visible symbols, the bookmark, was censored. It was at this time, too, that the bookstore distributed free mugs to administrators and members of the committee. Somehow, Lauren did not receive one. All of her colleagues were enjoying their coffee out of the mugs before Lauren ever knew they existed. When she requested one, a university official remarked that she would have to "mud wrestle for it." (True story.)

With this confluence of events—public censure from all sides, higher-ups impeding Lauren's doing the work she had been asked to do, a sense of being silenced—Lauren decided that it was time to write a letter to say that she needed clarification on the committee chair's job description. A response was not forthcoming. At that point, Lauren said that, as a result, she would continue to do the tasks linked to her original job description but would no longer complete the extra tasks that had been assigned to her because of her sex. In an e-mail, she listed the items that would need attention in both the short term and the long term. Within several hours, it was evident that the e-mail had drawn attention. Lauren received a call from a university official asking her to meet with two university officials that day.

STEPPING DOWN OR FIRING

When Yolanda, a student affairs dean, complained of a harassing supervisor, she was "offered the flexibility to step down" from her role. She could move to another division, without the same title, but this would at least alleviate the tensions in the office. "Flexibility" was the key word—Yolanda could stay in the position for the remaining year of her contract or she could "step down" a year early and move departments. Her cautious response was to read aloud the notes she had taken in the meeting to make sure she understood the terms of their oral negotiation and to say that she thought she needed a long conversation with the supervisor so that she could make an informed decision. When she asked the supervisor about the possibility of working together well enough for one more year, he shouted, "You know, Yolanda, not everything is about gender." And that's when Yolanda knew for certain that everything was about gender.

Unwilling to change her sex and unable to be seen as anything but her gender, Yolanda weighed her options. She believed that a contract is a contract, and that she needed to honor the terms of the one she had signed previously. She also believed that some of the institution's representatives had behaved themselves unprofessionally, unethically, and illegally, and that perhaps that demonstrated that her contract was already breached. When it came down to it, Yolanda knew that she would continue to be impeded from doing her job the way she believed it needed to be done and that this wouldn't help anyone. She stepped down, but she really believes that she was fired, forced out. The following fall, Yolanda received an e-mail invitation to a training session on the university's policy on discrimination, harassment, and retaliation. At the training, the session leader apologized for having to gather people together for the purpose of the training, attributed instances of discrimination and harassment to the "fact that Men are from Mars and Women are from Venus," and then said that the university's approach in these cases was to "remove the thin-skinned plaintiff." "Aha," Yolanda thought, "that's exactly how they perceived me and what they did to me. I was removed."

But she wasn't simply removed—she was disappeared. A supervisor decided that he needed to explain Yolanda's move to another department to all of the employees in the university unit, and so he crafted a letter about her "resignation." Five minutes before a scheduled meeting with all unit supervisors, this person brought the letter to Yolanda's office for her to read. She asked if this was just for her information, or if she was to suggest revisions. The supervisor gazed out the window as Yolanda instinctively pulled out a red pen to provide feedback. As she read the letter, her disbelief grew. The letter spoke of "negotiations about contract" and of wanting to "clear up rumors." Yolanda had never before seen a letter like this written about any employee—not when a person was fired for having child pornography on his computer, not when another person was fired for trying to film images of women up their skirts, not when another person was fired for embezzlement. The supervisor mailed the letter (the old-fashioned way) to every single person in one of the university units, even to a colleague who was in Japan on leave. These were the people with whom Yolanda had worked closely for years and with whom she had advocated tirelessly for resources. Yolanda still doesn't have a word for how she felt—violated, betrayed, smeared, humiliated, silenced, disappeared—a decrescendo of existence.

For a brief time, the letter was a lightning rod for further uproar concerning women on campus. A group of staff and faculty members got together to write a letter of protest, and over 300 students signed a petition to express their objection to the letter and to request Yolanda's reinstatement. Her office started to resemble a funeral home. Friends and colleagues came by with flowers and baked goods and to offer hugs. Yolanda reports that it was a very strange sensation, really, to have others sense in such a visceral way the death of something institutional—the death of hope for a fair work environment that would adhere to Title VII and Title IX mandates.

Yolanda's remaining time in her post was profoundly stressful. She continued to oversee and attend events she was in charge of planning, to advise student groups, and to oversee housing complaints, among her many other responsibilities. She held her head high in public and cried in private. She collapsed in a chair each night when she arrived home, wondering how she would get up and do it all again the next day. In the busy-ness of it all, she almost didn't notice getting hit with one more bit of shrapnel, contained in the institution's approach to replacing Yolanda in the administrative position. In one of the busiest of weeks of the year, potential candidates were sent to Yolanda's office to talk to her about the position. She had no warning that this would happen, just the impromptu drop-by visits that consisted of awkward questions and no small degree of measuring of drapes (well, really, of bookshelves). Through all of this, Yolanda tried to continue to respond to people and to e-mail promptly and politely. Her job was to continue to do her job well and to avoid as professionally as possible all contact with the harassing supervisor.

That was a busy month for everyone. It was the month in which the university named a person to a new high-level position in the institution. Many people believed that this new person would have the right under-standing of the university's many constituencies. The person's name was made public at about the same time Yolanda's firing was. Yolanda was impressed that he called her at the office to leave a message in which he expressed to her a sense of collegiality and support. She saved that message and one other from him on her voice mail. Coincidentally, months later, both messages were removed from her system. Only the time stamp was left, and all other saved messages were there.

After that month, Yolanda had two more months in the office until the end of the academic year. She knew they would be painful, but she also knew that much of her increased visibility from her current position would wane. There were several more incidents of gender shrapnel, and the institu-tion's removal of the "thin-skinned plaintiff" had begun in earnest. Yolanda had to give a speech about women students and women's philanthropy to a group of 250 Board members, alumni, and esteemed philanthropists. Her colleagues in the administration seemed to be on tenterhooks because she had not shared the text of the speech with them. No one had asked her to do so, and she had no way of knowing that she was supposed to. The speech praised the legacy of philanthropy at the institution, provided specific exam-ples of high-achieving female students, and said lofty things about the liberal arts mission. It could not have been more in tune with the administration's desires and was true to Yolanda's own beliefs. Nevertheless, it seemed evident that she was no longer to be trusted.

BITCH

On Yolanda's last day in the office, two people very kindly thought to give her going-away gifts. Unfortunately, even though the gifts were not intended as shrapnel, they were. One was a lovely flowerpot with a Katherine Hepburn quote about misbehaving, and the other was a baseball cap that said, "Bitch." These gifts might have worked well in a different context, but not on Yolanda's last day in a job for which she became a bitch (in the eyes of her supervisors) for calling people out for bad behavior. Yolanda, wanting to express thanks to two very well-meaning people, donned the cap and wore it out of the office. The bitch, that was Yolanda. The bitch walked herself and her laptop over to her new office in a different department, the place where she would be hidden away.

READING (AND UNREADING) GENDER IN OFFICIAL PROCESSES

When she was backed against the wall of the parking garage and asked what her contractual intentions were, Isabel knew she had to register a formal complaint. She was concerned about how legal issues seemed to enter the conversation more noticeably at this point. She could hear legal rhetoric at every turn. The institution appeared to be trying to protect itself from a lawsuit; it was maybe not trying to figure out how to do the right thing. Isabel spoke to two university officials about her potential complaint. As someone well versed in university policy, Isabel knew the system inside and out. It was unorthodox to assign two designated officers to a case. They seemed nervous. And these officials were both lawyers and both appointed by a higher-level official, not standard procedure at all. It turns out that one of them was in the running for a higher post, and so maybe was unwilling to get into hot water. The other was in a non-tenured position and might have felt the need to protect the job. Regardless, Isabel does believe that both were doing their jobs with her the best they knew how. She met with them, went over all the details of a previous meeting with a university official, and the fact that he said she would have to pursue a complaint to have the administration consider the whole issue. Isabel then discussed with the two officials/counselors several concrete examples of discriminatory actions she believed she had experienced. As they concluded the meeting, Isabel informed the two officials that she needed to sleep on the whole matter and that in the next several days she would let them know whether or not she would file a formal complaint.

Before Isabel ever had a chance to make a decision about whether or not to file a formal complaint, a high-level official told another one that she had filed a complaint against him. Isabel found this out in a meeting with the two counselors, during which she was asking them questions and probing the pros and cons of going forward with a formal complaint. One of them let slip in passing that the official in question already knew. Isabel recounts feeling clearly exposed, afraid, and vulnerable. She also remembers feeling an utter sense of shock, when you don't know what to say and you feel like you're watching yourself saying nothing. Now that she knows much more about how to protect herself, she looks back and thinks that that was the moment at which she should have ceased all contact with the administration. Isabel understands now that they were making every move to protect the institution from a lawsuit, rather than making any move to have a real conversation with her about real concerns. Nevertheless, at that moment, Isabel was still naïve and hoping that the institution could overcome this mistake and still do the right thing. When she learned that the person in question knew of a formal complaint that she had not yet filed, she felt extremely threatened, physically threatened, in fact. This person lived close to her children's school, and she felt unsafe for her kids. The institution had exposed Isabel, before she had decided she wanted to move forward with the complaint, and she felt like no one in her family was safe from the retaliation that could be heaped upon them. Isabel sensed that others viewed her fear of this type of retaliation to be extreme, but she was still trying to overcome the trauma of the parking garage incident and the uncertainty of the terms of a contract previously made.

Isabel called a high-level official, voice shaking, and asked to know why he had chosen to share any of her information with the other person. He had no answer and was clearly afraid to speak with her. The gag order seemed to be on. Isabel wasn't "safe," and anything said to Isabel could damage the institution. At that point, Isabel thought, "why not go forward with the investigation? They already think it's formal, although they neglected to tell you that." She learned several months later that the administration at that early point had already retained external counsel and a mediator. She was already the enemy—she just didn't know at the time to what extent. It is only in retrospect that Isabel developed the sharp visual image of the institution's officials lining up on one side of a line, battle armor on, weapons at the ready, with her alone on the other side. She didn't understand early on that the counselors—designated to help her put her complaint forward—were not on her side at all.

At this point in her story, Isabel becomes much less sympathetic about what the other side may or may not have been thinking, what may or may not have motivated them, and how they were or were not hit by gender shrapnel that was already flying through the air. She also becomes a tad less funny or full of flippant bravado because trauma is simply not funny. She was on a special fellowship, but the internal complaint at the institution became just that for her—an internal complaint, one that had her trying to work through formal and informal channels to make things right, and one that had her insides torn to shreds. Throughout the fellowship year, Isabel continued to write and to publish, and to pursue the complaint long distance, which took more hours than she ever could have anticipated at the beginning. The whole time she felt as though she had shrunk from a walking-tall professional person to a miniscule piece of mouse turd. The diminution notwithstanding, she still knew that there were people who did not belong overseeing a complaint system for discrimination and harassment, that the complaint she had filed was well founded, and that other people had keenly sensed the increased tension and vigilance of their surroundings.

As the internal investigation got underway, of course more people in the university community learned of Isabel's complaint. Isabel recalls that there was probably a general sense that she should have just let things go, that she was on a fellowship in another city, and that pursuing things further with the person in question was uncivil. She sensed that, to some, it was more important for her to speak with kind words than to point out illegal behavior. This might be just normal human behavior, or there might be a Southern sense of not airing the family's dirty laundry. Isabel is rather forthright about how she sees her relationship with her workplace. She says that she is given a contract, based on merit, to do a job that she should do meritoriously. Isabel respects the job and respects the concept of work in general, and she tries to show that respect in every way, every day. For her, this means working in a place that lives up to its high ideals and that, when it's unable to do so (as must happen from time to time), admits the wrongdoing, apologizes, and learns from the mistake. Isabel expects to do the same, both in the workplace and outside of it. Her filing the complaint was an attempt to live and work authentically in a place she could respect. She mostly tried to train herself not to talk with colleagues about the complaint unless they asked first. She didn't want to throw discomfort in their faces and didn't want to dwell on the complaint when there was other work to do.

One person told Isabel that she was sure she'd be happy to learn that the mediator hired by the university to investigate her case was a woman. More gender shrapnel—the assumption that Isabel prefers to work with women! Isabel looked at the person, attempted a weak smile, and said, "I enjoy working with men and women, as long as they are competent." Her case was being overseen by individuals who were very much a part of the gendered system, one of whom commented to her on another occasion, "You Northern women really know what you want. You're just not afraid of things."

As the hired mediator interviewed colleague after colleague, Isabel felt more and more like a pariah. Colleagues were understandably unsure about how to respond to questions about a possibly harassing supervisor. Many had not yet formed full opinions of this person, many were untenured, and many wanted to maintain a good working relationship with the administration. Supervisors hire and fire, decide whether additional instructors are necessary in any given department, determine who can apply for certain grants, decide who is eligible for paid and unpaid leaves, designate each year's raises, and put cases forward for tenure and promotion. This is a whole lot of leverage, and employees know that.

A combination of internal and external officials compiled a report of the internal investigation of the complaint Isabel had filed. She was allowed to read the report in the spring of that fellowship year. Isabel still does not understand the rationale behind her institution's handling of documents surrounding this complaint. For example, she was allowed to read the report, but not to have her own copy of it. She was allowed to bring a laptop to the room where she was to read the report, so that meant she was allowed to type the report herself. She still finds this a bizarre form of torture: When she had access to the report, she typed every word of it onto her laptop because that was the only way she would have the document, a document she would need to use to make her formal response. As Isabel read and typed word after word of a document that she viewed as uncritical and wholly cover-your-ass for the institution, her eyes tried to blink away tears of frustration and fury at the strangeness and the injustice of it all. While the report found that a supervisor did harass her and did create a hostile work environment, it did not find that it was based on gender (and, therefore, the university was magically absolved of all legal wrongdoing based on Titles VII and IX). Isabel understood this to mean that the institution's self-styled, pre-determined investigation had had the desired effect—the school could not be liable if there was no gender problem here.

The real problem in Isabel's eyes, though, was that the whole document itself was gendered from start to finish. The investigators refused to address the most gender-focused areas of the complaint. They simply ignored this gigantic part of her complaint, probably because it was the most dangerous to the institution. When the investigators acknowledged that other employees thought a supervisor harassed and was hostile to women, there was no record of the sex of these individuals. When the investigators quoted the supervisor, they used words like "confirmed," "stated," "declared," and they often neglected to use quotation marks for quotes from the supervisor, making his words blend with the supposedly authoritative voice of the document itself. All of the things Isabel said were set off by quotes and preceded by words such as "felt," "expressed," "sensed." Therefore, the language of the report itself suffered from gender shrapnel, with the man in the higher position as the voice of objective authority and the woman in the lower position being the weak, sentient being.

Isabel was given a limited time to generate a response to the report. The report was so riddled with factual errors, so unaware of its own gender problems, and so uncritical about Isabel's particular situation and the broader gender problems facing the institution that Isabel found writing a response to the report to be quite a daunting task. She wrote an 18-page response to the 18-page report. Isabel still says that it is significant that such a lengthy response was truly necessary—it basically indicated that there were two reports available and still two wholly different versions of the events that had transpired. Isabel also still says that she is tremendously grateful to have had a support system that allowed her to continue to do the right thing, despite the continued shower of shrapnel on and around her. She ended up with her own, self-typed copy of the now infamous report, a copy that was fundamental to her understanding of the institution's principal weaknesses—an inability to acknowledge gender problems, an unwillingness to deal with harassment and hostile work environment, whether based on gender or not, and a sustained self-defensiveness that would bring the institution more trouble later on. Her copy of the report was her only window into the university's priorities and strategies regarding both gender and her. Sometimes employers and employees don't understand that gender shrapnel, if uncontained, simply begets more gender shrapnel.

Isabel completed and submitted her response to the report to a high-ranking official and then awaited a response from him. Isabel always found that the "downtime" in between the institution's responses and her own proved extremely productive—to escape from the pressure and anxiety of the unrest between her employer and her, to think about her own relationship to the institution (she still thoroughly enjoyed the actual job, the actual students, her colleagues), and to produce scholarship. Several weeks later, Isabel received the terse letter from the official, who had determined that no further action needed to be taken, except to offer a university-sponsored mediation with the supervisor in question. What? Isabel was being "offered" continued interaction with the man who had backed her against the wall of the parking garage and threatened her contract. She felt as though she was supposed to stare down the person who raped her and convince him that he and she could be better people—that he could overcome his harassing tendencies and she could let go of her victimhood. This letter from the university official was the most extreme violation Isabel had felt up to that point. The trauma and retraumatization helped her to see sexual discrimination, harassment, and retaliation on a deeply problematic gender shrapnel continuum with sexual assault and sexual violence.

When Isabel e-mailed, in response to the letter, to ask two clarifying questions, she received an extremely angry, frightened (or so Isabel interprets it), and unprofessional e-mail from the university official. She printed out that angry response, which was a good thing, because at that moment, e-mails from this person started to disappear from her saved e-mail files. Isabel sensed that she was now, if she hadn't been before, an official "enemy of the state."

Isabel was allowed one last meeting with the official and two others (but no last meal, no final cigarette). At that meeting, the official remained stony-faced, already ossified in the legal pact he had made with the university not to speak to her or otherwise interact with her.

GENDER SHRAPNEL AS THE FIBER OF ACADEMIC INSTITUTIONS

Josephine was invited to submit a paper for the American Psychological Association (APA) Committee on the Status of Women. She was keenly interested in participating on this panel because this was exactly the type of committee she had been encouraging her university to form. If there were gender problems at her institution, then this type of committee would always be in place to attempt to fix them. If there weren't gender problems at the school, then this committee could form, analyze the status, and choose to disband or to sit idle until specific issues arose. It seemed truly harmless to Josephine; she thought the institution had nothing to lose and everything to gain. She had put the proposal for the committee together and had gotten people from all walks of university life to support it. But it had been a no-go, dead in the water. The institution seemed really afraid, in a way Josephine did not yet fully comprehend. Through this gender shrapnel experience, Josephine has figured out that she is a lot less fearful of what others think and less fearful of change than are most people. This has been a big lesson for her—a part of a second adolescence, almost—to try to understand that she is odd in this respect and that others are normal—not weak, not lesser, just normal. Josephine also wonders whether she is also a little less sentimental than many, and this means that she doesn't cherish tradition as much. Tradition often smells of privilege to her, and it's more of a stink than an aroma. This reveals a certain cultural dissonance between her and her institution, at least in the realm of these particular values.[2]

For the APA panel, Josephine presented a paper on the use of gendered language in academic settings, and this paper meshed extremely well with the other three papers on the panel. Josephine and her co-panelists were surprised and pleased to find that over 40 people attended the session, which was held at sleepy 8:00 a.m. on the last day of the conference. There was a very lively discussion afterward, and many women came up to the table to make comments and ask further questions. Being a part of the panel helped Josephine to envision healthy models for institutions that embrace positive change.

This experience confirmed for Josephine that much of the gender shrapnel that had hit her and others was flying around numerous other institutions as well. In essence, the session was an attempt for all present to start to generate terms and describe situations that contribute to the gender shrapnel concept as a way to think about the many intentional and unintentional injustices based on gender in the workplace. Broad interest in the panel uncovered the need to record stories, collect data, seek logical trends and tendencies, and pull the information together in such a way that working women and men could think more consciously about their work environments and the ways in which they contribute to work dynamics.

DISAPPEARANCE

Julia was forwarded an e-mail in which a supervisor referred to her, in a message to someone else, as "a petulant bitch." She wasn't sure whether to let it slide, to report it through the university's complaint system, or to discuss it directly with the person who had called her that term. A rather direct person, Julia decided to confront the official and talk it over. She asked the supervisor if he believed the term to be gendered, and he said he hadn't given it much thought. "If the e-mail had said, 'The N-word,' would that have been raced?" she asked the supervisor. The supervisor remained silent and soon dismissed her. From that moment and continuing for several years, the official did not speak to Julia, not when the two of them walked alone from a late-evening meeting on campus; not at local theater or sporting events; not even at formal meetings with others present. His Dumbledore-like silence (think Harry Potter, Book 5) helped to "disappear" Julia. More importantly, the fact that this person routinely ignored her as she carried out professional duties made it more difficult for her to carry out those duties well. She continued to work hard, to attend all meetings, to participate actively, but her presence was always prickly, and her participation was largely unappreciated by her superiors (although, Julia believes, it was valued by her colleagues who continued to nominate and elect her to committees that required strong faculty voices). Julia was supposed to put up and shut up; they are supposed to have "removed the thin-skinned plaintiff"; they were all supposed to move on, because everything was supposed to be A-OK.

He Said–She Said, Again?

After attempting to work through a gendered situation (constant references to her "being a lesbian," her style of dress, and use of various derogatory terms in this context) with her immediate supervisor, Teresa was told that she and her supervisor were to work through "their different working styles" through a mediator, hired by the university administration. Teresa was concerned about the "he said–she said" sound to the suggestion of mediation, but she felt like she had to work through and within the university, rather than outside of it. The official did not tell Teresa what the mediation format would look like and seemed deeply irked by the suggestion that he was to speak any more about this situation. Teresa agreed to meet with the mediator—just him and her, no one else—at least to hear the terms of the mediation as he saw them.

The mediator was tall, with a loud voice, and he communicated a certainty that "we're all reasonable people" and "we can come to an agreeable resolution." The problem with mediation in this type of case is that it gives too much credit to a person who has abused power and who has possibly broken the law. It treats the stories of the harasser and the harassed equally, placing blame at each door. It says that the time and effort put in will bear fruit. None of this was possible, because it would require that Teresa be in the business of rehabilitating her harasser—not a healthy position in which to place the survivor. In any case, she met with the tall, blond, confidently loud mediator, who had blocked all day for the meeting and casually remarked that lunch could be delivered if they needed it. It was only breakfast time, and Teresa had a funny feeling that they would not be making it to the chicken wraps and sliced apples. The mediator wanted to "get to know her," spend supposedly casual time asking her about herself, her partner, her years at the institution, and so on. Teresa was not interested in this type of discussion and quickly cut off the personal questions to inquire about the format of mediation: Will this person ever have to confront his wrongdoing? ("Well, I don't think we're talking in terms of wrongdoing here.") Will he be sent to retraining to understand how to treat all employees? ("I can't answer that.") Will I have to meet with you with this person present? ("Yes.") Teresa thanked the mediator for his time and bid him farewell. She had this funny, Monty Python-like image of him, mouth gaping open, insisting that mediation wasn't quite dead yet, that the chicken wraps really would be quite good.

At some point during the summer, Teresa learned by accident that one of the supervisors had been sent to some type of harassment prevention workshop. Finding this out proved to be one of the most painful moments of the ordeal. It meant that the institution agreed with her enough to send the person to rehabilitation, but that they refused to afford her the solace or comfort of knowing that she wasn't crazy in her allegations *and* that there was some hope that his treatment of others would improve. Had the administrators simply said to Teresa, "You make some valid points, and we have some work to do. We apologize for the wrongdoing. Here's what we plan to do to improve this situation," Teresa could have and would have left everything right there. It would have been so easy, and she could have attempted some type of reconciliation with the institution. Instead, the retraining was done in stealth, and none of the employees were permitted any sense of relief through the knowledge that something was being done.

WHO "OWNS" INSTITUTIONAL MESSAGES?

Michelle has worked for over ten years at her institution and has always been open about her activism for people of Color and women's rights. She sees the university as partially "her" university and is committed to the ostensible mission, curriculum, and her colleagues and students. After writing a piece for a higher education newspaper on Ferguson and (too) many related incidents, she was called in by an upper-level supervisor and asked to "curb her activist work." This was the first time Michelle sensed that her activism, fully linked to her scholarship, was called into question and the first time she felt her job security was threatened. She was quite taken aback and said little in the meeting.

At the same time, Michelle felt fully invested in having strong programs that helped students to progress as scholars, professionals, and citizens of the world. She appreciated (and still appreciates) the many opportunities afforded her to expand her research portfolio and to share her research across the university and beyond. In other words, she liked the nuts and bolts of her daily work and the overall vision of the university. The element with which she struggled mightily was being cast as a person who may be an effective teacher and scholar, but whose work and self were not to be appreciated because she did not toe the party line. In her mind, pointing out hypocrisies and refusing to be a part of them was the only right thing to do, and was an attitude that contributed to the overall ideals of the university. Nevertheless, the administrative hierarchy seemed too steeped in a legalistic, control-the-risk environment that too often fomented gender and intersectional shrapnel. They seemed to be more concerned about alumni dollars than about social justice. While she felt threatened, Michelle did not cease her activities of activism and public scholarship. At the same time, well-meaning but somewhat clueless colleagues offered to speak for her at meetings so that her voice would be heard.

How can we interpret what this means? It means that we'll look at issues of race and gender, but that we won't allow real-life race and gender people and issues to be visible or vocal. Those with firsthand experience of gender and race shrapnel on campus were to be silenced because what they had to say would be too frightening, maybe too radical, definitely too legally actionable. Michelle had numerous individuals coming to tell her that they would be happy to speak for her. This "academic ventriloquism" is simply the shrapnel of silencing the dangerous voices, hearing the safe ones, and tacitly encouraging the safe voices to take credit for the good ideas of the dangerous.

OUTSIDE HELP

After years of attempting to stop a colleague from making sexual remarks to her and her colleagues in the chemistry department, Christine finally went to the Equal Employment Opportunity Commission (EEOC) to file a complaint. She and her colleagues wanted someone outside the university to be aware of the gender inequities on the inside. Christine wanted the EEOC to ask her institution to admit specific wrongdoing in her case, to issue a specific apology, and to impose the creation of a group that would faithfully address gender problems in the workplace. This was all she wanted: to know that her institution would have to work toward an improved climate for women, and, by extension, an improved climate for all.

One of Christine's friends, a lawyer, counseled her not to face the EEOC alone. She heroically enlisted the help of colleagues of hers. This generous group of lawyers read through Christine's materials and agreed to meet with her. At the meeting, the small group ascertained that Christine had a real story, that it was well documented, and that she was a strong plaintiff because she had tenure and a clear record of accomplishment. The firm took Christine on *pro bono*.

The lawyers understood exactly what Christine wanted out of the case: the acknowledgement of wrongdoing, the apology, and the oversight committee, that was it. They agreed to help her to work with the EEOC, which, back then, had been somewhat neglected by the federal government, especially in terms of discrimination cases based on gender. Christine reports feeling strengthened by the support from the lawyers but, at the same time, disheartened by the EEOC's poor level of communication. The EEOC employee on the case neglected to inform Christine that the EEOC had received and moved forward on her complaint before they informed her university. All she knew was that she had filed a complaint and then had heard nothing more—no acknowledgement of receipt, no "here's our process going forward" from the EEOC. And then, bam, she heard from numerous colleagues throughout the university that they had received formal letters from university counsel telling them to hold onto all documents having to do with Christine and her employment at the university. This was the EEOC's mistake, an accident, but the shrapnel flew. No one at the EEOC meant to do harm, but the lack of communication surrounding her case made the work environment even more tension-filled.

Christine was at a meeting soon after her colleagues had received their letters about her case. As her committee chair asked the members to take on responsibilities for a group project, Christine volunteered for a task and then proceeded to write its due date in her agenda. The committee chair looked at her and said, "Christine, what are you doing? You do not have to write down every single thing that's said in a meeting." Christine's expression must have been one of utter disbelief, as she showed the chair exactly what she had just written, "Mission statement, due October 15." Christine then left the meeting, walked outside to get fresh air, and walked through the reality of the situation. She was *not* to be trusted, even at the level of this small meeting, located in a place where she had spent so many hours of her workday for so many years. Once she sorted through the implications of it all, she went back to the meeting. At the end of it, she politely asked the committee chair if they could meet briefly. She said, "Yes," and they met in her office. Christine asked the chair when she had stopped trusting her, when she had ever done anything that would make her wonder why she was taking notes in a meeting. The chair made a vague reference to the lawyer's letter, and, again, Christine knew there was no nuance, no gray—she was the enemy of the city (her own department) and state (the university hierarchy).

The lawyers knew Christine's story, had plenty of documentation, and understood at once how difficult it would be to go the long haul for one small case like hers, especially in a particularly conservative district of the state. Nevertheless, they were willing to stick with her. They helped her work with the EEOC. When the EEOC set up a mediation between the university and Christine (a preliminary step to determine if she would get a "right to sue" letter from them) and forgot to invite Christine to the mediation, the lawyers intervened and made sure that she was consulted on the date and time and that they and Christine would have plenty of time to prepare.

As Christine's lawyers consulted on and off with the external lawyer hired by her institution, several things became clear. First, the university did not seem interested in admitting wrongdoing, issuing an apology, or forming an oversight committee. This news dashed everything Christine was asking for. Second, the institution did not want to speak about any kind of settlement with her, unless it was "in the context of her separation from the university." Christine had been feeling so much stronger, so much readier to accept whatever happened, so sure that she was right and had support in her being right, that this information threw her for a gigantic loop. She was absolutely dumbfounded. Why would "they" (the university hierarchy) want to spend all this money and use all these resources to appear to make things right if they didn't really want to make things right? Wouldn't it be much cheaper for them to right wrongs, rather than pay damages *and* push her into leaving the institution? All they wanted, it seemed, was for her, the troublemaker, the whistleblower, to be gone. They wanted to "remove the thin-skinned plaintiff" permanently. Despite all she had been told about her superior job performance as a teacher, adviser, and scholar, Christine was learning that she was really worth nothing. In fact, that her absence from the university was far dearer than her presence. She really could not believe it. The third item she learned through the consultations between her lawyers and the university was that, they said, if Christine tried to sue the university, they would "make sure any other university she applied to which knew that she was a 'man-hater.'" Wow, a man-hater? That was gender shrapnel at its best. Turn the sex discrimination case into the fault and weakness of the classic man-hating feminist radical.

All of this information both made Christine falter significantly for some time and created some steely core within her. Okay, all they really wanted was a fight. If she wasn't going to leave the university, then she would have to pay (and so would many others, due to the university's unwillingness to admit that anything at all was wrong). If she left the university, the university would retaliate by making her an unhirable man-hater. Neither option was pretty, but she was at least going to tell her story to the EEOC. She wanted three things from the EEOC: that they hear her story, elicit a real, specific apology from the wrongdoers, and have the institution put into action a gender oversight committee at the university. It soon became clear that the only language the institution and the mediator would speak was that of money. This was the first time the question of damages came up as a real possibility because it had not been what the case was about. Christine learned that the US legal system has trouble operating outside of this mode. In other words, it ends up all being about money, even if that's not where you started or even wanted to start out.

Several months later, Christine met for hours with her legal team before the following day's mediation with the EEOC. That night, she went over her story again. She tried to convey her sincere desire simply to make the university behave, to create a better atmosphere for women and men workers, and to find a way back to working in peace.

The next day the EEOC mediator asked Christine to "tell her story." As she did so, the external lawyer hired by her university tried to interrupt at several points to disagree. The university's lawyer was not asked to tell a story, as Christine had been. Christine was deeply disappointed by this. After all, if the EEOC was really conducting a mediation, wouldn't both sides tell a story? This seemed inconsistent, and there seemed to be a move to protect the university from telling any more lies or committing any more acts of gender discrimination. Instead, the lawyer offered Christine a small sum in exchange for her silence surrounding the case. She said, "No, thank you," and that was the end. The next day, Christine recounts, she went out for an early-morning run in the winter cold and realized halfway through that tears had been running down her cheeks for she didn't know how long. How to keep on with this? How to let go? Neither option really seemed possible.

A month later Christine received her "right to sue" letter from the EEOC and then initiated a profound discussion with her partner about how they would manage a long-term suit. Could they be happy as Christine continued to be treated so poorly at her institution, as their social lives were affected by a pariah status, as they experienced the ups and downs of a possible five-year lawsuit? Knowing full well that dropping the suit, with its *pro bono* lawyers and solid plaintiff, was dropping the only opportunity to make her institution clean up its gender act, Christine dropped it. Dropping the suit made her feel incredibly vulnerable—there would be no more legal protection, and she had to keep working where she was, with no one able to move the university in the right direction. She felt violated, all over again.

REFLECTIONS OF GENDER SHRAPNEL

These stories reflect the ups and downs of the gender shrapnel experience. At times, it is possible to maintain a sense of dignity and humor and to work constructively for change. At other times, it is impossible to ignore the damage done to colleagues and to self through the effects of gender shrapnel—double or triple discrimination in the intersecting categories, inequity, erasure, silence, loss—and to feel anything but anger and frustration. That's why these narratives shift from what I hope is some degree of compassion and humor in certain sections to frustrated complaining and parsing of situations in other sections. A good friend of my partner has worked for many years on the management side of employment law. He has stated simply that employee handbooks and policies are only ever as good as the administrators who write and enforce them. Some do their jobs better than others, but it remains clear that institutions need to move away from an employee-as-risk (and in the case of rape, sexual assault, and sexual violence, from a student-as-risk) model of higher education. While it is excellent for institutions to hire women administrators, the "north" on many schools' compass is often a restoration of higher male representation. Nevertheless, hiring women just to have them become, out of necessity for survival, "yes men," doesn't do any of us much good. It does help in small ways, for sure, to have a woman at the table and to have others see women represented. But if that woman leader or those women leaders are strapped for political capital, then they will not be allowed to make much change for others. The same is very much true for hiring men and women who can advocate for change in terms of diversity and inclusion. They need political capital to be able to do their jobs and advocate for change.

We teachers might still believe that manners matter, that lessons can be taught, that bad behavior cannot be rewarded, and that there is hope for the future. We can be motivated by the possibility for change at our institutions with which we may well have long-standing connections, the places where many other hardworking people labor and hope for less hypocrisy and more equity.

STAGES OF CONFRONTING SEXUAL DISCRIMINATION, HARASSMENT, AND RETALIATION IN THE ACADEMIC WORKPLACE

1. *What the hell was that?* A supervisor stands above you, rubs your shoulder, and reads your computer screen. This can't really be happening, right? He's just being friendly. He's just a "touchy-feely" guy. I'm crazy, why do I keep thinking about this, this is nothing. Uh-oh, now he's challenging the terms of my contract. And now he's telling me that I "nurture" the faculty. This all just feels wrong, but why?
2. *Do I address the behavior or put up with it?* I've always addressed things directly, but I don't see how I can in this situation. Do I just let him rub my shoulders? Do I challenge sexist language? I talk to trusted colleagues, who make a variety of recommendations, from "put up and shut up" to "go talk to the guy's supervisor."
3. *Am I crazy?* There is no one, solid, consistent bit of advice that anyone has given me. People are all over the map on this. There is no solution. I must be the crazy one if there is no tried-and-true solution. Just get over it. Stay focused on the work. But, wait, this *is* the work…
4. *No, I'm not crazy. This person really is doing these things.* Yep, he really is rubbing my shoulders, reading my computer screen, putting his shirt and tie on in the main office, repeatedly threatening the terms of my contract. Admit it, this is really happening.
5. *Accommodate. Adjust. Get away from the situation.* Well, I can't really address this wholesale—it's just too big and scary a thing. Okay, so,

every time the supervisor walks into my office, I'll just stand up. That's what I'll do. Then his midsection won't be in my face as he leans over me in my chair to look at my computer screen. Then I'll be standing, too, and I'm tall-ish. I'm certainly taller standing than sitting. This is good. It alleviates the physical tension. But, darn it, there's still the gendered stuff he says to me.

6. *Doesn't help.* The less the supervisor can control me physically, the more he controls me verbally. He tries to dictate e-mails to me, he scolds me, he yells while interjecting my name way more times than is normal, excludes me from work meetings.

7. *Self-empowerment—address the situation.* I make the decision between putting up and disappearing altogether and confronting the sexual discrimination and harassment and at least standing up for my professional and personal selves. I stand up for myself. Okay, good, I'm empowered. I have not lost my voice. I can articulate what the hell is going on here. (I'm starting to understand what gender shrapnel is!) I have told the harasser why I feel harassed and what is hostile about the work environment.

8. *Doesn't help. Makes everything worse.* Gender shrapnel swirls as all the professional things I do surrounding gender are questioned.

9. *Self-empowerment—report the incidents.* I've documented everything. Wow, when I see it all in writing, it is irrefutable. There is some serious gender shrapnel flying. I've reported the incidents, first to supervisors, then through the employee complaint process.

10. *Optimism. The institution will recognize and correct wrongdoing.* Surely, the institution will read all of this documentation and understand gender at work, habitual discrimination, and the need to alleviate the hostile work environment for me and others. I haven't lost voice. I can still be myself—strong, knowledgeable, outspoken, keen on social justice.

11. *Disbelief. The institution protects itself.* What? It's a hostile work environment, but not based on gender. Oh right, I thought I was understanding gender shrapnel more before, but now I really get it.

12. *Talk to a lawyer.* Well, I didn't go through all of these stages to be quiet now, did I? It's time to talk to a lawyer.

13. *File EEOC complaint.* It's time to see if going outside the system works.

14. *Be "disappeared" from work environment.* I've become radioactive. People are afraid to talk things through with me. I won't be tapped

for posts/positions/service responsibilities that I used to be tapped for.

15. *Anger, frustration at the injustice.* Find voice. Consider writing cartoons or musicals. Comedy helps!

16. *Sue or don't sue.* This is an extremely fraught issue. Suing requires years of extra work, patience, and living with being the public enemy. An EEOC-based lawsuit in this region of the USA is very far from a slam dunk. Lawsuits are also all about the money and rarely about the apology for wrongdoing and the plan to improve. Not suing is giving up the formal possibility of having the institution change for the better, but it's also a healthier balance for the individual.

17. *Use voice and continue to advocate for change.* Write letters to editor, write to the governor, and write articles. Collaborate with colleagues who have had similar gender shrapnel experiences.

Notes

1. I am grateful to an anonymous reader for Columbia University Press for this cogent summary of the *Gender Shrapnel* project.
2. When my sister Molly Mayock read this section of my manuscript, she referred me to Brené Brown's TED talk on vulnerability. Dr. Brown's message in the talk is that, when we allow ourselves to feel and to be vulnerable, we also allow ourselves to be compassionate and to connect. We can make mistakes, say we're sorry, and we can forgive mistakes if we can allow ourselves to feel both vulnerable and worthy of connection and love. Dr. Brown's talk is both engaging and worth the watch.

PART II

Gender Problems in the Workplace

CHAPTER 4

The Enduring *Feminine Mystique*

There is a yearning out there for Betty Friedan, for a reconsideration of *The Feminine Mystique*, for an understanding of the climate for women in the workplace and the conditions under which women labor, conditions which, for some, have animated the creation of the equivocal term of the "opt-out revolution." Linda Hirshman's 2006 book *Get to Work. A Manifesto for Women of the World* is dedicated to the memory of Friedan and borrows heavily from the notion of the feminine mystique. Stephanie Coontz's 2011 *A Strange Stirring. The Feminine Mystique and American Women at the Dawn of the 1960s* examines the galvanizing effect of Friedan's work on (mostly White) women and men lulled into post-World War II, and 1950s expectations about gendered spheres, about where women and men supposedly belonged. Coontz updates Friedan's reading by including consideration of African-American women of the 1950s and 1960s and of working-class women of the same era. There is no doubt about it, *The Feminine Mystique*'s journalistic inquiry into the "problem with no name" is still highly pertinent because this "problem with no name" now has a name—gender shrapnel—and is in sore need of examination and solutions.

In this chapter, I am rereading Betty Friedan's *The Feminine Mystique* in order to examine how the author gives name and shape to the phenomenon of the disillusionment that women of the 1950s and 1960s felt both in the home and in the nation in general. In the 1983 edition, Friedan's new introduction, titled "Twenty Years Later," along with the epilogue, allows the reader a view inside the societal changes that occurred with

© The Editor(s) (if applicable) and The Author(s) 2016
E. Mayock, *Gender Shrapnel in the Academic Workplace*,
DOI 10.1057/978-1-137-50830-0_4

the Second Wave of feminism, along with Friedan's many ominous and insightful predictions for a backlash against women's increased access to the labor market and its implications for the traditional household. From Friedan's expansive work, I wish to look at the following concepts in order to conceptualize an evolving "professional mystique," or dissatisfaction with roles and cultures that women and underrepresented groups are experiencing in the academic workplace: (1) women's depiction in the popular press; (2) role crisis; (3) the "is this all?" phenomenon, the glass ceiling, and privilege envy; and (4) the structure and ambience of the work environment.

According to the US Bureau of Labor, in 2009, 59% of all working-age women were in the workforce, up from 43% in 1969 ("Women at Work" 12). The Bureau predicts that the number of women in the civilian labor force will increase 9% between 2008 and 2018 ("Women at Work" 15). Women are certainly in the workforce to stay. Women make up approximately 57% of college and university undergraduates and 62% of graduate students, while also moving into the majority of graduating doctors and lawyers (Kreamer 18). At the same time, despite the increased incidence of women at work, women and men are still not assured equal approaches to advancement and pay. Using data from many different areas of employment, Virginia Valian finds that data from academia are more plentiful and reliable, and also reveal more dire circumstances in terms of equity:

> Like the data for other professions, the data for academia are of two types—aggregate data and cohort data. Taken together, they show that in almost every field and subfield, in almost every cohort and at almost every point in their teaching and research careers, women advance more slowly and earn less money than men. The history of the profession in the past few decades suggests that the problem of women's lower status in academia will not dissipate in the fullness of time. (217)

A study published by Boraas and Rodgers in 2003 examines the role of gender in the earnings gap. The summary line for the published article is this: "Although personal choices, occupational crowding, and discrimination contribute to the gender gap, the higher share of women in an occupation is still the largest contributor" (http://www.bls.gov/opub/mlr/2003/03/art2abs.htm). The line is filled with information. While the authors acknowledge the importance of discrimination in the earnings pay gap, they emphasize the really important element of "the feminization of poverty," that is, the more women in a certain type of workplace, the lower the earnings in that sector will be. This revelation matters very much in the discussion of higher education and gender shrapnel. The disciplines with more women have a lower status than disciplines with fewer women. Given the stories that circulate about supervisors who seem to seek out the lowest-status person in the room, we can now recognize the vulnerability of these individuals, both in their daily interactions with a harassing supervisor and in their monthly interactions with their paycheck. In addition, women in the disciplines with more men might have more to say about *why* there are more men in their discipline—about what the levels of access are for women, about the inherent biases about women in mathematics and science.[1] For example, Forever 21 and JCPenney recently placed on the shelves T-shirts for young girls that say, "Allergic to Algebra" and "I'm too Pretty for Homework, so my brother does mine." In *Communicating Gender*, Suzanne Romaine examines the 1991 AAUW report's emphasis on the significant role of mathematics and science courses in the development of self-esteem in both boys and girls and highlighting that "girls who take and do well in these subjects are more likely to aspire to professional careers" (58). Putting more emphasis on biology and nature and less emphasis on encouraging women to access fields in which they are a rarity places girls at a disadvantage before they ever even begin formal schooling.[2]

An additional element of gender shrapnel in the workplace finds itself at the intersection of disciplinary programs (departments, usually located in academic buildings) and interdisciplinary programs (programs, often without their own turf). Let's dissect an example of individual versus disciplinary status or lack thereof. The conservative Intercollegiate Studies Institute publishes an annual guide to colleges and universities titled *Choosing the Right College* (emphasis on "right"). The text included on my own institution in the 2006 edition (http://www.isi.org/college_guide/sample/2006/washlee.pdf) warns of the encroachment of liberally bent interdisciplinary programs, such as African-American Studies and Women's and Gender Studies, and lauds the institution's perceived general adherence to conservative values. There is a section in which individual faculty members are cited for being the best in the department. What is so interesting about the list of 18 strongly recommended faculty members is that two of them are the founders of the African-American Studies Program, two are core faculty in the Women's and Gender Studies Program, another is an affiliate faculty member in Women's and Gender Studies, and another is an affiliate faculty member in Environmental Studies. The authors are gathering their information by soliciting student recommendations, but they are evidently not asking questions about individual faculty members' affiliations in interdisciplinary programs.

There is an interesting enigma here. The 18 faculty members included on the list are popular among students for their teaching in specific disciplines/departments. They are not linked to the significant administrative and teaching work they do in their interdisciplinary programs. Given the tension between discipline and interdiscipline, accepted scholarship and "new," "not yet tested" scholarship, and department and program, one might discern that departments carry traditional clout and have significant privilege. Interdisciplinary programs, whose quality or worthiness is felled with one swoop in the text of the guide, represent the untested, the "other," the lesser privileged.[3] The significance of this goes back to comments made in the introduction about how Women's and Gender Studies faculty are viewed and accepted on campus, *when they are considered as Women's and Gender Studies faculty*, rather than simply as members of their "traditional" disciplines. On campus, I believe that I carry more clout when I am associated with the Romance Languages Department than when I am associated with an interdisciplinary program. This is in part because the department has existed for centuries, while the interdisciplinary programs, principally allowed "only" to grant minors, have been around for only a little more than a decade. At the same time, I earn more automatic respect when I'm associated with the interdisciplinary program of Latin American and Caribbean Studies (LACS) than when I'm associated with Women's and Gender Studies. Clearly, one of the programs is perceived as less rigorous and, perhaps, more dangerous than the other. When the LACS program began in 2007, a university officer contacted the new program head to see if they could work with him on grant opportunities. It was exciting to watch the LACS program grow and succeed, and to see it supported by the administration. Nevertheless, as a participant in two interdisciplinary programs, I wondered why the older Women's Studies program had not generated similar collaborative interest among administrators. The "problem with no name," the invisibility of women and of academic research on women, gender, and sexualities, was clearly present in the workplace as well.

Friedan's extensive review of the popular press of her age reveals the repeated, stultifying image of the "happy housewife heroine":

> The image of woman that emerges from this big, pretty magazine is young and frivolous, almost childlike; fluffy and feminine; passive; gaily content

in a world of bedroom and kitchen, sex, babies, and home. The magazine surely does not leave out sex; the only passion, the only pursuit, the only goal a woman is permitted is the pursuit of a man. It is crammed full of food, clothing, cosmetics, furniture, and the physical bodies of young women, but where is the world of thought and ideas, the life of the mind and spirit? In the magazine image, women do no work except housework and work to keep their bodies beautiful and to get and keep a man. (36)

How different are the popular images of women today? Much of Friedan's description is sustained in the popular magazines and journals of our day, but the overall contemporary image might be an even more damaging one for women. Women are portrayed as too thin, weakened victims of sexual dominance, even as slaves. Women are depicted as wholly dependent on men's attention, which is portrayed as never fully forthcoming. Women of Color are either portrayed as faithfully as possible as White women, or they are portrayed as curvy and voracious. When women are portrayed in career roles, the image is usually of a harried, frantic, out-of-control White person who cannot handle the life she has created for herself and who still adheres to societal norms from before her own time. Even in the respected dailies, the rhetoric for women in general defaults to women's supposed failures in the "mommy wars," the "opt-out generation," and the "damaged daycare kids." This is all a fundamental part of the professional mystique for women. We are depicted in the press as weak, passive, and out of control and as heterosexual mothers who are not responsive enough to our husbands and children. These are portrayals that exist and function in our collective imagination, the imagination that each of us carries with us to the workplace.[4] Jennifer Siebel Newsom's 2011 release of "Miss Representation" is an astounding wake-up call to the USA about the limiting, sexualized, exploitative, and violent portrayal of women and men in our media. The film also signals the troubling stereotypes assigned at the intersections of gender and race/color, many of which are examined in *Presumed Incompetent* (see, e.g., Moffitt, Harris, and Forbes Berthoud's "Present and Unequal: A Third-Wave Approach to Voice Parallel Experiences in Managing Oppression and Bias in the Academy" and Flores Niemann's "The Making of a Token: A Case Study of Stereotype Threat, Stigma, Racism, and Tokenism in Academe").

What does the workplace do, then, with female laborers who are mothers (i.e. inferior laborers and inferior homemakers) or, even more difficult to pin down, with women whose sexuality is not overtly brought into the workplace through the known existence of a heterosexual partner and offspring? The simple answer is that the workplace writhes and withers before the uncertainty of the female workers' identities and then responds to the discomfort with a reassertion of White male privilege. In the meantime, several psychological studies, including Jeanine Silveira Stewart's "Mothering Out of Place" and several by Peter Glick and Susan T. Fiske, show that workers who are mothers are considered incompetent but warm, that women workers perceived as "career women" are considered competent but cold, and that male workers are considered competent and then gain "warmth" points when they are known to have children (Silveira Stewart 105; Friedan 46, 173). Linda Hirshman cites *The Career Mystique* to emphasize that male workers who have male children gain even more points than their counterparts who have female children (Hirshman 55).[5] As Valian writes in her thorough study on the slow pace of women's advancement in the workplace: "Independent of all other factors, gender appears to play a major role in people's ability to get ahead. Gender schemas are objectively costly for women. Relative to women, men have a leg up. Men look right for the job" (18). The professional mystique is embedded in this crucible of constricted perceptions of identity and forced identity performance. When women workers are perceived as women workers, they are eligible for fewer privileges. When women workers are perceived as manly, they may also be perceived as out of their proper place, thus inhibiting further their access to opportunities in the workplace. The question of "passing" or "covering" is less applicable in the gender schema than in the areas of race, religion, and sexual orientation. Nevertheless, in the gender sector, "passing" has much to do with parental status and the degree to which women can reveal that they are or are not mothers. As Kenji Yoshino writes, "Courts will protect traits like skin color or chromosomes because such traits cannot be changed. In contrast, the courts will not protect mutable traits, because individuals can alter them to fade into the mainstream, thereby escaping discrimination. If individuals choose not to engage in that form of self-help, they must suffer the consequences" (35). But, Yoshino adds:

> The flaw in the judiciary's analysis is that it casts assimilation as an unadulterated good. Assimilation is implicitly characterized as the way in which groups can evade discrimination by fading into the mainstream—after all, the logic goes, if a bigot cannot discriminate between two individuals, he cannot discriminate against one of them. But sometimes assimilation is not an escape from discrimination, but precisely its effect. When a Jew is forced

to convert to Protestantism, for instance, we do not celebrate that as an evasion of anti-Semitism. We should not blind ourselves to the dark underbelly of the American melting pot. (35)

Despite the bombardment of limiting portrayals of women in the popular press, I believe that many women who go to college (and possibly to graduate school) and who pursue careers do not anticipate that employers will have limited views of their roles and abilities in the workplace.[6] Many have spent their lives enjoying the fruits of 1960s and 1970s activism and of Title IX—equal access to opportunities in education, at least in written policy—and might have no reason to believe that workplace equity is hard to come by. The experiences that many women bring to the workplace collide with the traditional, entrenched values of their employers and create something of a "role crisis" (Friedan 75–77). Friedan describes the phenomenon in this way: "It is my thesis that the core of the problem for women today is not sexual but a problem of identity—a stunting or evasion of growth that is perpetuated by the feminine mystique" (77). Friedan later states unequivocally that, while it is useful to examine the formation of gendered identities and expectations of roles, it is essential that we offer alternatives to this type of gender role inculcation (132–37).

Capable women who arrive in the workplace are ready to have all their experience recognized and talents put to use, and this can happen in the early going. Nevertheless, with increased tenure in a post and an expectation of increased responsibility, many women experience in the workplace what Friedan attributed to 1950s and 1960s housewives: the "is this all?" syndrome (15). Many women find themselves in departments with few resources and in positions endowed with little authority to change the level of resources. Some women find themselves in the uncomfortable and little-rewarded zone between disciplines. Still more are temporary workers trying to "make do" at several different institutions or organizations at once—with no benefits, no power for change, and few formal ties to the institution(s). Even those women who climb the ranks might still find themselves bumping against the glass ceiling—glass through which they can see the privilege of male administrators above them and, sometimes, of female administrators whose "role" out of the office often looks nothing like that of those below the ceiling.

What is it that women are really seeing beyond the glass ceiling? It is not a series of floating penises, but rather an intricate web of authority, privilege, and social networking. As Friedan has so clearly stated, it is not the penis that women feel they lack, but rather the privilege bestowed upon the holder of the penis—simply stated, it is "privilege envy" (Friedan 114–17). Inequities in the workplace stem from a complicated process: Men have been leaders in the workplace for longer. It is therefore the image of the White man that is the image of the Leader. The Leader has power and authority and uses an extensive social and professional network that benefits him and those around him. Women are viewed as the "other," the ones without the penis, the ones with the penis envy. Women might view themselves in this socially formed way as well. We reinforce the stereotypes of leadership and forget to label privilege envy as exactly that— a desire to have privilege shared among all workers and thereby actually deconstruct the core meaning of privilege. In 1963, Friedan reminded us that, "The fact is, girls today and those responsible for their education do face a choice. They must decide between adjustment, conformity, avoidance of conflict, therapy—or individuality, human identity, education in the truest sense, with all its pains of growth" (175). This is true nowadays as well. Employees and employers must make a conscious decision to define problems based in gender and its intersected categories and to restructure programs and policies so that they can display therein the institutional core values of *consciousness of equity* and *realization of equity*.

In her introduction to the tenth anniversary edition of *The Feminine Mystique*, Friedan states that "if women were really *people*—no more, no less—then all the things that kept them from being full people in our society would have to be changed" (9). Therefore, the difficult question for institutions to ask as they confront entrenched gender problems in the workplace is simply, "Are women being kept from engaging fully at work?" Full engagement in the workplace would include having access to a variety of types and challenges of work, developing a work style that is accepted and maybe even admired, having equal access to additional training and opportunities for promotion, expressing ambition without penalty, being recognized appropriately for achievements and being credited for creative ideas, having a hand in making an organization a more efficient and effective one, and shaping the ways in which the organization evolves and welcomes other workers in years to come. The question of full engagement is the right one for underrepresented groups on campus as well. If the answer is "yes, women and underrepresented groups are facing barriers to full engagement," then the institution has to decide that it has real work to do in examining the professional mystique and finding ways to eradicate gender shrapnel. The ideal workplace recognizes and values in its workers the "unique human capacity to transcend the present, to live one's life by purposes stretching in to the future—to live not at the mercy of the world, but as a builder and designer of that world—that is the distinction between animal and human behavior, or between the human being and the machine" (Friedan 312). I contend that human beings also have the unique human capacity to use language—in oral and written forms—to convey a host of needs, desires, and emotions. This capacity brings with it an increased responsibility through and about language, both oral and written.

NOTES

1. See Christie Aschwanden's "Harassment in Science, Replicated" (*The New York Times*, 11-11-2014) for statistics on sexual harassment and sexual assault of women at field sites and for a call-to-arms to eliminate these illegal behaviors.

2. Suzanne Romaine cogently treats how women often become different because of the ways in which they have to navigate cultural and workplace inequities: "Feminist theorist Catherine MacKinnon has cautioned against regarding gender differences as an explanatory 'bottom line.' Instead, she advocates looking at the difference gender makes. It is no accident that the stereotypical female style of behavior shows the traits it does when the burden of caring for others has disproportionately fallen on women. Greater social sensitivity and politeness are the burden of subordinates in a climate when one has to pay attention to the nuances of the struggle for equality (see Chapter 6 on the linguistic hallmarks of politeness). Deborah Cameron (1992a) feels we should not unequivocally celebrate differences that have evolved and been sustained through limiting women's freedom of choice, and through keeping women in a subordinate and economically dependent condition. This does not mean, however, that we need to see women's behavior as being uniformly determined by and indicative of their subordination and powerlessness. Another implication of continuing to believe that men and women are opposites with different traits is that it absolves men from the responsibility of being caring, nurturing, and so on" (60).

3. See Chapter 5 of Maher and Thompson Tetreault's *Privilege and Diversity in the Academy* for a detailed examination of the power of traditional academic departments.

4. Elizabeth M. Chamberlain describes thoroughly the types of images that surround us in a daily barrage of media messages: "Middle level students and their teachers and parents are immersed in a larger culture in which sexual innuendo and sexualized comments are embedded in nearly all forms of media. Advertisements, televisions programs, music, video games, and even T-shirts present sexual images and messages in direct opposition to

mutual regard and respect between genders. [...] Images of sexuality in music, films, video games, and even cartoons are often nothing short of pornographic. Women are depicted as willing partners in their own mutilation and sexual invasion. [...]. Women's 'no' means 'try again,' and their protests of displeasure are interpreted as feminine wiles designed to encourage males to display more aggressive behavior" (9). In her article, Chamberlain provides this lengthy description in order to highlight the disjuncture between the official language of policy and actual cultural beliefs and practices.

5. See also Joan Williams' *Unbending Gender* (2000), Sharlene Nagy Hesse-Biber and Gregg Lee Carter's *Working Women in America: Split Dreams* (2005), Gornick and Meyers' *Families that Work: Policies for Reconciling Parenthood and Employment* (2003), Mason, Wolfinger, and Goulden's *Do Babies Matter? Gender and Family in the Ivory Tower* (2013), Hochschild and Machung's *The Second Shift. Working Families and the Revolution at Home* (2012 edition) and, Hochschild's *The Time Bind: When Work Becomes Home and Home Becomes Work* (2001) for examinations of perceptions of and realities for women and mothers in the workforce.

6. See Jennifer Siebel Newsom's documentary "Miss Representation" (2011) for an extremely elucidating, current view of the bombardment of damaging images of women in media.

REFERENCES

Aschwanden, Christie. 2014. Harassment in science, replicated. *The New York Times*, 11 Nov 2014. Accessed 14 Aug 2014. Web.

Boraas, Stephanie, and William M. Rodgers III. 2003. How does gender play a role in the earnings gap? An update. *Bureau of Labor Statistics Monthly Labor Review Online* 126(3): 9–15. http://www.bls.gov/opub/mlr/2003/03/art-2abs.htm. Accessed 26 Sept 2011. Web.

Coontz, Stephanie. 2011. *A strange stirring. The feminine mystique and American women at the dawn of the 1960s*. New York: Basic. Print.

Friedan, Betty. 1983. *The feminine mystique*. New York: Dell/Laurel. Print.

Gornick, Janet C., and Marcia K. Meyers. 2003. *Families that work: Policies for reconciling parenthood and employment*. New York: Russell Sage. Print.

Hesse-Biber, Sharlene Nagy, and Gregg Lee Carter. 2005. *Working women in America: Split dreams*. Oxford: Oxford University Press. Print.

Hirshman, Linda R. 2006. *Get to work. A manifesto for women of the world*. New York: Penguin/Viking. Print.

Hochschild, Arlie Russell, and Anne Machung. 2012. *The second shift. Working families and the revolution at home*. New York: Penguin. Print.

Mason, Mary Ann, Nicholas H. Wolfinger, and Marc Goulden. 2013. *Do babies matter? Gender and family in the ivory tower.* New Brunswick, NJ: Rutgers University Press. Print.

Siebel Newsom, Jennifer. 2011. *Miss representation.* Roco Films, DVD.

Williams, Joan C. 2000. *Unbending gender. Why family and work conflict and what to do about it.* Oxford: Oxford University Press. Print.

CHAPTER 5

Institutional Language(s) and the Enactment of Language

Several years ago, I was on my way to work, driving behind a university recycling truck. I saw the sign on the back, "{Our University} Recycles," and thought about the fact that certain academic disciplines are accustomed to the "Earth First" motto. This is a noble motivation and an effective motto. I work in the Humanities—I'm a humanist. It occurred to me on that day that my truck's motto would be "Humans First," which would align nicely with the work I do in language, culture, and literature and the personal commitment I have to respect in the workplace. In a sense, "Humans First" is a not-so-catchy way to think about tempered radicalism, which asks of laborers that they work on behalf of themselves and the institution in a steady, respectful way to make necessary change. My considerations about respect for humanity drive my work and my interactions, and my work feels less ethical, less authentic, if I am not zealous about having it take place in an environment that is welcoming to all and able to absorb a variety of perspectives. This sounds pretty non-threatening, right? Nevertheless, managers and administrators in many organizations fear deviation from the status quo to such a degree that they are less able to absorb new ideas or embrace the ideas of individuals who seem to promote change in an overly accelerated fashion. In my world view, humans matter, and our modes of communication need to express that.[1]

Language allows us to understand or misunderstand each other. Suzanne Romaine says, "The world is not simply the way it is, but what we make of it through language" (20). Language is the variety of discourses

© The Editor(s) (if applicable) and The Author(s) 2016   67
E. Mayock, *Gender Shrapnel in the Academic Workplace*,
DOI 10.1057/978-1-137-50830-0_5

in which we engage in order to interact with one another and with the work itself. It can be the reinforcement of the status quo or the suggestion of revolution. In the workplace, revolution, or just slow change, tends to be far less popular than maintaining the status quo. I often tell a colleague of mine that I wish we would suffer negative evaluations for *not* challenging the status quo.

In *Organizing Silence. A World of Possibilities*, Robin Patric Clair states that three types of discourse "may contribute substantially to the bureaucratization, commodification, and privatization of sexual harassment" (106). The first "Taken-for-Granted Discourse" tacitly defines the culture of the workplace by making consistent assumptions about stereotypes and authority. "Strategic Ambiguity" is the second type of discourse, and it allows individuals and groups in the workplace to send messages that conveniently can be interpreted positively (or at least not negatively) by different groups. With strategic ambiguity, Clair raises a significant question: "Does management use strategic ambiguity in sexual harassment policies, procedures, and brochures to preserve the existing power structure?" (108). The third type of discourse is "Exclusionary Discourse," through which minimization and trivialization help to "frame the issue in a limiting way by excluding pertinent information" (108). These three types of organizational discourse are embedded in the examples that follow.

In this chapter, I highlight the pervasive use of sexist language in formal workplace settings by examining recent linguistic theories on "communities of practice" and then providing seven examples of gender shrapnel in speech.

Lia Litosseliti reminds us that current linguistic theory stresses the analysis of multiple discourses, an analysis that takes into account the gender, race, class, status, and so on, of the speakers and the variability of "status" according to social context (47–58). This supplants older theory that focused on differences between men's and women's discourses and neglected to take into account the other important sociolinguistic factors mentioned above. Lia Litosseliti's *Gender & Language. Theory and Practice* examines our tendency to default to the question of gender, rather than to examine issues of context (often called "communities of practice") and status in the workplace. Most contemporary linguists have examined data which demonstrate that men and women are far more similar in their linguistic practices and behaviors than they are different (e.g. Cameron, Chapter 3) and that most human beings can work from a "wide-verbal-repertoire style" (Holmes cited in Litosseliti, 129). In addition,

Holmes and Marra introduce and employ the term "relational practice," defined as "behaviour oriented to the 'face needs' of others and aimed at mutual empowerment, self-achievement, solidarity in teams, consensus and good working relationships" (cited in Litosseliti, 131). In their research, Holmes and Marra found more examples of men using relational practice than women, even though the practice itself "is regarded as 'dispensable, irrelevant and peripheral,' but which 'serves to advance the primary objectives of the workplace" (cited in Litosseliti, 131). They conclude that relational practice becomes perceived as women's work, even if men are engaging in it. Depending on the context (the "community of practice"), this "feminine work" is either highly valued or stripped of its importance (132). Deborah Cameron's work reiterates that men and women share many discourses, but that the ones *perceived* as "feminine" tend to be valued less in the workplace. It is important to note, too, that data show more differences among women and among men than between the two groups (Cameron, Chapter 3).

John Gray's pop-culture work titled *Men Are from Mars, Women Are from Venus* made quite a splash in the USA in the early 1990s. Many people seemed reassured to be told that men and women really are different in the ways they speak and interact, that the differences are explainable, and that there are effective strategies to overcome the gender communication gap. When I read the work, I was amazed to find the lack of examination of the specific circumstances of specific men and women and the facile separate spheres sexism that was established and reinforced in the work. I remember, in particular, being horrified at being told that, when "my" man went into his "cave" to work out in his own way his hurt feelings, I should not bother with him and should keep myself busy with other things, for example, with shopping! The possessive adjective used with "man" did not speak at all to the type of relationships that I had had or was having, the interactional dynamic assumed between man and woman were not at all like the ones in my own relationship at the time, and I have never needed a prescription about what to do with leisure time. Nevertheless, this book somehow made its way into our culture's collective "wisdom" about men's and women's interactions. It was not until 2007 that renowned linguist Deborah Cameron deconstructed the popular culture obsession with Gray's *Men Are from Mars, Women Are from Venus*. Gray's "self-help guide" has remained in the popular imagination for over two decades, a dynamic time of pronounced change in the workplace.

At a meeting for university supervisors at an institution, the session leaders were providing training on the Policy on Prohibited Discrimination,
Harassment, and Retaliation. After apologizing for a few minutes for taking the supervisors' valuable time for this type of training session, the leaders began to talk about what constitutes sexual harassment. (In Chapter 6,
I will return to this example in the explicit treatment of the theme of
sexual harassment and discrimination in the workplace.) For the purposes
of this chapter, I wish to focus only on the fact that both session trainers resorted to the text *Men Are from Mars, Women Are from Venus* to
justify the existence of sexual harassment in the workplace. They did so
in a casual, we-all-know-this-to-be-true manner that seemed to be uni-
versally accepted by the individuals in attendance (at the very least, there
were more than a few attentive nods at this attempt at a justification).
I remain extremely worried that institutions are not only undoing any
previous good training or learning that has taken place in the realm of
fair workplace practices, but that they are actually reinforcing old-time
gendered-sphere notions *as they present themselves as the experts on prohibited harassment and retaliation based on the protected categories.* Who is
training the trainers? How are they deciding what language to use, both
on-script and off?[2]

In many organizations, the default mode is still man=universal and
woman=other. This dynamic manifests itself in a consistent linguistic pattern. Here I provide several examples so that readers can "hear" sexism
in language, keeping in mind Litosseliti's statement about "discourses of
femininity": "Discourses of femininity appear natural but in reality they
serve to maintain the status quo and 'emphasize meanings and values
which assume the superiority of males' (Coates, 1997: 292)" (132).[3]

Example 1: An executive at one institution once asked a professor to
"get her women's group together for a meeting." She heard the direc-
tive and wondered which group he would choose if asked to "get his
men's group together for a meeting." Would he even recognize that
nearly all of his authority-endowed groups were comprised predominantly of men? Leaving sarcasm behind, she then sincerely wondered,
"Which women's group?" She was core faculty in Women's and Gender
Studies and belonged to the Program Advisory and a group of women
faculty. And those were just the formal "women's groups" for which she
was working. The executive's implication was that there must only be
one "women's group" on campus because all women have the same set
of concerns. This casts women as "other" and as monolithic "other,"

that is, as one group of women with one professional woman indistinguishable from the next. This denies the very real intersectional concerns for many women in the workplace.

Example 2: As recounted in Chapter 3, a faculty member participated on a search committee for a large department comprised of all men and one woman. She was asked to serve on the committee for her expertise in area studies. Nevertheless, it became clear that the department members understood her placement on the committee (and on the three-person interview team) to be a purposeful move to "force the hiring of a woman on the department." In a meeting in which they deliberated over the candidates who had visited campus, one member of the department expressed preference for one of the candidates "who looked like the wonderful gentlemen who had been [his] professors when he was in graduate school." This statement was simply considered status quo—remember, default or universal = male. No one in the room blinked an eye, while the professor blinked both. To describe this type of occurrence, Litosseliti uses Riley's term "political nothingness," "where not taking any action at all is seen as the norm. Gendered differences that exist are buried by the production of alleged symmetry between women and men which obscures gendered differences in both experiences and expectations" (135). In other words, everyone in the room was supposed to be able to sympathize with the desire to hire men who look like the men who taught some of us decades ago. This is comfortable, familiar, easy territory for many.

When the professor participating on the search delineated the advantages and disadvantages of each candidate and used affirmative action language ("all other things being equal, choose diversity") to highlight her preference, another senior member of the department yelled across the table, "Why don't I come over there to your French department to make you hire more men?" Her mental response was, "Why do you assume I teach French? I don't. I am here because of expertise in another area. And, why do you assume there are more women than men in French? The opposite is true." This was a case in which a senior administrator, present at the meeting, could have made a public stand to point to the inappropriate nature of the exchange. Admittedly, in a patriarchal environment, taking a stand against patriarchal language is difficult. The academic workplace is very much in need of strong, committed administrators who consistently model appropriate communication and who point to inappropriate language in the formal work setting. In this case, language meant everything, and the masculinist dynamic carried the day.

This was the same group which, at a different meeting, thanked the professor for bringing the cookies that sat in the middle of the table. She hadn't brought cookies but was the only woman at the meeting. When she let them know that she hadn't brought the cookies, the response was, "Oh, well, you were the only maternal presence here." The committee seemed to decide that her presence on the committee was (1) to push a female hire and (2) to be a mommy to the group. Neither could have been further from the professor's actual desires. When she pointed out that she hadn't been "nurturing" or a "maternal presence" by bringing cookies to everyone, she probably lost points because she did not fulfill the role they perceived as appropriate and "natural" for her. This was certainly a lose–lose situation. The professor lost by having no credibility within this group for her expertise on Latin America, and she lost because she didn't bring the damned cookies. Had she brought cookies, however, she would have lost again, because she would have been perceived only as the nurturing presence. Instead, somehow, she just became a shrewish French professor.

Example 3: After a long and complicated conversation with two institutional leaders, one said to me, "It must be difficult to serve in your position and to be a mother with young ones at home." He then asked if he could hug me. These words and this action essentially erased the professional nature of the conversation which preceded them. It was clear that my co-workers could not separate my home role from my work role, although they did not appear to engage in such slippery crossover with male colleagues in similar positions. As a woman, and especially as a mother, I was in the wrong place. I was supposed to be at home, or at least back in my home department with many of the other women workers. And the hug represented the benevolent sexism inherent in the interaction. In Chapter 6, I will discuss the differences between quid pro quo and hostile work environment harassment to underscore how the former has become more clearly prohibited and the latter, connected in many ways to benevolent sexism, is more indulged in the academic workplace.

Example 4: A female administrator had an initial meeting with a new supervisor and another male colleague. This meeting took place several months before the supervisor was to begin his post officially. The meeting was scheduled for one hour but started 20 minutes late. The group of three then had 40 minutes to cover the agenda. They spent 40 minutes in which two of the colleagues did the apparently requisite "pedigree networking" (I see you got your PhD where I did. Do you know X and Y and Z? Did you used to go to such and such restaurant? etc.) and generalizing about life at a former institution and life in the new town. At the 40-minute mark, the female administrator had not yet spoken but needed to go to another meeting. She left a packet of materials so that her colleagues could familiarize themselves with the work that she was doing in the office.

The type of language that was used in this example is the discourse of networking. The two men in the conversation got to know each other through commonalities in their pedigrees and lifestyles. This could be fine and normal, if limited to the first two to three minutes of the meeting. For those outside of the "network" (usually members of the so-called "protected categories," those who are neither White nor male), the best way to create a group dynamic in the workplace is through the actual work. The extensive discourse of networking that took place at that meeting crowded out the discourse of work, and thereby crowded out the person from the underrepresented group. Essentially, their forgetting to include the woman, which was purely accidental, effectively excluded her. She was hit by shrapnel without anyone in the room even knowing that anyone was armed. It is difficult for people to realize that they must avoid accidents, rather than just avoiding purposeful misdeeds. This goes rather simply to something my mother always used to say. When we would get in trouble and say, "But I didn't try to," my mother would respond, "Did you try *not* to?" This one simple question is hard to ask and hard to accomplish, but it is the one that will lead to increased equity in the workplace.

Example 5: An outgoing male administrator gives advice to his incoming female replacement. He assures her that one of the keys to her success will be high visibility—that, in fact, she needs to make sure to be seen and heard at all faculty meetings. The incoming administrator is loath to speak publicly if she has nothing new to say and seeks other media through which to share routine announcements. This example highlights the "widely cited features of 'feminine' and 'masculine' interactional style," (Litosseliti 128), that is, that men are direct, aggressive, and competitive and that they dominate talking, while women are indirect, conciliatory, facilitative, collaborative, and talk less than men. Even if the female leader had followed the advice of her male colleague, her style might have been less well received because it might have seemed "masculine" and out of place for her. In this instance, the outgoing administrator viewed visibility as a significant means of climbing the career ladder, a view that influenced his self-esteem in the workplace. Buzzanell and Lucas look at these different approaches in the following way: "In this divide between winners and losers, workers engage in personal branding in which self-promotion strategies are turned into 'an ideological understanding of the corporate world capable of an embracing influence over workers' very sense of self' (Lair, Sullivan, & Cheney, 2005, p. 309)" (164). This means of advancing in the workplace was not available to the incoming administrator.

Example 6: A female administrative assistant is experiencing problems in her marriage. Her location in the middle of the office makes it difficult for her to have private conversations related to these problems, so the two male administrators in the office and one female administrator are somewhat aware of what is going on. At one point, the administrative assistant receives flowers at work from her husband. The male administrators seem keenly interested in knowing why the husband has sent flowers. The response is "because he's in the doghouse." This causes great amusement among the male administrators and female administrative assistant, but some consternation for the female administrator. The "doghouse" metaphor retrenches the gendered notions that "boys will be boys" and that "girls will be distracted by bad behavior with bright, pretty flowers." This gendered discourse from the home environment enters the workplace and reinforces the dynamics of male superiority and female abnegation in language and action.

Example 7: Rather than focusing on examples of individual, oral language used in the workplace, this example emphasizes written language that represents an institution in a more formally rhetorical manner. Chamberlain astutely comments on the gap between the law and our educational practices:

> In fact, relying on legal remedies alone, with their embedded presuppositions, may prevent us from getting to effective educational strategies. As we examine the presuppositions that characterize a legally correct policy, it becomes obvious that three significant elements are missing or not addressed: (1) the context in which behavior occurs, (2) the cultural influences that support and mask sexual harassment, and (3) the need for informed reflection by students and adults regarding current practices and the perhaps unintentional damage created by the latter. (7)

I share here my institution's preamble to its pre-"Dear Colleague" (2011) policy on prohibited discrimination, harassment, and retaliation and will then do a close reading of it to signal instances of the default patriarchy mode.[4]

> {This} University is a community based on trust and on respect for others. The quality of its life, academic and social, is shaped by the guiding principle of civility, and every member of the community is entitled to expect civil

behavior from all other members. Students, faculty and staff have the right to be free from prohibited discrimination, harassment, and retaliation within the University community. Specifically, the University prohibits discrimination, including harassment, on the basis of race, color, religion, national or ethnic origin, sex, sexual orientation, age, disability, or veteran's status in its educational programs and activities and with regard to employment. The University also prohibits retaliation against any individual who files a good faith complaint or is involved in a complaint process under this policy. Such conduct violates not only University policy, but may also violate state and federal law.

The preamble clearly contains official language that appropriately replicates that of Title VII. Nevertheless, the legal language is belied by the monolithic word "community." This word is certainly not negative in and of itself, but it does imply a monolith, a group of individuals bonded together by core institutional values. For those who, through day-to-day language, feel cast as "other," the one-body, one-mind approach to institutional policy might seem overly simple or maybe even downright false and inauthentic. Trust and respect are certainly excellent core values to list and to which to aspire. These are key words to use and to emphasize, as long as they are not cheapened by a false sense of unity.

The second sentence of the policy, the one that I would argue tries to make the greatest impact, underscores the importance of civility. The policy emphasizes explicitly that civility is at the center of all we do. Nevertheless, at an institution with a 260-plus-year-old honor system, civility has other historical and theoretical implications. When we use the words "civil" and "civility" on campus, we are hearkening back to a gentleman's code of honor—to a code that clarifies how men treat men in public, rather than how a heterogeneous group works together in both small and large settings. Honor sends traditional messages about men's ability to gain title, prestige, nobility, wealth, and goods and women's ability to lose chastity, purity, or "wholeness." For women who exist within a system of honor, then, "civility" is a behavioral code that discourages confrontation and movement toward change. For some women and men, such a code serves only to silence. The institution has removed the insistent repetition of the word "honor" in its formal policies, and this is a step in the right direction. Now it is time to consider how honor and civility are linked and why the repetition of and emphasis on the word "civility" does not encourage the full-bodied voices that should be emerging in a more pluralistic work community.

It is time to start talking about a "discourse of inclusion" so that individuals who enjoy privilege in the workplace will refrain from "dominant," "privileged" modes of conversation that focus on primarily White, male, monied territories. I come from a background that makes me comfortable navigating some traditionally male topics. Nevertheless, I have found myself avoiding such conversations (or feeling mildly embarrassed that I'm having them) when I know them to shut others out of conversations that are supposed to be focused on the work at hand.

Language, talk, conversation, meetings, rhetoric, discourse, text—these communication modes are all a part of the work we do, the actions we take, the decisions we make, and the ways in which we manage the work environment. When we start to understand language *as* action, then we can begin to understand its impact on human-friendly workplaces, personnel management, equity, and opportunities for improvement and optimism.

NOTES

1. The author thanks Editorial Fundamentos (Madrid) for permission to reprint in this chapter parts of a previously published article: "Gender Shrapnel and Institutional Language in the Academic Workplace." *Estudios de Mujeres. Volumen VII. Diferencia, (des)igualdad y justicia.* Eds. Antón Pachecho Bravo, Ana, Isabel Durán Giménez-Rico, Carmen Méndez García, Joanne Neff Van Aertselaer, and Ana Laura Rodríguez Redondo. Madrid: Fundamentos, 2010. 149–159.

2. Cronin and Fine speak to this point: "A further spurious premise of most diversity training is that male and female traits are inborn and static. The truth is that most of the characteristics labeled 'masculine' and 'feminine' are transient cultural concepts, as seen through the prism of the diversity trainer's personal perspective" (58).

3. Just recently I visited an intermediate Spanish class in which students were practicing vocabulary of the professions. Each time they responded with the feminine form of the profession, the instructor corrected them and supplied the masculine form. When the students gave the masculine form, no correction was offered. This is a small instance of reinforcement of power patterns in our speech, especially at a moment at which students could be learning more equitable use of language through their second-language acquisition experiences.

4. See http://www2.ed.gov/about/offices/list/ocr/letters/colleague-201104.html for the 2011 Office for Civil Rights "Dear Colleague" letter.

REFERENCE

Office for Civil Rights, U.S. Government Department of Education. 2011. "Dear Colleague" Letter. http://www2.ed.gov/about/offices/list/ocr/letters/colleague-201104.html. Accessed 4 Jan 2015. Web.

CHAPTER 6

The Cycle of Harassment in the Workplace

In this chapter, I aim to (1) distinguish between quid pro quo harassment and hostile work environment (HWE) harassment; (2) provide an overview of legal approaches to sexual harassment and delineate specific aspects of harassment and related workplace occurrences in the contexts of time, space, and identity; (3) examine cultural norms that help to sustain HWEs; (4) describe the notions of the "last straw" phenomenon and the "feminist fuse"; (5) discuss the concept of sexual harassment as a form of violence against women and explore the links between the cycle of harassment in the workplace and that of domestic violence; (6) briefly mention legal issues surrounding retaliation; and (7) consider the influence of compliance and progress, or lack thereof, on equity in the workplace.

Federal laws of the USA protect workers from sexual discrimination and harassment if they are members of one or more protected categories (age, disability, national origin, race, religion, sex, sexual orientation). Title VII, or the Civil Rights Act of 1964, prohibits employment discrimination based on race, color, religion, sex, or national origin. Title IX (1972) prohibits discrimination based on sex in a federally funded educational program or activity. In her 1979 field-changing work *Sexual Harassment of Working Women*, Catherine MacKinnon defines sexual harassment in the workplace in this way: "Sexual harassment, most broadly defined, refers to the unwanted imposition of sexual requirements in the context of a relationship of unequal power" (1).[1] In 1980, the EEOC further defined what constitutes sexual harassment, and, in 1986, the US Supreme Court,

© The Editor(s) (if applicable) and The Author(s) 2016
E. Mayock, *Gender Shrapnel in the Academic Workplace*,
DOI 10.1057/978-1-137-50830-0_6

through the *Meritor Savings Bank v. Vinson* decision, differentiated between quid pro quo sexual harassment (a supervisor's use of sexual demands in exchange for job security or perquisites) and HWE harassment, "which applies when the harassing behavior of anyone in the workplace—not only a boss or supervisor—causes the workplace to become hostile, intimidating, or offensive and unreasonably interferes with an employee's work" (Chamberlain 2–3).[2] Linda LeMoncheck cogently supports the protection of women under anti-discrimination law:

> I take the perspective that sexual harassment is a violation of sexual integrity, which violation is politicized by organizational hierarchies, gender expectations, and cultural stereotypes that inform sexually harassing conduct as a type of inequality. As such, women who are sexually harassed by men deserve special protection under antidiscrimination law that interprets sexual harassment as both a personal injury against individual women and a social injustice against women as a class. (165)

Despite increased social and legal attention to the problem of sexual harassment, "rates of victimization, at least in the United States and Canada, have remained remarkably stable" (Morgan 219). In 2001, harassment incidence was placed at 42%, with rates being significantly higher in male-dominated workplaces (Morgan 219).

Phoebe Morgan links an organization's culture to its potential to create a hostile climate: "Hostile climates are nurtured in any organization where values supporting gender inequality are legitimated and hostility against women is permitted. They thrive in workplaces and classrooms where masculinity is conflated with success and femininity is associated with failure (Messerschmidt, 1993) (211)." It is common for institutional training programs to define the two types of harassment but to provide examples or case studies that relate only to quid pro quo harassment. In the academic workplace, this situation urgently needs to be remedied, as HWE harassment is more common (Morgan 211), but far more difficult to detect, to deter, and to eliminate. Part III offers specific remedies to this point.

Buzzanell and Lucas base their examination of men's and women's careers on "discourses of time, space, and identity" (161). These three elements, as they relate to the workplace, are a useful starting point for an examination of the operation of harassment in the work environment. Time hinges on questions of tenure and seniority at an institution. Who has been in the organization longer? Who has sat in a more powerful position for more time? Who exercises authority? Who is most vulnerable due to junior and/or temporary and/or part-time status? What are the implications for harassment at different stages of an individual's career? How can we recognize the greater obstacles for individuals who are harassed based on both perceived sex and race? In the gender shrapnel sphere, much of this relates to the power dynamic involved in organizations. For example, the large majority of academic administrators are White males, and the greatest majority of female professors in the Academy are in the lowest ranks of the profession (see Valian, especially Chapter 11, for statistics). The mere fact of this time/power differential feeds into the gender shrapnel concept: If men in positions of power do not actively promote the creation of a workplace environment that is welcoming to all, women and members of underrepresented groups will be the first to notice the damaging consequences. In Chapter 2, I examined the analogy of the female worker's career stages to pre-adolescence, adolescence, and "maturity." On the career-time continuum, as women log more time in their organizations, they are effectively working themselves into a less powerful, more silent realm, even if they are actively acceding to power.

Much has been written in current literature in organizational management about the 24/7 workplace and the question of "face time." Of course, these issues can encourage flexibility for the worker labeled "different," but they can also pose significant problems. When I was selected to fill an administrative post, an older colleague who had served in the role a long time before gave me some advice. He said, "Your best bet is to stay past 5:00 or 5:30 every day. Things start to quiet down by then, and that's when you can get some real work done." I really like and respect the colleague who gave me this advice, but the advice was not at all possible in my own situation. I was a mother of one and expecting a second, and my partner worked full-time. The latest I could pick up my child was 5:00, and that was after an already very long day. My getting "real work done" would have to wait until after my son was in bed. Therefore, a worker who enjoys less privilege (no wife at home to take care of everything) might have to spend much more time on work in the home and on dependent care—and might have to do so at "key" moments in the workday or workweek. This limits the amount of "face time" available and can thereby also limit the ways in which the laborer is viewed as suitable for promotion.

In higher education, much of our work is flexibly scheduled, but all of it is never-ending. This point is an important one to consider in terms of women, availability, ambition, and advancement. For example, when I worked as an administrator, I was usually the first to arrive in the office, but others did not really notice. Nevertheless, when I had to leave by 5:00 p.m., I was losing out on what I soon realized was the valuable collective decompression at the end of the day. I was always back to work for three to four more hours at night, but electronic face time is not the same. These issues that are part of the professional mystique need to be considered more carefully as we look at women, ambition, and the glass ceiling. More importantly, in terms of the question of harassment, workers who cannot meet or choose not to meet the ever-growing demands of "face time" in the workplace need not be singled out as "different."

Harassment based on sex and/or gender works through space as well as time. For example, academic institutions are bound by physical realities that symbolize centuries of hallowed traditions, traditions that are steeped in White, male privilege. White columns, military façades, on-campus places of worship—these all become symbols of the college or university and usually speak to a long tradition of masculine values. I remember attending my institution's academic honors ceremony in the on-campus place of worship. While it was certainly the case that male and female students were honored, it was also symbolically and spatially "real" that two male administrators spoke to introduce the male guest speaker and that women students clad in black Robert Palmer dresses (think MTV in the 1980s) silently performed the "tapping-in" rites. The symbolism of place and gender sent strong messages about who was endowed with voice and who was viewed only as body. Very much to his credit, an administrator at our institution once asked me my impression of our formal ceremonies and, after hearing my view, started to incorporate more women speakers, to ask women faculty members to complete introductions, and to encourage more women students to take on leadership positions in the honorary societies. He worked on three fronts to make positive change and was successful.

Many feminist theorists (e.g. Abra Fortune Chernik) underscore how men are encouraged to occupy space in grand ways and how women are encouraged to occupy as little space as possible. This phenomenon relates to questions of actual physical form (e.g. anorexia), movement (e.g. passivity), and voice (e.g. volume and/or silence) and to more complex issues of power, domination, and abuse. A work space that is intimidating to the more vulnerable is one that is as fully occupied as possible by the supervisor. Examples of this range from actual office layouts in which women workers have less space to do their jobs, to assumptions about privacy, to physical artifacts that define the workplace, such as sexist posters and magazines. The semiotics of space influences how laborers feel valued or devalued in that space. I would argue that such items as sexist magazines or posters suggest strongly that quid pro quo harassment is perfectly acceptable and that, on the other hand, the domination of space of the male supervisor (e.g. free entrance into all office spaces, free access to all employees' computer screens) suggests strongly the acceptability of HWE harassment. Most workers recognize the first scenario, and far fewer are hip to the latter.

An additional space consideration is the location of meetings and the seating arrangement for meetings. Meetings are often scheduled to accommodate the person highest in the hierarchy. This is understandable, but consideration should be given to rotating meeting locations to respect all employees' busy work schedules. Some meetings, too, are arranged so that a core group can sit centrally to talk and do business and a more marginal group sits on the periphery to watch and remain silent. For example, in the last decade, my institution's Board of Trustees has welcomed elected faculty representatives to be present at each of the three Board meetings held per year. As an administrator, I had attended several board meetings and was all too familiar with how each of the meeting rooms was set up to foreground the participation of the Board members and to make non-Board members a kind of an audience. Even in meetings in which the Board members were seeking to have a broad, open discussion about hot-button issues, the room was set up in this theater/audience manner. A colleague of mine calls the non-speaker/non-participants at these meetings "the potted plants," a term that still makes me laugh to this day. Given the composition of the Board of Trustees (primarily White, well-off, middle-aged, and older), this room set-up fired implicit gender shrapnel, with the men front and center and the "others" populating the walls.

When I was an administrator, I made no waves about this because I didn't believe it was my place to do so. In fact, my input was never sought at those meetings, so I could not presume that I was there in a "talking capacity." Nevertheless, when I was elected three years later as a faculty representative to the Board, I decided that I had been elected because my colleagues judged that I would listen well and also provide insight when it was warranted. When I went to my first Board meeting as a faculty representative, I first checked to make sure that there were enough seats in the main section for everyone, and then I grabbed one, too. This put me in the midst of the discussion, allowed me to be a more dynamic listener, and allowed me to participate more easily at key moments. It was soon the case that the other faculty reps were taking these prime seats *and* participating more and better. I strongly believe that everyone around the table sees the conversations as both more varied and more productive when everyone in the room is a participant (or at least a potential participant). Divided set-ups, which are much more common than you might think, should be either avoided or explained to all present beforehand.

Universities should also examine the possibility of inequities in the space devoted to the accomplishments of their employees. Are men's accomplishments more visible, more publicized, more generally celebrated than women's? If so, institutions need to decide how this issue can be consistently and fairly addressed.

Identity is a third key element regarding harassment in the academic workplace. Communication theorists Buzzanell and Lucas state that "scholars try both to expose the ways in which career systematically excludes anyone who does not fit the profile of the ideal entrepreneurial worker and to create a vision for workplace change" (165).[3] The emphasis on the politics of exclusion and the limited profile for the "ideal" worker echo much of what has been written on "mobbing," the phenomenon by which the person or people in the workplace who are publicly identified as "different" are subjected to a group bullying dynamic that causes long-term negative effects both for the target and for the work environment itself.[4] In the mobbing paradigm, a worker can be labeled "different" because she or he approaches the job in an ostensibly different manner than those around her or him, because she or he is more accomplished, and/or because she or he belongs to one or more of the categories protected under discrimination law. Mobbing allows and encourages a bullying dynamic in the workplace. This dynamic, if it goes unrecognized and uncorrected, becomes part of the sustained workplace environment, part of the status quo.

Harassment in the workplace occurs when an individual or group makes unreasonable demands that have a disturbing, threatening, nonproductive effect on the individual receiving the abuse. Mobbing is intimately connected to harassment in that an individual's ability to get work done is impeded by the work environment. Both concepts are connected to discrimination in that the person labeled "different" is usually a person who the majority do not expect to find in their midst, that is, a member of one or more underrepresented groups in the specific context of the specific workplace. In order for individuals labeled "different" to fit in and to be able to do well in unwelcoming environments, they often have to perform a specific identity—either one that is akin to the dominant norm or one that is "expected" of their protected category and therefore plays to the potential prejudices of colleagues.[5] Morgan appropriately points out that (1) "the term *sexual harassment* effectively summarizes a core experience associated with work or school" (212) and (2) that the term itself might be less useful for lesbians and women of Color, whose experiences with sexual harassment are based not only on gender, but also on sexual orientation and/or race (212). Audrey Murrell signals three areas in which work on sexual harassment of women of Color must distinguish itself from research about White women's experience of sexual harassment: frequency, labels (sexual racism or sexual discrimination that involves race), and the effects or consequences of sexual harassment for the victims (such as in career outcomes or psychological well-being) (53).

I have used legal language in this chapter in order to demonstrate where our nation stands in terms of legal remedies for sexual harassment in the workplace. It is essential to note, however, that legal remedies are not nearly sufficient for colleges and universities to tackle the problem of harassment and discrimination. Robin Lukes and Joann Bangs have emphasized this point in their excellent article on anti-discrimination law and microaggressions in academia. Chamberlain reinforces the need for education on this issue, in addition to legal functions: "Many schools have taken the stance that sexual harassment is a legal issue, not an educational concern. [...] It has, in such a case, only been legally addressed; the students and staff have not been engaged in any process of critical thinking that would support their ability to make the sort of informed, reflective moral judgment that is key if we are to fully address sexual harassment" (15). Chamberlain's emphasis on education and critical thinking pushes institutions to think beyond the law and their own liability and toward cultural norms, practices, language, and behaviors.[6] Educational institutions must model appropriate behaviors if they want their students to understand and be a part of their mission.[7] My institution has done good work of late on the issues of sexual violence (the same kind of work colleges and universities have had to take on due to more stringent interpretations of Title IX), but it still often neglects to address cultural norms that encourage sexual discrimination and violence. The school has sponsored performers who sing insistently about the lack of value of women in general, college women as chattel, and college women as prime candidates for sexual assault. After requesting and being denied intervention on these issues from our university administration, I staged a public protest. Stemming from this situation and others, students, staff, and faculty started a Gender

Action Group (GAG), whose principal aims are to nip sexist actions and events in the bud and to maintain an online forum for discussion of local and national gender issues.[8]

Hosting such a blog, in its own small way, helps an institution to address cultural issues. At the same time, ironically, such a group that protests institutional inaction and lack of response to issues of sexual discrimination, harassment, and retaliation and of sexual violence also can contribute to the reduction of institutional risk. In "The other side of the compliance relationship," Gray and Sibley establish that most studies on compliance address only "the relationship between the firm and the state regulatory apparatus" (126). At many colleges and universities, then, the focus is on the Department of Education's and the EEOC's relationship to individuals in the upper administration. These government agencies and institutions of higher learning often forget to include "frontline workers" (term used by Gray and Sibley in their work) in conversations and actions surrounding compliance. In addition, Gray and Sibley state, "The ability of organizations to mask simple violations from inspectors, and the lack of enforcement of minor violations contributes, in many cases, to the persistence of hazards in the workplace (Gray, 2002, 2006a)" (130). In this study and others (see Gray and Sibley, 130), the principal idea is that a lack of enforcement allows minor infractions in the workplace, which then communicates the message that these infractions are not actually against code or policy. I am convinced that this permissiveness surrounding "microinfractions" establishes and reinforces a culture of sexism (and other concomitant–isms) and foments a greater permissiveness around bigger infractions.

An organization that turns a blind eye to sexual harassment, discrimination, and retaliation is telling its female and male employees (and/or students) that the prevailing attitudes and behaviors are acceptable and repeatable, thus contributing constantly to a cycle of cultural affirmation of patriarchy. The "blind eye" phenomenon actually *foments* the belief in masculine superiority and the acceptance of harassment and discrimination based on gender. This is another element of gender shrapnel: While it appears that no single individual intends to ignore the problems of harassment, the institution consistently turns a blind eye and thereby creates more opportunities for the shrapnel to fly. Nan Stein eloquently warns of the dangers of the blind-eye phenomenon:

In schools, harassment often happens while many people watch. This public enactment of sexual harassment may have more damaging ramifications than harassment that happens in private because of the potential for public humiliation, the damage to one's reputation, the rumors targets must fear and combat, and the strategies that the targets implement in an effort to reduce or avoid the encounters. When sexual harassment occurs in public and is not condemned, it becomes, with time, part of the social norm. (231)

As seemingly simple as this concept is, we ignore it all the time. I would argue that the lack of public condemnation of sexual discrimination, harassment, and retaliation is the single most important factor in confronting these legal and cultural issues. Everyone sees the incidents. No one says anything. And then the harassed individual feels crazy and out of place if she addresses the incidents either publicly or privately.

Institutions that have and do not confront an environment of pervasive sexual harassment, who suffer from the "blind-eye phenomenon," cannot bridge gaps that often occur in work organizations—gaps between management and the labor force and gaps between and among individuals of different categories. The result is a lack of trust in the organization and a frustration with a work environment that is, at best, simply unwelcoming and, at worst, possibly hostile and abusive. Individuals *learn through the environment itself* that it is neither beneficial nor revolutionary to confront the issues of the negative environment. This is a *learned silence*, a phenomenon that will be addressed more fully in the next chapter.

In the end, those who have been harassed generally do not speak of or report specific harassing events, but the distress surrounding those events accumulates.[9] Of course, these events are now commonly and appropriately called "microaggressions" (coined by Chester Pierce and popularized more recently by Derald Wing Sue). Eventually, there is what I call the "last straw" moment, when a harassing incident occurs that the individual simply cannot abide. The individual, who has ignored, "let go," or repressed a series of harassing moments in the past, reacts and attempts to confront the "last straw" event. At that moment, the onlookers view the individual as overly sensitive, since they likely have been unaware of or not critically thinking about the environment and the incidents that have occurred in the past. The collision of the onlookers' view of "something minor" with the victim's knowledge of a whole heap of events exacerbates the feeling of alienation of the victim, the inability to confront the specific event and, especially, the overall, generalized patterns of harassing behavior(s). In addition, women can arrive at the "last straw" through a combination of others' harassing experiences and their own. In one institution, one woman experienced significant and highly public sexual harassment. The harassment came from male workers both above and below her in the hierarchy. Six months later, one of her female colleagues began to experience a period of harassment that was similar in scope and severity. The second woman had witnessed not only the lack of remedy for the public harassment but the entrenchment of the victimization of her colleague. When it was her turn, the accumulation of collective events—a serious contribution to the phenomenon of gender shrapnel—brought the "last straw" to bear perhaps sooner than it might have in other circumstances. This concept is a fundamental part of the individual and collective *cycle* of harassment that becomes entrenched in organizations that rely only on policy and rarely on practice.

The repression of feelings and confrontation surrounding harassment can create what I have dubbed the "feminist fuse," which plays into the stereotype that feminists have no sense of humor. While some in the workplace are unaware of the jokes, comments, exclusions, and impediments that define the environment for certain women, the women in question tire of the repetition and the abuse and can no longer have even the mildest of sense of humor in harassing contexts. In welcoming work environments, the fuse is lengthened and the sense of humor can be restored. At my workplace on several occasions, when I have been talking in a public place with a group of female colleagues, a male colleague has walked by and jokingly asked what we're plotting. This could be funny (maybe?) one time, but the joke and its repetition become quite tiresome. By the fourth or fifth time we hear the same joke, the same implication that women don't belong together in the workplace, it's just not very damned funny, and our response becomes less gracious.

In "Theoretical Explanations for Violence Against Women," Jana Jasinski enumerates varieties of behaviors that are considered elements of violence against women. These include emotional, sexual, and physical assault, murder, genital mutilation, stalking, sexual harassment, and prostitution (5). Given the ways in which sexual harassment is perpetuated in the workplace through general patriarchal structures, fear, and silencing, it is useful to consider it as part of a more publicized and theorized body of work on violence against women, as Phoebe Morgan has done in her book chapter titled "Sexual Harassment. Violence Against Women at

Work" (*Sourcebook on Violence Against Women*, Ch. 11) and as Cleveland and McNamara have done in "Understanding Sexual Harassment: Contributions from Research on Domestic Violence and Organizational Change." Morgan believes that sexual harassment continues to be a major element of violence against women (210) and notes that "sexual harassment is a form of woman control" (Morgan 211).

The general trend in sexual discrimination, harassment, and retaliation cases in the workplace is the following:

1. Men prevail in positions of power and privilege. Few women accede to those positions. Women prevail in subordinate positions. A patriarchal culture exists and is reinforced. Morgan states that women who are especially vulnerable to sexual harassment are women who depend on men for employment (214–15) and women (and men) who challenge male dominance (215–16).
2. Some women (and men) experience harassment (any kind from the lists provided previously).
3. Those who are harassed develop a sense of the culture and pattern of harassment and navigate this culture either by not reporting incidents of harassment or by reporting them. The former affirms the validity of the culture of harassment, while the latter exposes the complainant to further victimization (being considered disloyal to the institution, rejection from the environment through control of work flow, alienation, and possible need to abandon the specific work environment), which in legal terms is the institution's way of retaliating against the complainant. Workers begin to expect the "discrimination du jour" (the "microaggression"), and women are treated as if they are wearing the proverbial short skirt.
4. Those who report harassment are subject to loss (of job, promotion, personal dignity, trust, links to the workplace community), to distress (humiliation, anger, isolation, depression, physical ailments, feelings of dissatisfaction), and to trauma (creates a need for escape and avoidance, a fear of retaliation, lack of resources for redress in federal agencies and legal outlets) (Morgan 216–19).
5. Some laborers who have been harassed actually attempt to speed the cycle of harassment by making self-deprecating comments before habitual harassers can. This aligns with the cycle of domestic abuse commonly treated in the literature on violence against women.

6. The lack of prohibition of and remedies for sexual harassment reinforces harassment's existence and power in the workplace. The vicious cycle operates on both individual (employee–employee) and collective (corporate culture) levels.
7. In some organizations, great employee benefits tie the employee more closely to the work environment, thereby making it more difficult for a harassed employee to leave. In the academic workplace, benefits and the tenure system reinforce these ties that become ever more difficult to sever. This relates well to clinical work done by Nancy Johnston on webs of unhealthy relationships in her 2011 book titled *Disentangle*.
8. The cycle of harassment can be further complicated by the omnipresence of communications technology. Supervisors can repeatedly send harassing e-mail messages that interrupt the flow of the workday and further retrench the employee in the threatening dynamic of sexual harassment.

In an academic environment, it is especially important to examine cycles of harassment between and among students, staff, faculty, and administration. The incidents of sexual discrimination, harassment, and retaliation in all of these groups are linked to each other and very deeply to the culture of which they are a part. Clearly, to break the cycle of sexual harassment, especially of discriminatory hostile environment harassment, it is necessary to examine each step in the cycle and explore multiple remedies for each. Furthermore, scholars and administrators need to do more work to see sexual violence on a continuum with sexual discrimination, harassment, and retaliation. These are profoundly linked phenomena in that colleges and universities that are unable to address sexual discrimination, harassment, and retaliation appropriately are highly unlikely to be able to create climates, systems, and procedures to handle cases of sexual violence on campus.[10]

Employees and employers also need to be aware of the employee's protection from retaliation. When an employee files an internal complaint and/or an external complaint (e.g. with the EEOC), the employee should have the right to due process (which is a fraught concept; see last section of this chapter) without fear of retaliation. Employers can retaliate by direct dismissal, but most are much more astute than that these days, and so retaliation can take the more subtle form of issuing repeated derogatory comments, isolating the complainant, removing the complainant from the general flow of work, and ensuring that the complainant has no access to pay raises or promotion. The managerial strategy of "removing the thin-skinned plaintiff" is an unjust way to manage risk and a retaliatory response to internal and/or external complaints.[11] Lauren B. Edelman and Shauhin Talesh describe this experience: "Complaint managers typically chose to remedy employee grievances with managerial solutions such as training programs, transferring the grievant and providing counseling rather than formal recognition of legal rights violations" (108). A major limitation for the resolution of complaints of this type is employers' hesitation to admit wrongdoing and/or utter denial of wrongdoing.

The changing Title IX landscape, especially in the realm of sexual violence on college and university campuses, has become an extremely complicated compliance issue—more complicated, perhaps, than its appli-cations to athletics in the 1970s and 1980s, due to the cross-over issues with law enforcement. The US Department of Education (and specifically the EEOC and the Office of Civil Rights, OCR) and the Department of Justice since 2008 have participated much more actively than in the previ-ous decade in questions of equity and safety on college campuses. This fact has transformed the legal landscape, but, I would argue, has had less of an impact on the cultural landscape of our campuses. Many colleges and universities have hired Title IX officers (in a much more explicit way than in the past, when most Title IX coordinators served in that role primar-ily as an "add-on" to their main job) and have created Title IX offices.[12] Some colleges have employees of the Department of Education installed on campus to enforce compliance of Title IX law.

Discussions about Title IX, and especially about rape, sexual assault, and sexual violence, happen everywhere—in the major media outlets, among Boards of Trustees, and in dining halls and dormitories. Nevertheless, the question of employer liability still can promote an alliance among upper administrators that is all about protection and too often about conceal-ment. General counsel still moves heavily behind the scenes, and Title IX officers now simply take the heat that Title IX coordinators were taking before. Edelman and Talesh see a tension between the due process of a "liberal legal regime" (105), which allows workers to hold the powerful, accountable, and managerial discretion and authority, which are the domain of "business or managerial logic" (105). They add that, "Organizations struggle to find rational modes of response to legal complexity and ambi-guity and to devise strategies to preserve managerial discretion and author-ity while at the same time maximizing the appearance of compliance with legal principles (Edelman, 1990, 1992)" (106). Ultimately, Edelman and Talesh conclude that when institutions create "symbolic or ineffective structures and policies" (115), they often weaken or subvert legal ideals (115). I interpret all of this to suggest that institutions might be better off by admitting wrongdoing and rectifying the wrongs, rather than creating labyrinthine processes that often are ineffective and retrench the problems of gender shrapnel.

NOTES

1. See Crouch, Chapter 5, for a critique of MacKinnon's conceptualization of sexual harassment in the workplace.
2. Morgan provides a useful summary of EEOC and Office of Civil Rights (OCR) definitions of sexual harassment: "The EEOC defines sexual harassment as any form of uninvited sexual attention that either explicitly or implicitly becomes a condition of one's work (U.S. EEOC, 1999). Along the same lines, the OCR conceptualizes it as a form of unwanted sexual attention that becomes a condition of one's educational experience (U.S. Office of Civil Rights, 1999). The types of behaviors that fit EEOC and OCR definitions include but are not limited to unwanted talk about sex, jokes about sex or sexualized horseplay, uninvited physical contact, requests for sexual favors, pressures for dates or sex, sexual abuse, and sexual assault." (210). For additional information on application of Title VII and Title IX law to higher education, see Dziech and Hawkins' *Sexual Harassment in Higher Education. Reflections and New Perspectives*. For the text of the decision of *Meritor Savings Bank v. Vinson*, see *Applications of Feminist Legal Theory to Women's Lives. Sex, Violence, Work, and Reproduction* (740–748). For histories of sexual harassment law, see also Peirce, et al., and Crouch (Part 1).
3. Timothy Macklem theorizes about the perception of women as different and the resultant denial of human rights and opportunities: "What women are entitled to, and what a misconception of their character may deny them, is the opportunity to make a success of the projects of their lives. That opportunity is not one that is owed to women in particular, as a special entitlement born of their special condition, but one that is owed to all human beings yet finds its particular meaning in its application to particular human beings, in this case, women. The particular character of what women are owed is simply a consequence of the fact that human beings can develop and pursue the projects of their lives only on the basis of the particular qualities of character, distinctive and nondistinctive, that they happen to possess, and more important, that not only they but the societies in and through which those projects are pursued understand them to possess.

It follows that if a society misunderstands what it means to be a woman, either comprehensively or in some respect that is critical to the success of the project of a woman's life, as I have contended we now understand women, it thereby denies them the opportunity to which they are entitled as human beings" (192).

4. See *The New York Times*' 2008 "bullying questionnaire" for a useful way to audit the work environment through a series of pointed questions.

5. See Yoshino for a fuller examination of identity politics and performance in the workplace. See Chamallas for analysis of the "reasonable person" standard in sexual and racial discrimination and harassment law.

6. Additional recommended references include Sandler and Shoop's *Sexual Harassment on Campus: A Guide for Administrators, Faculty and Students* (1997), Paludi's *Sexual Harassment, Work and Education: A Resource Manual for Prevention* (1998), and Gruber and Morgan's *In the Company of Men. Male Dominance and Sexual Harassment* (2004). The "Know Your IX" website (http://knowyourix.org/) is a particularly useful resource for college students who want to understand Title IX in the context of sexual violence. See the US Department of Education website for abundant information for Title IX Coordinators (http://www2.ed.gov/policy/rights/guid/ocr/title-ix-coordinators.html). Finally, the Feminist Majority Foundation has created a very useful "Education Equity" website: http://feminist.org/education/FMFprogram.asp.

7. See Hill and Silva's *Drawing the Line. Sexual Harassment on Campus* (AAUW, 2005) for an extremely useful guide to how sexual harassment plays out specifically on college and university campuses and especially how it affects students.

8. See the Gender Action Group (GAG) website at http://gag.academic.wlu.edu.

9. Morgan cites loss, distress, and trauma as the primary areas of impact on women who have been harassed (216–19).

10. See *The Chronicle of Higher Education*'s "Reader's Guide," titled "In Context. Campus Sexual Assault" for a summary of articles published on this topic in the busy fall of 2014. The PDF is available to subscribers through a web request form.

11. See John Mahoney's website Workplace Fairness. It's Everybody's Job (http://www.workplacefairness.org/generalwhistleblowing) for more information on retaliation.

12. Edelman and Talesh state that, "Neo-institutional organization theory emphasizes the process through which common systems of meaning, values and norms develop among the community of organizations that make up an organizational field (Meyer and Rowan, 1977; DiMaggio and Powell, 1983; Powell and DiMaggio, 1991; Scott, 2002)" (104). In the

organizational context of colleges and universities, this means that college presidents and their leadership councils observe the legal landscape, analyze risk, follow what peer institutions are doing, and often follow suit. Higher education institutions therefore often respond to change by replicating what others do, which is often to circle wagons and respond to the most immediate risks. Edelman and Talesh also comment upon the tendency of organizations to create new offices to respond to federal regulations while at the same time attempting to maintain "unfettered discretion over employment decisions" (107).

REFERENCES

Gruber, James E., and Phoebe Morgan (eds.). 2004. *In the company of men. Male dominance and sexual harassment.* Boston, MA: Northeastern University Press. Print.
Hill, Catherine, and Elena Silva. 2005. *Drawing the line. Sexual harassment on campus.* Washington, DC: AAUW. Print.
Paludi, Michele A., and Richard B. Barickman. 1998. *Sexual harassment, work and education: A resource manual for prevention,* 2nd ed. Albany, NY: SUNY Press. Print.
Parker-Pope, Tara. 2008. Have you been bullied at work? *The New York Times,* 24 Mar 2008. Accessed 8 Feb 2012. Web.
Sandler, Bernice R., and Robert J. Shoop (eds.). 1997. *Sexual harassment on campus. A guide for administrators, faculty, and students.* New York: Allyn and Bacon. Print.

CHAPTER 7

On Emotion, Silence, and Shutting Up

Audre Lord says, "Primarily for us all, it is necessary to teach by living and speaking those truths which we believe and know beyond understanding. Because in this way alone we can survive, by taking part in a process of life that is creative and continuing, that is growth" (189). Lord clearly advocates for an expression of emotion and opinion as a mode of survival and growth, and these principles can and should be recognized and applied in the academic workplace.

Similarly, Verlyn Klinkenborg writes poignantly in *The Chronicle of Higher Education* of his invited visit to a small college at which he was to talk with students about approaches to writing. In several conversations about women and writing, Klinkenborg encouraged the young women students to be themselves, to be sure that what they think and write matters. His interlocutors responded fearfully, believing that assuming a position of importance or, quite literally, "authority" would make them too manly. Klinkenborg translated this anxiety as, "Won't the world punish us for being too sure of ourselves?" and concluded his piece by stating, "I realize how much has been lost because of the culture of polite, self-negating silence in which they [the students] were raised." As a professor in the humanities, I understand this lament. It is my job to get my students thinking, analyzing, talking, and writing. They can do none of these tasks well if they are afraid of their own intellect, afraid to express their own thoughts, or afraid to appear too "other." It is my job to encourage healthy silences—contemplative moments, spent alone or with others, that

© The Editor(s) (if applicable) and The Author(s) 2016
E. Mayock, *Gender Shrapnel in the Academic Workplace*,
DOI 10.1057/978-1-137-50830-0_7

lead to effective synthesis and more profound analysis. But it is also my job to move students and classes away from fearful silences. In fact, loosely translated, this is the overall mission of most colleges and universities—to provide the tools for students to share ideas, research, and products in an environment based upon respect. What Klinkenborg had found at that small Minnesota college were the seeds of women's silence in the professional realm, that is, the fear of being visibly and audibly smart, of being noticed, of being too "out there." The professional mystique for women starts early in the school system, where it finds an easy training ground for later silences and acceptance of gender shrapnel. I have seen this at my own institution, where there have been lengthy meetings in which people have expressed concern that the women students have suffered sexual assault, have manifested severe eating disorders, and have been extremely reticent to put themselves in the public light to run for office on campus. (While I link these issues together here, they are not always examined together at my institution.)

This chapter on silence follows the two on language and harassment specifically because language used in a harassing manner causes many different types of silence. Language is, of course, an intrinsic part of harassment. When harassment continues unchecked and/or worsens, institutions tend to silence processes and outcomes. The Jerry Sandusky/Joe Paterno case at Penn State illustrates all too well this phenomenon. In essence, this silence surrounding processes and outcomes "disappears" those who have complained of sexual harassment. Rudman, Borgida, and Robertson see concerns about procedural justice (e.g. fear of retaliation) and processes of gender socialization (e.g. the notion that women prioritize empathy and education, rather than confrontation and punishment) as the principal causes of women's unwillingness to report incidents of sexual harassment in the workplace (520–21). Susan C. Wooley sees these same processes at work in the Anita Hill–Clarence Thomas case. In "Anita Hill, Clarence Thomas, and the Enforcement of Female Silence," Wooley writes that, given our culture's propensity to show violence against women, the aggressive attacks on Anita Hill "seemed entirely routine," while, "in contrast, men and women came together in their will to avoid what almost no one has yet learned to endure: the sight of a man in emotional pain" (5). Wooley believes that there is a "reflexive instinct to protect men from uncomfortable feelings" (5). In the Hill case, gender socialization was operating on all sides, as "Ms. Hill was essentially charged with having victimized the nation with her utterances" (Wooley 7).[1] In addition, the case, as Kimberlé Crenshaw has analyzed with such nuance, forced spectators to start to see the overlap, the double-bind experiences of Black women: "The particularities of black female subordination are suppressed as the terms of racial and gender discrimination law require that we mold our experience into that of either white women or black men in order to be legally recognized" ("Whose Story" 827).

In the words of Krolokke and Sorensen, Anita Hill's voice was "rendered deviant" (156). "As in other forms of violence against women," writes Phoebe Morgan, "secrecy shrouds the face of sexual harassment victimization (Fitzgerald & Ormerod, 1991). Sexual harassment is practiced in public at many workplaces and inside classrooms. It is common; yet, talk of the experience is taboo. Women have been socialized to keep the details of their victimization private. Thus, the pain that sexual harassment brings often goes unnoticed, and the suffering of its victims is greatly underestimated" (212). Silencing the victimization causes suffering, and so does speaking of it. The only thing to be gained from speaking about being harassed is getting it off your chest, but there are certainly other forms of punishment for speaking out. I believe that individuals who speak out against sexual harassment and hostile work environments (and, especially, those who have survived sexual violence in these environments) are brave because they know they risk being completely ostracized in the workplace for having uttered the truth.

These two major concerns surrounding harassment in the workplace—procedural justice and gender socialization—are at the heart of the seven themes related to the overarching phenomenon of silence analyzed in this chapter: (1) "talk-as-action," (2) emotion (fear), (3) survival, (4) "professional rubbernecking," (5) "rhetorical anorexia" and the physical analogs of silence, (6) "professional ventriloquism," and (7) being Sisyphus—continuing to speak, despite the damage it can cause, so as not to be completely erased.

A healthy work environment makes room for all voices to the degree possible. Why hire people if you don't want to hear from them? When a person or a group of people no longer speaks, then we can assume that their voices are not heard, are not welcomed, or are actively silenced. Of course, silence is intimately linked to gender shrapnel in that we often don't know whence it came, we can't always place blame for it on one individual person or event, and we know it's not healthy for the individual or those surrounding her. It is no coincidence that much of the literature on sexual discrimination and harassment addresses the issue of silence.

In fact, many of the articles and books written on these themes contain the word "silence" in their titles (e.g. "the dome of silence," "breaking the silence," "suffering in silence," "enforcement of female silence").[2] Silence is the single most difficult topic to write on, precisely due to its negation of oral or written language, its inherent link to emotion, and its implications regarding power and control. The consistent use in this book of Friedan's term "mystique" is intimately associated with the concept of silence. The professional mystique is a phenomenon of unarticulated disillusionment in the workplace. The lack of articulation or description of the underlying causes of disillusionment (the gender shrapnel) is based on silence and foments silence. The idea of gender shrapnel itself has that "Ow, it got me" feel, but the questions left unanswered to date are "what got you?" and "where did it come from?" Shrapnel flies out of nowhere and does random, but expansive, damage.

In their poststructuralist discourse analysis, Krolokke and Sorensen cite feminist conversation analysts who study the concept of "talk-as-action" (158–59). "Talk-as-action" is increasingly important in the contemporary workplace, where "talk" is largely how the work gets done, whether it is oral talk—face-to-face conferences, meetings, dispensing of instructions—or written talk—memos, reports, e-mails, tweets. This means that the ways in which we talk *and don't talk* increasingly affect how we operate in the workplace and how efficiently the work gets done. Krolokke and Sorensen cite Judith Butler on this point, saying that it is she who elucidates the notion of "agency in speech" and how this agency is related to "performativity as a conceptualization of the constant tension between performances and the underlying conventions and the ways words and bodies are involved in both" (161). As discussed in Chapter 6, this "performativity" can, in a sense, be a mode of shutting up, as the employee who is an outlier at work performs her difference according to the expectations of those who surround her. In effect, she is shutting up her true self in order to please others' preconceived notions of who she is or should be.[3]

Silence is packed with emotion. Anger, frustration, fear, and amusement inhabit silence. Anne Kreamer, author of *It's Always Personal. Emotion in the New Workplace*, addresses the presence of emotion in the workplace and our attempts to deny its very presence. She examines specific cases in which a person's shouting, cursing, door-slamming, crying, joking, or laughing has influenced others' behaviors and feelings in the workplace. We all bring our own feelings surrounding our personal and professional experiences into the workplace, and we all interact daily with our co-workers' bundles of feelings. When a worker has been harassed or discriminated against, her or his choices are to seek legal recourse, respond firmly that this behavior cannot continue, or be quiet. In some cases, workers have attempted one, two, or all three of these responses. When the worker determines that silence is the only recourse, that silence is filled with fear—fear of losing the job, fear of public humiliation, fear of speaking out and being shut down, fear of loss of self-esteem, fear of slowing the work flow, fear of the silence itself—and then the workplace itself has hit rock bottom. I think we would all agree that we do not want our co-workers to feel this way, that we want, in fact, quite the opposite. Nevertheless, research out of Northwestern University's Kellogg School of Management reveals that "not only do women lose work-related status when they express anger but that men actually *gain* status. Data from our JWT Emotional Incidents in the Workplace Survey supports these findings: 42 percent of younger men believe that anger is an effective management tool" (Kreamer 55). At the same time, as Anne Kreamer states, citing research done at Drexel University, "On average, people in good moods solve 20 percent more word association puzzles than a control group given the same amount of time" (108). It is evident that happiness yields more production than anger, frustration, and fear, *but* anger is valued as a management tool by men in men, and men dominate the higher ranks of most professions. And so the cycle continues: Men can express anger and gain points; women who express anger lose status; underlings often must be silent about the anger expressed by their superiors or lose their jobs. These factors can easily contribute to a hostile work environment, which, as we know, is based on hierarchy and privilege. Those at the bottom must put up or shut up. Silence begets more silence and, quite possibly, less work productivity.

Individuals who have experienced sexual harassment and discrimination cope, or survive, by attempting to compartmentalize work experiences— separating the good from the bad and then attempting to avoid the bad— so that they can function in the hostile environment. In order to continue to work, they shut themselves up, which serves as a temporary coping mechanism that is not beneficial for either the victims or the institution itself. Silence ignores the underlying problems. Silence assures some that all is well, when precisely the opposite is the case. Silence avoids necessary confrontation and potential improvement. Silence is a fundamental piece of the gender shrapnel puzzle. Krolokke and Sorensen propose that silence is a dangerous two-way street:

> For instance, within a patriarchal framework, silence is a significant practice of submission and domination, respectively: When women fall silent, it is both a sign of their oppression and the creation of it, and when men fall silent, it is both a mark and form of domination. Thus, feminist conversation analysis reads communication as a gendered societal pattern, and within this pattern, women are more readily muted and men engage in muting. (159)

This double-edged sword of women's silence—that women's silence is both a sign of oppression and the *creation* of oppression—plays into why I have included the phrase "shutting up" in the title of this chapter. Gender shrapnel, effected through general gender discrimination and/or through specific sexual harassment, operates on the victim in such a way that she must endure the dominance of others' silence (manifested in any number of ways, such as actual lack of oral communication, shunning, mobbing, withholding of necessary documents, or just plain old *forgetting*) and at the same time seeks to protect herself by shutting up, by not inviting any attention, by making unwanted comments or behaviors go away through her own disappearance.[4] Spanish speakers use the verb "ningunear," which literally means "to nobody," or "to make a nobody out of a somebody." This powerful verb has crossed my mind many times as I have watched outspoken women be silenced and then disappeared. These "somebodies"—highly accomplished, effective people—became "nobodies," and sometimes the individuals themselves contribute to this process because it's just easier to disappear. In my estimation, this factor is the most disheartening for both the worker and the workplace. Shutting oneself up doesn't move the work along and does have a negative impact on the group of employees and on the individual.[5]

Colleagues often cast the quiet, silenced worker as sullen and unapproachable and then avoid that person, both personally and professionally. The silenced worker herself refrains from making key comments that could help advance the work. This worker ends up horizontally silenced—impeded from moving and speaking in the day-to-day activities of the workplace—and vertically silenced—unable to be heard by superiors and unable to advance. This silence becomes her way, ironically, both to survive and to wither in the workplace. I see this survival technique as strongly linked to Gondolf's "model of survivorship" (quoted in Jasinski, 8) and as an important alternative to the repeated use of the term "victim." Gender shrapnel in the workplace is akin to the realm of violent relationships in many ways. Jasinski writes that the model of survivorship "suggests that women are active survivors who try to escape violent relationships but are often limited by the unavailability of resources. In other words, women respond to abuse by attempting to seek help that does not exist. Rather than blaming the victim, this model places blame on the social structure that prevents access to needed resources" (8).

As the harassed worker becomes increasingly alienated in the work environment, many co-workers experience a desire to "rubberneck"—to witness the accident and to see the individual hit by shrapnel. We have all done it; each of us has passed an accident on the highway and turned our heads in horror at the violence of it, the bloodshed, and the injury. And we have each guiltily thought, "Thank goodness that's not me," and then, as we speed down the road, we dutifully add, "Oh, I hope that person's okay." This happens in the workplace as well. A female employee gets silenced at a meeting, or she is not consulted on the restructuring of her own office, or her name is left off a work product, or her idea is taken without attribution. Occasionally a co-worker will create more shrapnel by speaking out against the slight. More often, co-workers watch in horror as they speed through their days. They observe the slight (or the outright aggressively illegal action), make a mental note of it, and then move on. If they pay any more attention to the incident, they fear that they'll be the next, that the gender shrapnel might come their way. And then there is another group of co-workers who are so certain that gender shrapnel, as unfair as it may be, will never touch them. They're so certain of this that they don't *mind* talking to the victim. Talking to the victim demonstrates their compassion and their being above-it-all. It makes them feel better to think that they have made the victim feel better. Some members of this group even offer to speak for the victim, who they're sure is destined never to speak again. In offering to speak for the victim, the above-it-all co-workers further entrench the victim in her silence. In being certain that they will never be victims of gender shrapnel, they imply that there is blame to be placed, and that that blame must clearly be placed upon the victim. In other words, she asked for it; she brought the gender shrapnel upon herself; she wore the short skirt. Just as there is nothing positive about a highway accident, there is nothing positive about gender shrapnel. Gender shrapnel does take its victims and does create an unwitting dynamic in the workplace of haves and have-nots—those who have professional capital and those who do not.

The individual who has been hit by gender shrapnel attempts to go through her day—teaching, advising, writing e-mails, grading, preparing for class, conducting research, running meetings, meeting with students, clients, and patients—and she experiences repeated incidents of being silenced and of shutting up. In an uneven work environment, gender shrapnel is all around us. Those who have been hit by gender shrapnel and/or those who won't tolerate the spread of shrapnel among colleagues and students must pick and choose which events matter enough to address, which ones merit the attention of the community, which ones deserve the worker's further loss of professional capital. The opportunities to point out the inequities caused by gender shrapnel are few and far between. If you say too much, you'll be told that, "Not everything's about gender." I translate the innocent connotation of this as, "I don't get what you're saying and I can't see why it's important," and the more pernicious connotation as, "Nothin' we can do about it. You've gotta put up or shut up."

Each time we choose to "shut up"—and there are many good, self-preserving reasons to choose to (see Chapter 6)—we are silencing ourselves and indulging our environments in the practice of gender inequity. A certain rhetorical anorexia develops in which the person who has experienced gender shrapnel allows her voice to have less and less volume, to take up less and less space, to shrink in size and importance, almost to disappear. This concept of a woman's decision (or reaction) to occupy as little space as possible so as not to draw attention to herself and not to attract unwanted shrapnel is at the core of the identity questions raised by women's and gender studies. It is the result of gender socialization so firmly inculcated that many of us don't recognize physical or rhetorical anorexia when we see it. If the healthiest recovery for a person with anorexia involves the development of a higher degree of self-esteem and a regime of healthy eating and exercise, such is also the case for a person whose voice has shrunk. The person needs to gain enough confidence to speak often and to be heard well, understanding the repercussions of gender shrapnel and overcoming them.

Another workplace phenomenon related to silence and voice is what I call professional ventriloquism.[6] Even if a woman who has been hit once or repeatedly by gender shrapnel has the courage to continue speaking out at the same types of moments at which she would have before the shrapnel (the guideline I have always used—What Would the Pre-Shrapnel Ellen Have Done?), it often happens that she is simply not heard. The workers have been trained to rubberneck—to look but not to hear—and they're not going to be prepared to tune in again easily. Sometimes the person hit with gender shrapnel is simply not heard, no matter how many times she has made a suggestion and no matter the many different ways she has made the suggestion. At other times, nevertheless, a careful listener might catch that the victim of shrapnel is onto something, that her suggestion is an excellent one. These co-workers sometimes use the exact same words of the original suggestion, pitch the idea, and are heard. Instant heroes! I call this "professional ventriloquism," and this example is the kind in which the victim has not agreed to being ventriloquized or plagiarized.

It can also happen that the woman who has been hit by shrapnel uses professional ventriloquism strategically to get her point across somehow, with someone. When I had felt disappeared, I considered myself to be radioactive. I felt like my advocating for a person or an idea would surely sink that person or idea. At that time, a colleague of mine who I respect profoundly was up for promotion to full professor. What would the pre-shrapnel Ellen have done? She would have written a knowledgeable and appropriately glowing letter of recommendation for his file. So, that's what I did. And then I realized that my words of praise might not reflect well on my colleague *simply because they came from me*. I shared the letter with a colleague at another school, and she borrowed heavily from my letter to write her own. This was a clear case of professional ventriloquism—everything I had written in the letter was from years of observing the actions and accomplishments of my colleague. I had written from the heart and the mind. Nevertheless, my words appeared more easily accepted when written or uttered by someone else.[7]

In the end, the person hit with gender shrapnel must make many small, daily decisions. When to speak? When to shut up? When is a meeting important enough that you attend, despite the attendance of the individual who has harassed you? When do you write on behalf of a colleague because it's the right thing to do? When do you speak out about the institution's inertia surrounding gender socialization and rape among the undergraduate population? Once I felt strong enough to speak again, my decision was exactly what I've repeated here several times—just speak out (and write) at exactly the moments you would have before. Even if you're not heard, even if it brings on more gender shrapnel. Recovery from rhetorical anorexia is a victory, no matter the consequences.

I recall clearly the announcement that a high-level official had formed a search committee to hire a new administrator. The job description insisted that the administration was looking to hire from outside our institution. We employees understood clearly the message—that the administration did not want to count on an experienced insider for this important post, and, most probably, that he already had someone very much in mind for the hire. I viewed this as an effort to "silence the locals" and thought it particularly unfair that, at the moment when we had an internal female candidate who seemed very prepared for the position, the administration was choosing to ignore her deliberately. At that point, I wondered, why even have a search committee? Just hire your person, if she or he is qualified. Why drain hundreds of hours of labor if you're just going to ensure the outcome of the process before it has even begun? I also thought, well, if we're going to have a search committee, and we have a very strong internal candidate, I am going to nominate her. I am going to use the process fairly and see where we end up. I wrote a detailed letter of nomination and sent it to the search consultant. I then went to one of the open forums held by the search committee to get input from the university community. As I listened, I got the sense that no one from the search committee who was present at the forum had ever seen the nomination letter I had sent. I raised my hand, asked directly if they had seen it, and their shocked faces gave me the answer—no, they were not aware of an internal nomination.

I remember just feeling lost in the knowledge that institutions often do not follow through on any of their own processes, that every search, every decision, big and small, can be controlled from above in a twisted, unnecessary way. It made everything seem inauthentic. It made me feel like I was in a dictatorship, with a heavy-handed state propaganda machine in place and a whole lot of empty gestures. Nevertheless, I did not regret my decision to do the right thing and nominate the qualified candidate. At that point, I started to call myself Sisyphus. I kept pushing that gender shrapnel back up the hill, knowing that it and I would fall again, but knowing, too, via Camus, that Sisyphus is happy. I related Sisyphus' actions to my activism, his busy-ness to my own.

Feminist scholarship helps us to speak out on the subject of inequity and gender shrapnel. I took to writing short, non-fiction pieces to help me sort through what I was experiencing. This was when the term "gender shrapnel" occurred to me. Several years later, I began working in earnest on the *Gender Shrapnel* manuscript. I made the conscious decision to be up-front about working on feminist activist scholarship while also advancing my work in Hispanic Studies. In each year's official Faculty Activities Report, I listed *Gender Shrapnel* as one of my projects and reported on the progress I was making. In addition, a colleague from my department and I started to collaborate on a co-edited volume eventually to be named *Feminist Activism in Academia*, which was published in 2010. I don't know if the excellent support I have received for these projects from the university is motivated by the administrators' care against retaliation in order to manage risk or simply by their customary support of my research. I would love to think it's the latter, but gender shrapnel has taught me that it must be some strange combination of the two.

NOTES

1. Anita Hill has since become one of the leading legal scholars on sexual discrimination and harassment in the workplace. See her essay "Thomas versus Clinton" for a fascinating look at the state of the public discussion and the law in the early to mid-1990s. In addition, see the 2014 documentary *Anita. Speaking Truth to Power* for a more contemporary view of the Hill–Thomas case and its consequences.

2. See De Welde's and Stepnick's *Disrupting the Culture of Silence. Confronting Gender Inequality and Making Change in Higher Education* (17 essays from a variety of viewpoints) for a thorough examination of gender inequality and silence in the Academy.

3. In "Sexual Harassment: A Problem Shielded by Silence," Kathy Hotelling emphasizes the association of sexual harassment with silence: "In 1978 the Project on the Status and Education of Women (1978) called sexual harassment on campuses a 'hidden issue.' In many ways, despite the prevalence reports, court cases, establishment of policies and procedures, and other publicity, sexual harassment remains an invisible and elusive problem because its victims are extremely hesitant to report its occurrence to a university official. For example, Adams, Kottke, and Padgitt (1983) found that none of the victims that they surveyed reported their experiences. Only 4% of the participants of Johnson and Shuman's (1983) study reported incidents to a department head or other administrator, and 20% told a faculty member. Singer (1989) surveyed deans and directors of graduate programs in social work and found that while 54% of these administrators had knowledge of sexual harassment occurring at their schools within the last 5 years, only 22% of the situations were reported directly to them" (499). This phenomenon is particularly distressing when we consider that those who do report often have a negative experience, thereby retrenching the no-reporting tendency and further sullying, through the rarity of reporting, the professional names and reputations of complainants.

4. See Cheryl Glenn's *Unbroken: A Rhetoric of Silence* for an outstanding treatment of gendered power dynamics in the varied silences we create.

5. See *Sexual Harassment. Theory, Research, and Treatment* (Ed. William O'Donohue) for a thorough discussion of sexual harassment and its effects on those who have experienced it.

6. The UC Hastings College of the Law Center for WorkLife Law created in 2009 a game titled "Gender Bias Bingo." Individuals who submit stories pertaining to three of the nine squares on the bingo card receive a free T-shirt. The areas for submission include "Double Binds" (sanctions for self-promotion, hostile prescriptive bias), "Maternal Wall" (attribution bias, role incongruity), "Double Jeopardy" (intersectionality; women who experience bias that is shaped by their race as well as their sex), "Prove-It-Again!" (leniency bias, recall bias), "Gender Wars" (conflict, rather than support, among women), "Frigid Climate for Fathers" (discrimination against fathers in an active parenting role). Many of the stories submitted reveal how in some workplaces, "now it means something because he said it." Joan C. Williams, of the Gender Bias Bingo project, and Rachel Dempsey have organized the project into an extremely useful book titled *What Works for Women at Work. Four Patterns Working Women Need to Know*. I would argue that working women *and* men need to know the four patterns analyzed in the book ("Prove-It-Again!," "Tightrope" [double bind in prescriptive bias], "Maternal Wall," and "Tug of War" [balance between assimilation and resistance to gendered norms in the workplace]).

7. In his article "Faking It for the Dean," Carl Elliott cites the term "bureaucratic plagiarism" (coined by Gavin Moodie) to talk about how often in colleges and universities, thoughts, ideas, and projects are committed to paper by an anonymous underling and then used by employees in communications and/or by upper-level administrators.

CHAPTER 8

The "Glass Ceiling" and Hiring, Training, and Promotion

August 31, 2008: "Girl Power at School, but Not at the Office"
December 9, 2008: "Where Are the New Jobs for Women?"
September 16, 2009: "How the 'Snow-Woman Effect' Slows Women's Progress"
October 28, 2009: "New Game Plays on Women's Experiences of Gender Bias in Academe"
August 29, 2010: "Equity for Women—Still"
November 18, 2010: "Damning With Praise"
November, 2010: McKinsey Global Survey Results: "Moving women to the top"
March 9, 2011: "The Pyramid Problem"
October 29, 2012: "More Gender Diversity Will Mean Better Science"
October 31, 2013: "Fixing a Gender Pay Gap Can Lead to Faculty Discord"
October 27, 2014: "Don't Let the Gender Gap Overshadow Deeper Racial and Economic Disparities"
January 14, 2015: "Coming Out as Academic Mothers"
February 6, 2015: "Is the Professor Bossy or Brilliant? Much Depends on Gender"
February 6, 2015: "Madam C.E.O., Get Me a Coffee. Sheryl Sandberg and Adam Grant on Women Doing 'Office Housework'"[1]
April 23, 2015: "Black Women Want Top Jobs (but They Aren't Getting Them)"

© The Editor(s) (if applicable) and The Author(s) 2016
E. Mayock, *Gender Shrapnel in the Academic Workplace*,
DOI 10.1057/978-1-137-50830-0_8

July 20, 2015: "Un alcalde del PP llama 'puta barata' a una dirigente socialista" ("A Mayor from the Popular Party Calls a Socialist Party Spokesperson a 'Cheap Whore'")
August 13, 2015: "Let's Expose the Gender Pay Gap"

I have provided here just a sampling of titles of articles from *The Chronicle of Higher Education*, *The New York Times*, and *El País* from the last several years, along with the McKinsey survey referenced in a *Chronicle* article. The titles of the articles themselves reveal a deep anxiety, both in the USA and internationally, about women's work and women's access and station, specifically in the academic workplace, but certainly in other work sectors as well. Even *Cosmopolitan* is getting in on the action. In their March 2015 issue, they featured a piece on what to do if (when, for one out of three women) you are sexually harassed at work. The article, surrounded by ads showing women in weak (and sometimes deadly) positions and other articles on topics such as breast reduction, "50 lip looks we love," and "worst dates ever!" contains useful statistics, quotes, and tips for dealing with what surely now is considered a mainstream problem. Federal Bureau of Labor Statistics (cited in Chapter 4) seems to reveal that the pipeline for women to access the workplace is open (except for severe problems in the Science, Technology, Engineering, Mathematics STEM fields). Women are attending high school, college, and graduate school and are completing their degrees at an equal (PhD) or higher (BA or BS) rate than men. In a 2010 piece in *The New York Times*, Nicholas Kristof wrote:

> The yang of America's labor force is this: over a 40-year career, a man earns $431,000 more than a woman on average, according to the Center for American Progress.
> The yin of America's labor force is this: in this decade, for the first time in American history, men no longer inevitably dominate the labor force. Women were actually the majority of payroll employees for the five months that ended in March, according to one measure from the federal Bureau of Labor Statistics. (July 21, 2010)

Although Kristof recognizes that women seem to be "catching up to men," he warns that, "catching up is easier than forging ahead."[2] His final, pragmatic, and fair-minded point is that "men have typically benefited as women have gained greater equality," with examples being unemployed men who are married to employed women and women who work in the social sector and provide programs that are of benefit to jobless and/or homeless men. Nevertheless, the McKinsey survey, Valian's 1999 *Why So Slow?*, numerous articles from *The Chronicle of Higher Education*, and US Bureau of Labor Statistics themselves demonstrate that women are still facing significant barriers in acceding to higher-level jobs (e.g. beyond minimum wage, hourly jobs) and advancing in the organizations in which they work. In some arenas, women seem to be "catching up," while in many others, there is still great stagnation.[3] Furthermore, according to Boraas and Rodgers, "although personal choices, occupational crowding, and discrimination contribute to the gender gap [in earnings], the higher share of women in an occupation is still the largest contributor" (9).[4] Linda Hirshman asserts that,

> "Men enjoy a 'marriage premium' of at least 10 percent! Even holding constant for their education and experience, married men earn more than single men. One explanation to date is that their wives are picking up the socks, but one can never completely discount the power of the ideology of gender. Married men may get paid better, because they are doing the job of a man, supporting a family. According to *The Career Mystique* fathers of sons even enjoy a premium over fathers of daughters" (55).

Access to equal pay and advancement are still problems. The "glass ceiling" still looms large.[5]

Of course, the term used for this complex set of barriers is the "glass ceiling," coined in 1986 in the now famous *Wall Street Journal* article by Carol Hymowitz and Timothy Schellhardt and subsequently the object of study in numerous university and governmental (The Glass Ceiling Commission of 1991) research projects. The 1990s seems to be the golden era of research on the glass ceiling effect, with a relative dearth of research on the subject throughout the 2000s. This might be due to the perception of women's advancement in the workplace, coupled with the reality of the stagnation in the statistics.[6] (If the statistics stay the same, there appears to be nothing new to report.) Linda K. Kerber says that progress has been made in the areas of equal access to education and training, equal pay for equal work, and equal promotion to leadership positions in all fields. Nevertheless, Kerber adds, "These accomplishments are real, but they are incomplete. Moreover, those accomplishments rely on a definition of equality that is rooted in sameness—same access to opportunities and rewards—but it is the less-understood idea of equity that will be most bedeviling and vital during the next decade" (*Chronicle* 8-29-2010).[7]

Kerber's point is really important and signals an overreliance on the notion that women can simply act more "like men" in order to advance and succeed. We know from the dynamics discussed in *Gender Shrapnel* that there are many factors in the workplace that affect women and men differently, and/or to a different degree. In the US workplace, there are still significant pay gaps, there are still far fewer women in "fast-track," high-level jobs than there are men and far more women in temporary and part-time positions (Mason, "Manage Your Career"), there are still significant barriers for women of Color and lesbians, and there is a documented, increased bias against women with families (Mason, "Manage Your Career"). Mason calls this the "pyramid problem," which relies on data on men's and women's representation on the faculty, pay, and family formation as a measurement of gender equity at a given institution in order to draw attention to the high number of women in the lowest strata of the pyramid, with women with children found at the very bottom.[8] Mason states simply, "That pyramid is unlikely to change its shape without serious structural transformation" ("Pyramid").[9] On this topic, Kerber states, "The feminist visionaries of the 1970s named what were then new harms: quotas masquerading as preference; sexual harassment; and criminalized abortion when it was known to be a safe medical procedure. The visionaries of our own time need to focus on new harms, like family-responsibility discrimination. The struggle won't be pretty." In *Why So Slow?* Virginia Valian says the following about the career paths of female and male academics: "The data show that women are considerably less successful in academia than men are. Women earn less money, are promoted and granted tenure more slowly, and work at less prestigious institutions" (220). With abundant data from across the USA, Valian effectively demonstrates the ways in which women are at a disadvantage in academia and anticipates what Mason a decade later calls "the pyramid problem." And, yes, as Kerber says, we have a long way to go to level the playing ground, and "the struggle won't be pretty." People with privilege are not fond of surrendering parts of it, and it takes purposeful, fair-minded, hardworking administrators to attempt to boost the number and types of opportunities available to lesser-privileged groups.

Litosseliti mentions McConnell-Ginet's notion of the "glass elevator": "The invisible barrier that seems to keep even some exceptionally capable women from ascending to the top in the many professions dominated by men. Its companion, the glass elevator, is the invisible leverage that propels even relatively mediocre men upward in female-dominated occupations (McConnell-Ginet, 2000: 260)" (140). While women can only see opportunity through the glass ceiling in a male-dominated work environment, men are more easily handed opportunity in a female-dominated work environment. The issue is even more acute for women of Color. Buzzanell and Lucas make clear that the glass ceiling in the context of minority women is really a concrete wall (168–169).

My institution is over 265 years old and was founded upon and then bolstered by the ideals of the southern (White) gentleman. Even with the advent of co-education in the 1970s (law school) and 1980s (undergraduate), the institution has found challenges in hiring, training, and promoting people of Color. In the 2000s, the school successfully hired ten women of Color. In 2011, half of them remained. The record is worse for hiring men of Color. Many of the same factors that contribute to gender gaps in hiring, training, and promotion also plague people of Color, but there remains much research to do in this intersectional zone.[10] Of course, this problem is not unique to my institution, but my institution could do more in the areas of EEOC language in job ads, composition of hiring committees, and equity in programming. For example, featuring Robert E. Lee as the ideal pedagogue upon whom we should model ourselves doesn't make women or people of Color too confident that they will have a key role in institutional development.[11]

In "Paycheck Feminism," Kornbluh and Homer make clear that government labor policies were devised many decades ago, when there were far fewer women in the workplace and that, with women's increased representation in the labor force, it's time to revisit these policies and find ways "to better value women's work" (28). These five ways are: (1) stop making unemployment, retirement, and other benefits contingent on steady, full-time work; (2) don't make flexible hours a barrier to health insurance, and *do* stop charging women more for health insurance; (3) guarantee workers paid family and medical leave; (4) provide high-quality child care; and (5) stop taxing women's income unfairly/disproportionately (28–32). Individual employers can certainly decide to make effective changes on a micro-level, particularly in the areas of benefits and part-time work, health insurance, flexible hours, paid family and medical leave, and high-quality child care. In fact, much to its credit, my institution has worked hard over the last several years to understand and improve benefits for people in different work arrangements and to examine and institute better and more child care.[12]

Hiring, training, and promotion operations in the workforce are profoundly influenced by the gender shrapnel concept. Lauren B. Edelman reminds us that, "Law causes certain organizational routines (including procedures for hiring, firing, and promotion and rules regarding leave, dress, language, or accent) to appear natural and normal" ("Legal Lives" 237). Oftentimes, we refer to the "firm," the "company," the "institution," the "university," the "organization," assuming all the while that these are impersonal, objective entities somehow capable of making highly personal personnel decisions. We forget that those who hire are human beings, many of whom must make a concerted effort in order to think beyond their own sphere and therefore to hire beyond their own sense of familiarity and comfort. Organizations *are* people and are therefore subject to many of the same foibles and stereotypes to which human beings are subject. This means that those in a position to hire might, consciously or unconsciously, tend to hire people who look, sound, and act like they do.

When I briefly told my own gender shrapnel story at the beginning of this book, I did so chronologically so that readers could understand how the shrapnel gathered and grew and turned into an unwanted gender battle. I offered others' examples of gender shrapnel, examples to which I return in subsequent chapters in order to emphasize vocabulary and definitions for gender shrapnel phenomena, analyze cases of specific areas of gender shrapnel (language, harassment, silence, access, and advancement), and provide texture so that these areas can be understood based on real, human stories. One of the stories I recounted was a professor's involvement on a search committee in another department of her institution. The story exemplified some of the dangerous Title VII territory that can manifest in hiring in the academic workplace. Twelve men and two women participated on the search committee, and one of the women was not in attendance at most meetings. The professor in question was the departmental outsider, the only person not from the hiring department. She was also younger by at least a decade than the youngest member of the department. Therefore, she was an outsider for being from a different department, for her age, and for her sex. Triple jeopardy! These factors do not have to matter, but they did, a lot. They influenced the ways in which her colleagues could or could not listen to her, could or could not respect her comments about candidates and her choices in the search. In the end, her advocating for a female candidate seemed to her colleagues just a reflection of her own sex, not of her expertise in the field or her experience on job searches. The hiring shrapnel, thus, played on both sides of the process—the perception of the outsider as "only" a woman damaged the perception of one of the candidates also as "only" a woman.

Furthermore, the overwhelming predominance of male professors in that particular department at the time promoted the perception that that discipline was for boys, that male candidates would "fit," and female candidates would be anomalous.

The composition of hiring committees plays a fundamental role in successful hiring. Especially in the academic workplace, where tenure-track jobs often go to individuals with freshly minted PhDs, departments and administrators must consider carefully whom to include on the hiring committee. Including employees with a variety of backgrounds and opinions allows job candidates to get a sense of the full department and of where she or he might fit in the range of areas of expertise, academic backgrounds, and personal and professional interests.

Institutions' employees often do not reach consensus about the EEOC language for the commonly used sections of job advertisements. This can give a dissonant, mixed message about the employer and can reveal inconsistencies between and among hiring departments. For example, a simple statement that "women and minorities are encouraged to apply" stems from EEOC language but offers a lukewarm invitation to individuals from these groups. So lukewarm, in fact, that women and minorities might actually get the sense that they are not encouraged to apply or maybe even are actively discouraged from applying. Stronger, more welcoming language across the board can stabilize an institution's hiring processes and create an efficient and consistent system for years to come.

Much has been written about hiring men and women and how the two groups negotiate for salary and benefits. Men ask for what they want, believe they will get it, and often do. If they don't, there's no harm, no foul; they can ask again on the next go-round. Women are pleased to be considered for the job and are socialized to behave obediently and graciously. Hard-driving negotiation might lose a woman the potential job or besmirch her reputation (as too aggressive or too masculine) as she begins in the post. Women are supposed to be glad to have something and to be happy to accept what they've been offered.

When I was hired at my institution, it never occurred to me to negotiate my salary. I had never had a conversation with anyone about such an approach, and I don't believe they would have recommended that I negotiate. I was delighted to be offered the job and to be asked if I needed a PC or a Mac. Of course, we all know that starting with a lower base salary affects all potential earnings for the rest of one's time in the job. Especially in academia, where many of us spend our entire professional careers, not negotiating from the start affects every subsequent salary decision, every percentage raise. In addition, having a lower lifetime salary brings less prestige, and so candidates might appear lesser in the eyes of their deans, provosts, and presidents and, as a result, be passed over for other types of promotion, such as ad hoc posts or endowed chairs. Virginia Valian says that, "Most advancement comes from having a small to medium edge over other employees. Our way of evaluating women puts them at a disadvantage, compared to men, in acquiring that edge" (144). She adds, "On the surface, everyone is in the same organization, but the underlying reality is that men and women work in different organizational environments. Women work in an environment that is less likely to offer them the rewards they deserve" (144). One useful strategy is to say consistently to job candidates, "The starting salary is X, and that is firm." This simple move effectively levels the playing ground for female and male candidates *and* sets a proper tone about equity.

An additional piece of the hiring puzzle is the content of the job recommendation letters for the candidate. A November, 2010 article in the "On Hiring" segment of *The Chronicle of Higher Education* cites a study published in the American Psychological Association's *Journal of Psychology*, which states that letters that describe the collaborative abilities of a candidate (most frequently in the case of female candidates, even if the female candidates were not actually more collaborative) are "less highly regarded by search committees" (Montell). The study, out of Rice University and the University of Houston, also finds that strong adjectives (e.g. "aggressive," "independent") are more highly regarded and are much more frequently used for male candidates. Montell goes on to say that the study found that more tentative terms were more frequently used for female candidates and that strong language in recommendation letters is more apt to help land the applicant the job, especially for high-level positions.

The same principles apply to training employees. As Human Resources directors well know, employees must go through a common core training about the workplace. When I worked in administration, I met with all of candidates for jobs in academic administration and for non-permanent academic positions. I quickly learned in that role that employee training begins at the moment the job candidate meets with an official representative of the institution. This is the moment at which the representative can provide a brief history of the institution, a summary of "where we are now," a rationale for how benefits are assigned, and an idea of the job candidate's potential trajectory in the position. If this is done well, the candidate who is hired will already be prepared for official employee training and perhaps be open to being assigned a mentor. The candidate might feel more willing to ask questions pertinent to her or his unique situation (research needs, Americans with Disabilities Act [ADA] questions, partner benefits, family responsibilities, first person at the institution to fill a certain role, etc.). In addition, the institutional representative can set the tone by using language that doesn't assume one situation or another, language that allows the candidate to choose an identity or identities without having them dictated from the get-go.

Creating a common training experience for all employees allows people in different job sectors to meet and get to know each other, ensures a consistent institutional message, and creates a base for future, more sophisticated training opportunities. In addition, institutions can establish an optional mentoring program (optional so that it is not overly paternalistic or presuming of an individual employee's needs) so that employees may choose to get informal and formal advice from other co-workers. As administrators consider employees for new opportunities and/or promotion, they should keep their eyes on all employees, thinking beyond the "usual suspects" and examining what each employee brings to the table. I remember a moment when a supervisor asked me to go through a stack of summer grant applications to select one of the "usual suspects" for a particular, statewide grant opportunity. I remember thinking, "Usual suspects? Usual according to whom?," and then carefully reading each of the proposals for the one that seemed the most brilliant—the best written, the most original, the most promising. The author of that proposal was brand new to the university and so could not yet figure on the list of usual suspects. This is certainly a case in which gender shrapnel has an effect. If we are always accustomed to the handpicked "winners" to come from the same upper-level administrators, then we might forget to consider the group at the bottom, that is, the group most populated by women, according to all data presented here.

Administrators (provosts, deans, department and program heads) also need to encourage actively their co-workers to say "yes" to committee nominations and even, if they're comfortable doing so, to create a smart, appropriate lobbying effort on their own behalf. At my institution, men are often appointed to committees such as finance, first-year admissions, employee benefits, and capital projects. Even with abundant reminders to consider appointments more broadly, men still predominate in these arenas. Therefore, elected committees may be the only area in which women can advocate for themselves. Of course, we know the dangers for women of too much self-promotion, so this, too, becomes a delicate task. Formal and informal words of encouragement by administrators can help to overcome some of these obstacles. It is also important to keep in mind that members of underrepresented groups should not be expected to do more service than their colleagues or constantly be called upon to represent a particular group.

Institutions must approach training about gender socialization and sexual harassment in a frank, open way. A 2009 EEOC report shows that, of the sexual harassment charges filed over the past decade, 14–16% of them were filed by men and 84–86% of them were filed by women. The data clearly show that sexual harassment continues to be a much more acute concern for women as a group than for men as a group. This fact, profoundly linked to Title IX, affects how we should be looking at women's access and advancement in the workplace. *The same is true for treatment of the women students who populate the academic workplace.* Phoebe Morgan reminds us that "sexual harassment" can be a useful term to describe "a core experience associated with work or school" (212), but that it might not be an apt term in the case of lesbians and women of Color. This again speaks to the overwhelming maleness, whiteness, and purported heterosexuality of the supposedly objective, impersonal organizations and institutions for which we work.

Phoebe Morgan very cogently declares that there are pernicious effects of sexual harassment (and its yet-to-be-defined counterparts to address the intersectionality of race and sexuality with gender) on women's attachment to the labor force in terms of "job turnover and slower career advancement" (212). Valian states that her "explanation for why women are underrepresented at high levels of professional achievement has focused on gender schemas and the accumulation of advantage" (303). An institution's individual and collective understanding, prevention, and public intolerance of sexual discrimination go a long way in signaling gender schemas and leveling the playing field for men and women.

Numerous studies (e.g. Valian, Siebel Newsom) have shown that it is culturally acceptable for boys and men to brag about real and perceived accomplishments and that it is unacceptable for girls and women to do the same. This gender paradigm affects the awarding of formal and informal promotions in the workplace. For example, at my institution, our merit pay raises are ostensibly based on the "faculty activities report" that each faculty member generates and submits at the beginning of each new calendar year. The supervisor of the unit provides the lengthy base questionnaire, and faculty members complete it. Senior colleagues in some departments give sound advice to junior colleagues about the importance of the document and the ways to complete it, while others relatively new to the system remain in the dark. I had a happy and productive first year at the institution, but I was woefully unaware that I should enumerate every achievement and highlight the big ones. At the same time, maybe it would have been harmful for a female employee to come off as too boastful, too "self-promoting."[13] This presents a real obstacle: The report is intended for an individual to report to her or his department head about her or his activities and accomplishments and to be fairly judged for a merit raise. But, at the same time, it is more acceptable and laudable for the male employees to list and highlight accomplishments than it is for women, and so the process quietly and covertly helps men to accumulate advantage. Again, every subsequent pay raise is determined from a percentage of the base. If a person's base salary starts low and *also* increases more slowly, the damaging effects are sustained throughout that person's career.

The fair evaluation of employee performance does not depend only on encouraging female employees to delicately boast about themselves; it also requires that the evaluators understand gender schemas at work at the institutional (employer) and individual (employee) levels. In other words, they have to sort through their own potential biases as they attempt to judge their employees fairly. They will succeed in this if and only if they meet with employees about their self-reports, communicate clearly what the rating system is, provide careful feedback on each element of the review, and follow up appropriately in formal (evaluations, letters) and informal (checking in by e-mail, phone, or personal visits) ways. Secret evaluation and merit pay systems are secret for a reason—they attempt to hide accidental or deliberate gender bias and to allow one group to continue to accumulate advantage, either knowingly or unknowingly. In a phrase, administrators and managers should not have anything in employees' files that they would not want the employee to have access to.

Another common imbalance in the promotion of female and male employees is the unequal sharing of job opportunities. If a department head, dean, or provost creates or comes across a job ad, grant opportunity, or consulting position (internal or external) that seems perfect and exciting for a specific person, then the administrator should widen the net and decide who else might like to be aware of the opportunity. Maybe it would be all employees, who knows? Singling out one person who is deemed worthy of such a notice can have two unwanted effects: the exclusion of other employees from access to an opportunity and the possible message to the one, singled-out person that he or she is no longer welcome in the present work environment.

In the promotion arena, recognition and praise matter. We learn about people's accomplishments in this digital age with the click of a mouse. Our supervisors need to be increasingly aware of how they visibly promote one person or another. At my own institution, many female employees have had to do significant promotional work for other female employees because the communications/publications machines tend to dwell more on our male colleagues. Several years ago, a female colleague of mine had a new novel and a new scholarly monograph come out at the same time— two gigantic and hugely noteworthy achievements. The day that I saw the press releases (from the publishing house, Amazon, Barnes & Noble, etc.) about the early success of my colleague's novel, there was nothing, and still had been nothing, on our institution's website. Nevertheless, that very same day, there was a hot-off-the-presses release of the news of a male colleague attending an important conference over the weekend. He attended the conference but did not present a paper at it. Indeed, somehow conference attendance trumped the release of one person's two major books. In this instance, I fully believed that our communications office *wanted* to be aware of and promote equally each successful student and employee, but they didn't even realize how short they were of that mark. To this day, I still pay attention to gendered "air time"—on the website, on the printed university calendar, in the alumni magazine, everywhere. After all, our alumni base is mostly male, and the alumni dollars come in when the alumni are pleased with the university's message. Nevertheless, we could take the tack that it is easy and fun to promote all of our hard-working colleagues; it just takes a little thought to do it fairly.

Informal communications of praise or recognition are also really important. Senior colleagues, supervisors, deans, and provosts can easily see a notice of a student's or an employee's great accomplishments and send a quick e-mail or write a little note. They just need to appreciate different types of achievements (not all sports, not all service, not all the arts) and to try to stay in tune with work across campus and across the constituencies. Such awareness will allow a broader swath of individuals to be recognized when it's time for nomination for bigger awards and rewards.

In *Closing the Leadership Gap*, Marie C. Wilson encourages women to embrace the four A's—authority, ambition, ability, and authenticity—in order to help themselves to level the playing field in a world with separate organizational structures for women and men. A part of women's success in the workplace depends on women's ability to recognize their own potential and to take pride in their own achievements, and on men's ability to "allow" women to be loud and proud, both in and out of the workplace.

NOTES

1. See Adam Grant and Sheryl Sandberg's four-part series on women at work in *The New York Times* (2014–2015).
2. Catherine Rampell's 2009 article in *The New York Times* points out that women's potential to surpass men in the job force "has less to do with gender equality than with where the ax is falling," stating that the recession has affected first male-dominated industries, such as manufacturing and construction. Rampell adds, "A deep and prolonged recession, therefore, may change not only household budgets and habits; it may also challenge longstanding gender roles."
3. See Claudia Goldin's "A Grand Gender Convergence: Its Last Chapter" for suggestions for tangible change in the labor market to effect tangible change in the gender pay gap.
4. Boraas and Rodgers conclude the following: "We find that, for men, the most important measurable factor in each year is the industry of employment as opposed to personal characteristics such as education, age, and region of residence. It is well known that particular industries pay more than others, and our results show that these industries, on average, have higher concentrations of men. The opposite occurs for women. Education and age are the most important factors for explaining the wage- and percent-female relationship. If education and age capture personal preferences that influence occupational choice, then solely focusing on expanding occupational choice will result in a small narrowing of the gender wage gap. This is because, as shown in our Oaxaca-Blinder decompositions, even after we add the concentration of women in an occupation to the model, the overall gender wage gap is still largely unexplained" (14).
5. Dean W.H. Knight uses National Association of Law Placement statistics from 2005 to support the following statement: "According to the National Association of Law Placement ('NALP'), men and women are employed overall at the same rate after graduation. Relatively fewer women enter private practice, with more entering government and public

interest organizations compared with men. Women who do enter private practice tend to leave at each benchmark in their professional lives in greater numbers than men do. For the most recent year for which NALP has data [2005], women constituted nearly 48% of summer associates, 44% of law firm associates, but only 17% of partners. These statistical disparities in the trajectory of women from law school to partner suggest that the glass ceiling remains a major barrier for women in the profession" (470–471). See also *The Chronicle of Higher Education*'s PDF compilation titled "The Gender Divide in Academe. Insights on Retaining More Academic Women."

6. In "How the 'Snow-Woman Effect' Slows Women's Progress," Mary Ann Mason provides the following statistics regarding this stagnation of progress in glass ceiling arenas: "It is not surprising that we still find few women at the top. More than 20 years ago, *The Wall Street Journal* used the phrase 'glass ceiling' to describe the apparent barriers that prevent women from reaching the highest leadership positions. In 1995 the government's Glass Ceiling Commission reported that women held 45.7 percent of American's jobs and received more than half of the university master's degrees. Yet 95 percent of senior managers were men, and female managers' earnings were, on average, a scant 68 percent of their male counterparts'. A decade later, in 2005, women accounted for 46.5 percent of America's work force and represented less than 8 percent of its top managers (although at large Fortune 500 companies the figure is slightly higher). Female managers' earnings now average 72 percent of their male colleagues' wages. Since 1998, the figures have stagnated. Over all, the trajectory is not promising" (*Chronicle*; web).

7. See the AAUP's January–February, 2015, issue of *Academe* for a thorough history of the organization's "Committee W," the Committee on Women in the Academic Profession. The AAUP will celebrate its centennial in 2017. The lengthy, informative article covers Committee W's history, along with a summary of the states of salary discrimination, family issues, widespread contingency, legislative efforts, retirement and health care, and sexual harassment and assault. Author Mary W. Gray concludes: "Over the AAUP's first century, women have made enormous gains in graduate education, in medicine, and in the law. This makes the scant progress for academic women in hiring, pay, promotion, and tenure discouraging. Lobbying higher education institutions, Congress, and state legislatures to protect individual and institutional academic freedom while prohibiting discrimination is a task for Committee W and the AAUP in general in its second century. Perhaps by the committee's own centennial in 2018, a few small miracles will occur, aided by the diligent, devoted efforts of faculty women and men" (52).

8. Mason adds, "Most women, it seems, cannot have it all—tenure and a family—while most men can" ("Pyramid"). In 2007, the EEOC amended Title VII text by adding the prohibition of discrimination against employees with caregiving responsibilities. The background information recognizes the following: "The prohibition against sex discrimination under Title VII has made it easier for women to enter the labor force. Since Congress enacted Title VII, the proportion of women who work outside the home has significantly increased,[2] and women now comprise nearly half of the U.S. labor force.[3] The rise has been most dramatic for mothers of young children, who are almost twice as likely to be employed today as were their counterparts 30 years ago.[4] The total amount of time that couples with children spend working also has increased.[5] Income from women's employment is important to the economic security of many families, particularly among lower-paid workers, and accounts for over one-third of the income in families where both parents work.[6] Despite these changes, women continue to be most families' primary caregivers[7]" (http://www.eeoc.gov/policy/docs/caregiving.html).

9. In her article in *The Chronicle of Higher Education* titled, "Title IX Includes Maternal Discrimination," Mary Ann Mason states that, "President Obama should be aware that Title IX does not just cover blatant gender discrimination—such as bias that women are not as competent as men in science or math. It also protects women against sex discrimination on the basis of marital, parental, or family status, and on the basis of pregnancy. Those provisions come into play over the issue of retaining female scientists in science, technology, engineering, and mathematics, the STEM fields."

10. See Deirdre Royster's *Race and the Invisible Hand: How White Networks Exclude Black Men from Blue-Collar Jobs* (2003) for a nuanced analysis of the work dynamics for Black men.

11. Over the last several years, the institution where I work has struggled more publicly with its association with Robert E. Lee and, in particular, with the question of flying Confederate flags and whether or not to formally recognize Martin Luther King Day.

12. See *The New York Times* Editorial Board's recognition of Equal Pay Day in its piece from April 14, 2015.

13. Mary Ann Mason tells of the tricky advice that she provided to a female colleague in her law school: "'Speak low and slowly, but smile frequently,' I replied. This advice (which did help her next presentation) was based on my observation that women must adhere to a narrow band of behavior in order to be effective in mostly male settings. Women who speak too fast, or in too shrill a tone, are overlooked. Women who act in a highly assertive manner, which might be acceptable for men, are attended to,

but not invited back. Women must be friendly, but they cannot be too friendly or a sexual connotation may be inferred. After meetings, women are frequently marginalized when they are left out of job-related social networking" ("How the 'Snow-Woman' Effect Slows Women's Progress"). This is probably good advice for someone in the short term, but in the long term, it may encourage too much of a gendered performance that simply adds to and supports some higher-ups' already overly developed gender schemas. In another advice column of *The Chronicle of Higher Education*, "Ms. Mentor" responds to a tenure-track woman faculty member's plea for advice about a dean making unwelcome overtures by telling her to pretend not to hear the dean, pretend to misunderstand him, be mildly apologetic, and say "thank you" a lot (Ms. Mentor, "I'm OK, He's Sleazy"). These half-measures, again, seek short-term compromise and protection but ignore the long-term damage of not confronting matters head-on.

REFERENCES

Editorial Board, *The New York Times*. 2015. Women still earn a lot less than men. *The New York Times*, The Opinion Pages, 14 Apr 2015. Accessed 14 Apr 2015. Web.

Gray, Mary W. 2015. The AAUP and women. *Academe* (January–February):46–52.

Kerber, Linda K. 2010. Equity for women—Still. *The Chronicle of Higher Education*, 29 Aug 2010. Accessed 2 Sept 2010. Web.

Kristof, Nicholas D. 2010. Don't write off men just yet. *The New York Times*, 21 July 2010. Accessed 22 July 2010. Web.

Rampell, Catherine. 2009. As layoffs surge, women may pass men in job force. *The New York Times*, 6 Feb 2009. Accessed 6 Feb 2009. Web.

Royster, Deidre. 2003. *Race and the invisible hand: How white networks exclude black men from blue-collar jobs*. Berkeley, CA: University of California Press. Print.

Valian, Virginia. 1999. *Why so slow? The advancement of women*. Cambridge, MA: MIT Press. Print.

PART III

Solutions

CHAPTER 9

To Be PC or Not to Be PC, That Is
the Question

"Politically correct" language really pissed a lot of people off in the 1980s
and 1990s. As a teacher of language, I am a huge fan of colorful language. I believe that all vocabulary matters and that a broad, rich vocabulary makes for broad, rich speaking and writing. I don't believe in the
total control of people's speech, but I do deeply appreciate that the move
toward "politically correct" made people think more about language, feel
on the defensive (whether admittedly so or not) when they used derogatory terms, and influenced much of the language we use informally and in
the workplace today. "Politically correct" made us all but eliminate informal usage of the "N-word," which many, maybe even most, would say is
a victory. Although many friends and colleagues of mine, especially from
outside the USA, think that "politically correct" usage just makes for two-
faced nice statements/mean thoughts, I believe that recognition of politically correct language has made the US culture more aware of language
choice surrounding race, religion, and sexual choices. I do not believe in
the least that it has done the same for sex/gender. In fact, I think that the
more some people feel controlled in their language choices, whether by
press pressure or peer pressure, the more they employ some kind of outlet
to let out all of those fancy, fun words they're no longer allowed to say in
other arenas.

The Urban Dictionary's initial definition offered on the term "politically correct" is: "A way that we speak in America so we don't offend
whining pussies. Only pathetically weak people that don't have the balls

© The Editor(s) (if applicable) and The Author(s) 2016
E. Mayock, *Gender Shrapnel in the Academic Workplace*,
DOI 10.1057/978-1-137-50830-0_9

125

to say what they feel and mean are politically correct pussies" (accessed 10-20-2011). I actually think using the term "balls" is extremely entertaining, but it certainly does, even in its jokey way, set up an us/them, strong/weak, balls/pussy, stoic/whining gender dichotomy that implies, at least speaking in loose cultural terms, that choosing "politically correct" language is for pussies—that is, for sweet little cats, women's genitalia, women as represented by their genitalia, or men who aren't behaving "as men should." The website also claims that the push for politically correct speech came from left-wing liberals. Interestingly enough (and as a very basic sketch), Linder and Nosek's 2009 research on the links between social and political tolerance find, at least in a preliminary way, that political liberals are more likely to favor protected speech than are political conservatives.[1] As I argued in Chapter 5, increased awareness about the ways in which gender shrapnel strikes both formal and informal language usage should at the very least start to make people think before they speak. In other words, "politically correct" does not have to be equated with censorship or dogmatic leftiness; it can just be a reminder that language matters and that, given the choice whether to offend or not to offend a group of people, it's possible to choose the latter.

In this chapter, I aim to look at the ways in which institutions attempt to strike a balance between protecting First Amendment rights and protecting individuals who are often verbally attacked for belonging to a particular group. I argue that, instead of using the fraught term "politically correct," we can advocate for a profound cultural competence that informs workers' speech actions and that observably and positively affects equity practices within an organization. Although I still outline some of the problems here, I seek to offer concrete solutions that will contribute to the training principles delineated later in this book.

Dennis Poole's article takes exception to the use of "politically correct" language and offers a different term. Of the term "politically correct," Poole states the following:

> This much is clear. I do not want my students to be politically correct. "Political correctness," Drucker (1998) observes, "is a purely totalitarian concept" (p. 380). Stalinists first made use of the term in the late 1930s and early 1940s. They used intimidation, character assassination, and denial of freedom of thought and speech to suppress all but the "party line." Current use of the term is different. Political groups use political correctness to denigrate people who have a progressive orthodoxy on issues involving race, gender, sexual orientation, and the rights of marginalized people. (No pagination)

Poole suggests that, rather than trying to impose a new set of terms or vocabulary, we can impose upon ourselves and our students a "cultural competence":

Providing an open, vibrant, and intellectually challenging atmosphere for my students is the first challenge. The second is equipping them for culturally competent practice. Culturally competent professionals recognize similarities and differences in the values, norms, customs, history, and institutions of groups of people that vary by ethnicity, gender, religion, and sexual orientation. They recognize sources of comfort and discomfort between themselves and clients of similar or different cultural backgrounds. They understand the impact of discrimination, oppression, and stereotyping on practice. They recognize their own biases toward or against certain cultural groups. And they rely on scientific evidence and moral reasoning to work effectively in cross-cultural situations. (No pagination)

Poole goes on to say that effective, analytical thinkers need five types of cultural competence: knowledge (micro- and macrocosmic), skill, policy, research, and values. I would argue that this recipe aligns with the majority of US college and university mission statements in this day and age. I want to strike here a balance. I firmly believe that we as individuals—students, staff, faculty, administrators, managers—and as groups—employers and employees—should strive toward and eventually achieve real cultural competence. At the same time, I think some strong suggestion of values "from the margins" can get us more quickly to cultural competence. Free expression of the N-word doesn't really help anyone, and so politically correct language did its job there. Free derogatory expression of "bitch" doesn't help anyone either. For me, it remains the single most damaging word for women because of all it implies in terms of the animal world (bad for women, bad for dogs), status, and lack of privilege for women, gender codes for submissive behavior, racist and sexist prison language, and so on. And yet this is a term that we hear on television, that we hear our students call each other, that I have called myself ("I don't mean to be a bitch, but"), and that we hear always as a poundingly derogatory term for girls and women, and for men who are "less than men." It has infiltrated the household and the workplace, and I believe that this is one example in which a little dogmatic, politically correct inculcation might have us wonder 20 years from now how we ever talked about women in this way.

This all has to do with the workplace because the work environment has always demanded a certain protocol that, granted, varies from workplace to workplace, but that certainly speaks volumes about how the actual work gets done. If protocols are in place, if we have employee handbooks, websites with policies and procedures, hearing processes, federal and state laws about the workplace and employment practices, then we are saying that how we treat each other at work matters. And, as I insisted back in Chapter 5, talk is action! Especially in our current technological world in which many of us no longer exert ourselves physically, but rather get the work done through meetings, written reports, e-mail, even Facebook, talk is action. Our protocols therefore must dictate to some extent *how* we talk, what we say to each other, what is fine and what is not fine, what the consequences are for not using language of respect. These protocols are dictated in large part by federal laws, such as Title VII and Title IX, which of course impose a certain degree of political correctness, if we can deign to call it that. For Title VII, individuals in protected categories are supposed to be protected from adverse work actions and decisions that are predicated on their belonging to a protected category.[2] For Title IX, women and men in educational environments are supposed to have fair and equal access to resources (yes, in athletics, but also in the classroom, the band-room, the cafeteria, the sorority, or fraternity house). Letting institutional speech/talk get hit repeatedly by gender shrapnel violates both Title VII and Title IX and is good for no one.

Several years ago at my institution, students printed in one of the two main student publications a piece called "The Bracket," a local version of the National Collegiate Athletic Association (NCAA) bracket for the basketball playoffs—"March Madness," which at our school has come to mean something markedly different from "hoopla" and pageantry surrounding college basketball. The two male authors of the piece created bracket categories such as "pretentious slut" and "in the closet" and referred to our institution as a "cuntry club."[3] They listed a number of students in each of the categories. The result was significant outrage among many constituencies on campus. What should a university administration do in this case? The big debate among us was whether what the two students wrote should be considered free speech, protected by the First Amendment, or whether their speech, in fact, violated Title VII and Title IX and created a hostile work environment for staff, faculty, and students alike. Our debate was parallel to the national legal debate on free speech versus sexist and/or racist speech:

> Racist and sexist speech generates much debate about the proper balance between freedom of speech and the protection of historically disadvantaged

groups from verbal abuse. First Amendment absolutists argue that speech cannot and should not be legally restricted (Post 1990, 1993; Strossen 1995). Critical race theorists argue that racist speech results in substantial harms for its victims (Matsuda, Lawrence, Delgado, and Crenshaw 1993), perpetuates inequality, and must therefore be legally limited to realize the equality guaranteed by the Fourteenth Amendment (Lawrence 1990). Cultural theorists contemplate how the performative aspects of speech translate into harms (Butler 1997). Feminist scholars identify sexist street harassment as a source of women's disempowerment (West 1987), investigate the harms associated with sexually suggestive public speech (Gardner 1980, 1995), explore potential legal remedies (Bowman 1993; Davis 1994), and question if pornography is a legally actionable harm (MacKinnon 1993). (Nielsen 10–11)[4]

Seven faculty members at my institution took issue with some expression of desire for protection of the students' right to free speech and, when unable (or, in some cases, unwilling) to have the student editors accept their letters to the editor against the free speech argument, established a website titled "Speaking Freely" (http://home.wlu.edu/~mayocke/ SpeakingFreely/index.htm). When do we determine that the derogatory use of the words and phrases "sluts," "in the closet," and "cuntry" establishes a social hierarchy and influences how certain groups are treated or mistreated? How do we understand the Titles VII and IX implications of the accepted use of this type of speech? The major issue at stake, still, today, is who wins this battle? It is a cultural war between the dominant and the seemingly marginal (or very definitely marginalized, depending on your point of view), and, in an organization still entrenched in tradition, the marginalized do not win. Nielsen makes the significant point that "different groups of Americans have very different attitudes about the law, which are rooted in their experience with the law. In the specific context of offensive public speech, white women and people of color are reluctant to turn to law for help, either because they do not believe the law can help or because they fear the law would be used against them" (2).

With the launch of the "Speaking Freely" site, two of my colleagues and I were asked to meet with an administrator, who took issue with our mode of free speech and attempted to admonish us about our approach. Seven of us had worked together to launch the site, but the three of us on the Women's and Gender Studies faculty were the only three invited to this conversation. These types of experiences do not foster trust in the law, being, in this case, the decisions and actions of the upper administration. I have read Nicholas Kristof's and Sheryl WuDunn's *Half the Sky* and thought about the deep trauma they describe in three areas of women's oppression: sex trafficking and forced prostitution; gender-based violence, including honor killings and mass rape; and maternal mortality (xxi). These profound issues have their less profound, but still significant, analogs in the workplace. Kristof and WuDunn recount how, time and again, women who manage to escape forced prostitution are subjected to many of the same abuses when they report the crimes to the authorities. "Speaking freely" isn't always free. Attempting to right wrongs for oneself and on behalf of others by speaking against the status quo, against speech deemed allowable by the First Amendment, can heap more abuse upon the individual engaged in the struggle.

Free speech is always the safer victory because it protects the damaging statements of the *perceived* majority. I'm not saying that all wealthy, White, male students are slinging this kind of language around, just that they are a part of a dominant culture that is White and male and that condones this use of language. Nielsen warns that women who experience stares, comments about women being less capable than men, and sexually objectifying comments "may lead to women's 'self-objectification,' a process whereby women internalize the outsider's view of themselves (Fredrickson and Roberts, 1997)" (169). Of course, we know from ample mental health evidence that this type of spiraling downward can cause eating disorders, depression, and underperformance (Nielsen 169–70). In addition, as Nicholas Kristof put it, "catching up" is much easier for a marginalized group than is "forging ahead" ("Don't Write Men Off"). In the free speech versus Title VII/IX cases at my institution, marginalized groups have not caught up. Bristling against the status quo can still seem dangerous and damaging. As Nielsen says, "This doctrinal treatment in effect grants a license to harass. The judicial protection of offensive public speech works to normalize and justify such behavior" (3). Nosek, Banaji, and Jost examine "intergroup attitudes" by looking at two factors that they have found to distinguish political liberals from conservatives: resistance to change and tolerance for inequality. These factors, as they relate to free speech and protected groups, and to the status quo versus institutional movement and progress, might influence training principles for administrators, whose job tends to be a balancing act between supporting the traditions of an institution (the status quo) and competing in the "marketplace" with new ideas, innovative programs, and the like (equality, equity, innovation). Recently, one of my students of Color was thinking about the fear many women experience in confronting negative workplace experiences and said, "Well, segregation is just intimidating." This statement simply and elegantly sums up the alienating effects both of being sexually and/or racially harassed and of trying to do something about it.

While we know that staff, faculty, and students have made valiant efforts to speak against the administrative lack of action, or status quo party line, what can administrators do? How can they intelligently and publicly contribute to debate on these issues, a debate whose contours they are nervously watching members of the university establish? How can they demonstrate that they are engaging with both sides of the issue, seeing points well made, and then taking a firm stand based on all the evidence before them? It really is a question of valor. I heard a Spanish author say informally that bravery is having your actions meet your ethics. We need to see university administrators and business executives bolstered by Title VII and Title IX employment law, not cowed or threatened by it. What I am proposing is that workplace leaders count on their training—their real, documented cultural competence—to guide them through these issues of free speech. I believe that administrators fortify their positions in the work-place by publicly weighing information that supports conflicting sides, making a strong, well-considered judgment, and articulating the factors that influenced the decision. Administrators who hide behind legal coun-sel and who are afraid to make strong, clear statements about expectations do not become real leaders. Administrators who appreciate strength, even divergent, possibly competing types of strength, in their employees also exhibit real strength, for they are modeling the type of intellectual debate that their organizational mission statements are promoting.

Research by Ranganath and Nosek published in *Psychological Science* in 2008: ...demonstrated immediate and automatic evaluation of little-known social targets based on evaluations of associated individuals. An encounter with one member of a group can have lasting effects on evalu-ations of other members of the same group. In social judgment, general-izing evaluations from one person to others provides a simple heuristic for assessment. However, the potential cost is that individuating information that would enable more accurate assessment may be missed because of a propensity to generalize qualities that group members may not hold in common. ("Implicit Attitude" 254)

The implications in terms of workplace attitudes and generalizations vis-à-vis speech and assumptions about certain groups are huge. If our implicit tendency is to carry over a judgment from one individual we have connected to one certain group to other members perceived to be in that group, then we are forgetting to allow individuals to have unique characteristics in this regard. The message here is that actions taken based on these implicit judgments must be carefully considered *and* vetted by others so that there is an external check on the implicit, individual judgment. In my workplace, I am one of three outspoken Women's and Gender Studies faculty of the same generation. The three of us have extremely divergent viewpoints on just about everything, from lifestyle to gender politics. Nevertheless, we are quite often lumped together as if we were just one (not even three-headed), monolithic, feminist.

I'd like to illuminate this idea further with an example from an e-mail that all employees of my institution received from our Human Resources office. The e-mail, possibly generated by a retirement agency but certainly added to and sent out by Human Resources, was an invitation to a women-only session on investment practices and strategies. Adorned with pictures of autumn leaves and offering refreshments to all female participants, the invitation invited female employees to learn more about investment strategies "without all that intimidating jargon." After speaking with ten other employees about the invitation, I was able to offer the following reactions to it: Some men didn't know that the invitation was sent out to women, some men were amused by the invitation, and some wondered why they were not included in it. It would have been easy and fair just to extend the invitation to all employees. Many women staff and faculty were both amused and insulted by the flowery design (assumptions about the sensibilities of women) and the assumption that financial strategies and vocabularies are intimidating to women. This assumption reinforces the "Math-is-Hard-Barbie" idea about women and ignores the expertise that the institution's women employees have in the areas of mathematics, science, accounting, economics, and finance. In one fell swoop, expertise is erased and ideas about group membership and characteristics are promoted. Women are included in the invitation because they're supposed to stink with money, and men are excluded from the invitation because they're supposed to be the powerful money managers.

What should have been done differently? In this case and, if this case is any indication, in all cases, a careful vetting process is required. Run the invitation by a few employees first. See what the reactions are. What are the pros and cons of offering such a workshop and of targeting only one group of employees? What's the possible fallout? What's the solution? In the case of the financial workshop, a simple invitation to all employees, female and male, would have sufficed. If the crafters of the invitation wanted to insist upon clip art, well, then, some dollar signs or stock exchange images might have worked well. It's fine to offer refreshments; just make sure to do it for everyone. This approach is not necessarily "politically correct," but it does reveal cultural competence, that is, an awareness about the employee population and the various areas of expertise of many of the employees.

A few years ago, our institution made the decision to terminate the use of the term "freshman" and to actively promote the use of "first-year student." My first impression was that this was politically correct overkill, but my second and lasting impression is that it was the right thing to do. If "man," "mankind," and the pronouns "he/him" really don't include women, which they don't, then "freshman" doesn't either. I have been really interested to see how our school achieved this lexical change in a short time. Without any formal, global announcement of the change, the administrators in academics, student life, and the registrar's office all adopted the change in their own oral speech and their offices' written documents. New first-year students became quickly accustomed to the "first-year" term because it was all they had ever known. In the end, the term "first-year" is wholly descriptive and wholly inoffensive, and the term "freshman" is much less descriptive and inclusive, so why not adopt the change? A simple decision was made and communicated, and the new language became the norm.

One area in which our institution has not made great strides but *could* employ the same strategies is the use of the phrases "gentlemanly behavior" and "conduct unbecoming to a gentleman." Of course, these Robert E. Lee-infused phrases are holdovers from over 150 years ago, a bit of tradition that continues to breathe through our honor and conduct systems. Nevertheless, it would be relatively easy to broaden the language to include women (and not "ladies") and to undo the race and class assumptions proposed by the terms. I would suggest simply writing a clear code of behavior without any reference to ladies or gentlemen and then adjudicating breaches through the judicial and honor committees and making clear that sanctions mean that an individual has not adhered to the behavior principles. There's no need to cast "gentlemanly" hues and thereby alienate significant parts of the current student, staff, and faculty populations.

Elizabeth Chamberlain has enumerated examples of student-to-student harassment, including speech acts, such as sexual jokes, demeaning portrayals of women in school skits, rating of girls on sexual desirability, and comments related to sexual orientation or sexual preference (5 [of web version]). In these areas, too, institutions need heightened awareness about free versus harmful speech issues to decide fairly which speech acts cause an inhospitable climate and impinge on equal access to learning. At my institution, the "Bracket" brought all of these issues to bear, and the students got a firsthand look at the tension between free speech and groups protected by Titles VII and IX. Chamberlain recommends an institution-wide (staff, faculty, students) examination of legal remedies, but also recognizes that "relying on legal remedies alone, with their embedded presuppositions, may prevent us from getting to effective educational strategies" (7 [of web version]).[5] While institutions undoubtedly benefit from having carefully and thoughtfully framed policies on sexual harassment, Chamberlain asserts that three elements are often not addressed: "(1) the context in which behavior occurs, (2) the cultural influences that support and mask sexual harassment, and (3) the need for informed reflection by students and adults regarding current practices and the perhaps unintentional damage created by the latter" (7 [of web version]).

These three elements relate well to Poole's notion of "cultural competence" as a tool that manages inter-group tensions better than a vaguely prescribed "politically correct" language. Therefore, for example, at my institution, if we had understood better the context of "the Bracket" (a yearly, "traditional" time for student journalists to use derogatory language about specific groups of people as a "class") from both an academic perspective (gender studies, journalism, law) and a social one (fraternities, sexual harassment and assault, gender imbalance), we might have been able to talk up-front, before the mad month of March, about the context and the cultural influences of sexual harassment on our campus. Had we successfully and openly prevented this "tradition"—in the very public arena of the student press, and maybe even also in the more underground arena of e-mail and/or Facebook—we (and I mean all of us, not just the same old, same olds advocating for equity in student access to education) would have sent a message about how cultural norms can be shaped and changed, even if slowly.[6] If we can keep cultural competence as the fundamental goal—in the classroom, in the meeting room, on the playing field, in the orchestra pit, and through study abroad—we can slowly build a safe environment for respectful speech and frank disagreement.

Solutions

1. Embrace moments of discord on campus and/or in the workplace as opportunities to increase knowledge about Titles VII and IX and to encourage critical thinking.

2. Create open forums in the workplace to discuss heated issues. These can include electronic forums, panels, moderated discussions, and written exchanges through the newspaper(s).
3. Have a campus-wide or organization-wide media review board that understands the organization's mission statement, meets regularly, and carefully oversees media production, especially of neophyte journalists.
4. Have the curriculum speak to the extracurricular issues. Include courses on First Amendment law and politics through the lenses of Titles VII and IX. Cross-list, when appropriate, with Women's and Gender Studies, Sociology, African American Studies, and Latin American and Caribbean Studies.
5. Hire and retain managers and executives who are culturally competent and who underscore the value of cultural competence in the workplace. Such values are inherent to most organizations' mission statements, so this is really just matching institutional rhetoric to the actions of the workplace leaders.
6. Hire and retain managers who consistently use their own speech acts to set the tone for other speech acts in the work environment. Do not place the onus upon the members of protected categories always to have to protect themselves from harmful speech.
7. Consult with the experts in the workplace. If there is a question of race, religion, sex, and so on, in campus activities, brochures, or speech, include the scholars (students and faculty) in the related departments on the question. If there is a question about sex/gender, consult with the students and faculty of Women's and Gender Studies.
8. Protect Title VII and Title IX in the organization by openly demoting or firing those who consistently violate them.
9. Be aware of the rhetoric of "zero tolerance." Only use this term if it aptly describes the environment, which it likely won't or can't for a long time.

NOTES

1. See Linder and Nosek's "Alienable Speech: Ideological Variations in the Application of Free-Speech Principles" for a full discussion of the links between social and political tolerance regarding Constitutional protections. As Nielsen has stated (10–11), we might see this, in the case of race, as a battle between the First and Fourteenth Amendments. I would add that, in

the case of gender, this issue begs further analysis on the at times contradictory protections of the First Amendment and Titles VII and IX.

2. For an excellent history of how the question of sex and gender was challenged in Title VII law, see Chapter 4 ("Women Challenge 'Jane Crow'") of Nancy MacLean's book *Freedom is Not Enough. The Opening of the American Workplace.*

3. See Robin M. LeBlanc's brilliant essay, "Teaching to Spite Your Body," for an examination of the implications of the students' use of the word "cunt" in the university-sanctioned student publication.

4. Nielsen later discusses how to understand hierarchy, power, and privilege from a socio-legal perspective: "It [contemporary social theory] suggests that a phenomenon like street harassment and the hierarchical systems reinforced by it are accepted as 'social facts'—real, uncontestable, and inevitable. In this framework, assumptions and ideologies about gender relations, the law, and street harassment become naturalized and taken for granted. Social norms about law, gender, and public interactions work together to create and reinforce these interactions as 'normal.' Law works with existing systems of hierarchy (based on race or gender) to render these interactions invisible and uncontestable" (33). Although Nielsen's focus is street harassment, her statements about how laws interact with social assumptions to influence speech acts are an important element of how institutions determine what is "allowable" speech within their walls and on their grounds.

5. Kathy Hotelling signals how the organization and campus climate of colleges and universities make these types of workplaces, despite their reputation for being different from the outside world, "potentially ripe ground for sexual harassment to occur. According to Dziech and Weinter (1984), the complexity of the issue, however, extends even further in that other factors converge to delay, ignore, or refute any sexual harassment charges that are reported. The diffused institutional authority can result in a lack of accountability and role conflict at all levels of the university that allow one to deny authority and responsibility. The concept of professional autonomy or academic freedom is sometimes used to defend behavior and avoid responsibility; eccentric behavior is tolerated (i.e. the absentminded professor). In an environment where politics are harsh and segments of the university openly vie for power, collegiality may be used to be "supportive of colleagues and unsympathetic to women complainants and their advocates' (p. 49)." (499).

6. See Kelly J. Baker's "Writing About Sexism in Academia Hurts" for a description of the overwhelmingly convicting data and narratives on gender bias and sexism in higher education that she has encountered in her research *and* for an understanding of the "activist fatigue" that sets in when individuals confront microaggressions and gender shrapnel in the workplace.

REFERENCES

Linder, Nicole M., and Brian A. Nosek. 2009. Alienable speech: Ideological variations in the application of free-speech principles. *Political Psychology* 30(1): 67–92. Print.

The Urban Dictionary online. http://www.urbandictionary.com/. Accessed 20 Oct 2011.

CHAPTER 10

Thinking About Institutional Language in New Ways

A high school friend of mine named Susan used to spell her name "Sus3an," but, she reminded us, the "3" was silent. I remember seeing her write her name that way and trying to get a "three" sound into the middle of it. I remember feeling the challenge of a nomenclature system that permitted the mixing of letters and numbers, long before we had that type of username and password for many of our daily operations. And I remember clearly laughing from the gut when I was told that the "3" was silent. Just one small change in the spelling of someone's name got everyone thinking differently about names, about language, about personal preferences, about identity. Just that one small change got everyone trying to spell and pronounce Sus3an's name correctly, with "correctly" being exactly as Sus3an would want it.

In the context of the workplace, we might ask ourselves how language can strike us as new, innovative, different, and thought-provoking; how certain combinations of signs and symbols might for one or more reasons seem incongruous together, out of place, off-putting, or even insulting to our sensibilities. This chapter aims to examine shifts in student population that signal the need to redirect schools' focus to Title VII and Title IX, to discuss elements of these two laws that can influence our everyday language use in the workplace, to consider Joanne Martin's concept of deconstruction in organization management, and to provide examples of this type of deconstruction in the workplace and in literature on sexual harassment.

© The Editor(s) (if applicable) and The Author(s) 2016
E. Mayock, *Gender Shrapnel in the Academic Workplace*,
DOI 10.1057/978-1-137-50830-0_10

In her brilliant article, "Deconstructing Organizational Taboos: The Suppression of Gender Conflict in Organizations," Joanne Martin suggests that the image of the pregnant executive can help us to break taboos and think innovatively about language. The image of a professional woman, sometimes considered an "honorary man" (Martin 348), with a visible pregnancy gives many employees cause for pause. As Martin says, "In a male-dominated organization, a pregnant employee is just such an alien element, (*especially when she is a 'token,' that is, one of few women holding a relatively high ranking organizational position usually reserved for men, as in the Caesarean story)" (348). Martin adds, "Pregnancy removes the option of ignoring a working woman's gender: 'Honorary men' don't become pregnant" (348).

In a way, the pregnant executive becomes the "Sus3an" of the work-place. Employees, in varying degrees of comfort and discomfort, are "confronted" with the pregnant body and must make an effort to restore the image to something mentally and emotionally acceptable. The relative taboo on high-level female employees (both a sexist and a classist taboo) offers one possibility for thinking of institutional language in new ways, of getting the high-level executives and all the employees more aware of the many different human variables in the workplace. I still laugh when I recall the skit on Saturday Night Live that featured a very pregnant, very rapping Amy Pohler. As an audience, we were not only not used to seeing comedians on stage in the latest stage of pregnancy but also certainly not accustomed to seeing such comedians singing and dancing. This is really funny *and* offers the opportunity for co-workers (and audiences) to remember that pregnant women are workers (and vice versa). In other words, breaking taboos allows for more equity in the workplace. As the only woman at her institution to be pregnant and have a baby during her tenure as an administrator, Jessica (see Chapter 3) felt freakish as she attended meetings, visited campus construction sites, advised students, and submitted budgets with her body changing daily. It was almost as if she had been pregnant' and rapping her way across campus, even though she had no desire to be any more of a spectacle than she usually was. It would have been helpful to have had more people around who took it all in stride, who didn't care that she was or wasn't pregnant, and who understood that the work was getting done in all the same ways. In other words, it would have been helpful if Jessica's visible pregnancy had simply become part of the signs and symbols that were the language of the workplace. Instead, I'm convinced that Jessica's visible mother status contributed to increased gender shrapnel down the line.

Joanne Martin reminds us that:

> Recent efforts to alleviate gender inequality have made it socially, and in some contexts, legally, inappropriate to express overt gender prejudice. Of course, open and direct expressions of gender prejudice do still occur. However, gender conflict in organizations is often unspoken or hidden "between the lines" of what people say and do, like the more subtle forms of modern racial prejudice (e.g., Pettigrew and Martin 1987). Such suppressed conflict is easier to deny, harder to detect and combat, and more difficult to study. Deconstruction offers one way to address this problem. (340)

Indeed, an awareness about language and a keen ability to deconstruct its use in the workplace is a key element in creating an environment that embraces the values behind Title VII and Title IX.[1] Mumby and Putnam have astutely asserted that employees can be strongly influenced by the inculcation of an organization's values over time. They write, "For many members, emotions are embedded in symbols such as myths and stories that transmit the organization's values and ideology. The orchestrating of symbols extends beyond emotional displays because it can control both the expression of and the interpretation of members' feelings. That is, the management of an organization's culture is aimed at controlling feelings of loyalty, identification, and solidarity that bind a collectivity in a particular way" (473). To its credit (in part), my institution is fervently trying to undo, I think principally on the public relations level, its local and regional reputation of spreading gender shrapnel. Certain employee programs, like the wellness program, and human resources newsletters are designed to bring us together as a community and to feel a communal happiness or satisfaction about our institutional bonds and allegiances. If we're not all on the same page about whether or not to celebrate Robert E. Lee as eternal icon of the institution, then maybe we can be if we just all attend the wellness fair and have our blood pressure taken together. The wellness fair might help to keep people physically well, but it will not solve the problems of gender or race shrapnel in the workplace. One element that might contribute to a solution is this open, more innovative approach to language and imagery that will, over time, influence how we treat one another in the workplace. Mumby and Putnam's work serves to revamp organizational theory by examining the interplay between "bounded emotionality" and "bounded rationality" (474):

> This contrast, however, does not treat bounded emotionality and bounded rationality as mutually exclusive constructs. Instead, "the different powers of

both voices [are used] to generate a sense of opposition, difference, and creative tension. The resultant third voice, retaining the personal power of the first and the intersubjectivity of the second, might thereby open a window on as yet unimagined, ungendered possibilities of speaking, knowing, and living" (Dimen, 1989: 35). Hence, the two concepts are engaged in "play" to produce an understanding of the organizing process (and theorizing about organizing) that neither term can capture alone. (474)

The Western Interstate Commission for Higher Education in 2008 released data that revealed that, "By 2022, almost half of all public high-school graduates will be members of minority groups" (Ashburn, "New Data Predict"). Sarita E. Brown of Excelencia in Education told *The Chronicle*, "This really isn't new. But it's going to be a much greater proportion of students than we've seen before, and the downsides of not addressing these issues will be felt much more keenly" ("New Data Predict"). Therefore, colleges and universities should expect a differently composed student population in years to come. Furthermore, a 2011 national study of 7th to 12th graders conducted by the AAUW reported that "girls reported being harassed more than boys—56 percent compared with 40 percent— though it was evenly divided during middle school. Boys were more likely to be the harassers, according to the study, and children from lower-income families reported more severe effects" (Anderson, "National Study Finds Widespread Sexual Harassment"). These are the students, those already exposed broadly to in-person and online sexual harassment, who populate our colleges and universities and will continue to do so over the next several years. These data on demographics and on experience with sexual harassment tell us that the academic workplace must be more focused on formal questions of equity through Titles VII and IX and on informal questions of equity through language selection and use and its consonance with college and university mission statements. As I've stated several times in *Gender Shrapnel*, most colleges and universities have sound, forward-thinking mission statements. The challenge, therefore, for these institutions will be to put their mouth where their mouth is. Thinking about "Sus3an," institutions will need to understand how informal and formal communications are capable of offending, on one level, and of violating civil rights, on another level, and how deconstruction of prepared pieces will be a step in the right direction toward creating a welcoming environment.

I want to write briefly now on the harm that institutions can do when they are sincerely trying to clear gender shrapnel by forming committees and offering workshops but do not think consciously about or deconstruct the language they choose to use for such actions. An example from a recent article from *The Chronicle of Higher Education* reveals how even when an author is "gauging gender" (the title of the piece) in an apparently respectful way, there can be pitfalls. The author of this piece is exhorting colleagues in the humanities to school themselves better on advancements in the biological sciences in order to understand the ways in which biology offers much more nuanced evidence about sex and gender than the dangerous essentialism of the 1990s. The author mentions sex versus gender, the feminine brain and the masculine brain, and the ways in which biology and gender studies have attempted to undertake the study of these issues. I'm always amazed in studies by experts and even on governmental forms that "male" comes before "female," given that, alphabetically, the reverse should be true. In the "Gauging Gender" article, the author states, "The solution is not to argue that there is no such thing as 'male/female' or 'normal/abnormal' or 'typical/atypical'." In creating these dichotomies, even if the author is going to knock them down, the author wittingly or unwittingly again aligns "male" with "normal" and "typical." Male again becomes universal.

In the book titled *Developing & Maintaining a Sexual Harassment Free Workplace*, David Bassham makes several similar mistakes. Like many of the handbooks currently on the market to counsel individuals and organizations on creating "harassment-free workplaces," Bassham's guide is very much targeted at businesses that simply want to protect themselves from lawsuits, rather than actually create a work environment that is just and promotes equity. Most of these are simply "risk management" guides, which I frankly see as Cover Your Legal Ass guides that do nothing to help actual employees and, therefore, do little to manage real risk in the workplace. Bassham's guide starts with a heterosexist quote by Henry Kissinger: "Nobody will ever win the Battle of the Sexes. There is just too much fraternizing with the enemy" (7). The quote gets its own page and sets the tone for the entire guide. Nevertheless, the quote is never given any context, never deconstructed, never dissected by the author and, therefore, it gains way too much power as the anchor of the guide itself. It tells us that Kissinger is important and invites us to accept the superficial assertion about the "Battle of the Sexes" (note the capital letters) and to indulge the "reality" that everyone in the workplace should just want to have sex (but not really engage in having sex) with employees of the opposite sex. This sexist, heterosexist rhetoric goes absolutely against the spirit of Title VII and Title IX and immediately tells the intelligent reader that this guide only serves to apologize that we all have to be trained on this silly old thing called sexual harassment and that, if we just pay attention to a few little legal remedies, the whole darned thing will go away. All other quotes at the beginning of new chapters are by men. All of the photographs show White men in charge, with two photos of White women in business suits who have fearful looks on their faces. The guide reinforces, rather than deconstructs, all of the signs and symbols of gender and race shrapnel.

At my institution, what could have become "a standing committee on the status of women," as had been done successfully at so many other colleges and universities, became the "task force on women." Not the status of women, just "on women," because using the word "status" implies a lack of equity, a caste system within which women find themselves at the bottom. The use of the phrase "status of women" would have aptly addressed the problems of gender shrapnel among those who actively inhabited the university workplace (rather than those who flapped around it with great and sincere interest, but without having to live with the daily realities on the shrapneled campus). The term "task force," as loaded in its military might as, perhaps, is "gender shrapnel," implies that one strategic strike will eradicate all of the problems, that the problems have no roots, and that they are easily swept away with one plan. It belies the reality of the deep-rootedness of tradition, culture, risk, and the status quo. Had the administration created back then a standing committee on the status of women, it would have now much more buy-in from many of the employees and students and might have by now cleared some of the shrapnel. The "task force" terminology made the "women's issue" a very temporary front-burner issue that fizzled out quickly with no real resolution, while a "standing" committee would have brought forward the notions of both an active (standing, not sitting) committee and a desire for long-term solutions.

Another factor that made the "women's issue" more diffuse was the assignment of the duties of the typical one-person Title IX officer to three different people. I came across this unique situation through my role as the university's faculty athletics representative. We had to complete and submit to the NCAA a Title IX report. When I went about ensuring that we were consulting with all the right people on campus by trying to ascertain who our Title IX officer was, my phone calls met with suspicion. When I discovered that three different people were assigned different aspects of Title IX policy on campus, I was sincerely surprised. How could three different very busy people with three markedly different job descriptions cover this responsibility clearly and efficiently. I have been pleased to see that the university has now placed Title IX responsibilities in one person's hands, which is a move in the right direction to demonstrate good-faith compliance and real interest in the educational equity issues at hand. The symbolism of one person in charge sends the message that the institution might at some point prioritize these questions of access and equity. At the same time, that one person carries great responsibility and liability, especially on a more fraught Title IX landscape. Institutions need to ensure that the Title IX officer is excellent at her or his job, open to change and suggestions, and well protected.

It is particularly important for the individuals and groups in charge of setting the college or university's course and publicizing its mission to think about institutional language in new ways. I served for two years as a faculty representative to our Board of Trustees. In this role, I attended plenary sessions and specific committee meetings of the Board. I developed great respect for how knowledgeable many of the Board members were, especially in the areas of finance, real estate, and capital investments, and for how very much they cared about the institution. At the same time, I was able to observe centuries-long cultural influences that impeded innovative thought about languages and symbols. The plenary sessions still begin with a Christian prayer delivered by a senior, White, deep-voiced member of the Board. While the melodious sounds of the prayer seem innocuous enough and maybe even soothing, the Christian prayer sets a certain tone for the entire day's meetings. If the day sometimes began with a Christian prayer, sometimes with an Islamic one, sometimes with a Jewish one, and sometimes with nothing at all, then I'd have a little less of a problem with it. But, why is it actually necessary when it might serve to alienate any one of the 50+ individuals in the room?

During my two years with the Board, I learned that they were good listeners on controversial issues, in particular when the issues had to do directly with the student body. They were appropriately concerned about the lack of women running for elected positions on campus, the sexual assault statistics, alcohol abuse, eating disorders, the lack of sober interaction between women and men on campus, and the language used in student publications. I also learned that, while they were able to run through budget and finance at a high level, they seemed unable to synthesize, summarize, or analyze the deep problems of gender shrapnel, both in the student body and among the staff and faculty. Their principal weakness was a lack of consultation with real experts on gender issues. The gender shrapnel within the student body had turned into a generalized physical and metaphorical anorexia, but the Board members could not find the language to pull the ideas together and to devise a series of discrete *and* unified solutions. So, the Board listened well on these issues, for sure, but became unsure and lacked confidence regarding how exactly to act on what they had heard.

One particular experience with the Board might help to illuminate this point in a somewhat humorous way. On one of the big Board meeting days, the Lesbian, Gay, Bisexual, Transgender, Questioning (LGBTQ) group on campus was sponsoring their annual "Gay? Fine by Me" day, on which members of the campus community were asked to wear their brightly colored LGBTQ "Gay? Fine by Me" T-shirts. One of my favorite students specifically asked me and several other professors to wear our T-shirts through our daily activities for the day. I agreed and donned my bright orange T-shirt with business-style pants and a fancy orange scarf. I tried to look dressed up enough for a meeting of the Board of Trustees while also honoring the day by wearing the T-shirt. What I found was that the Board members saw the T-shirt, really didn't seem to mind that I had worn it, but were afraid to ask about it. One even commented to me, "Hey, I like your scarf!" This cracked me up to no end—there we were, with the perfect opportunity for a real conversation about how this traditionally marginalized group could feel more welcomed on campus, and I was just wearing a nice scarf.

An additional word to the wise on institutional language includes the problematic conceptualization of sexual abuse and harassment as featuring two individuals, the perpetrator and the victim (Chamberlain 11 [web version]). Chamberlain notes, too, that victims often feel such guilt surrounding the actual victimization that they take responsibility for it, encouraged to do so as well by others around her: "She/he will not feel empowered to effect a change or develop a plan to change the prevailing customs of harassment; the only option that presents itself is to restrict her own movements, dress, and interactions" (11 of web version).

This is another instance in which we as a nation have insufficient vocabulary to describe the people and circumstances of sexual harassment. As we know, those who have been sexually harassed and/or assaulted often are forced to "share the blame" so that the harasser can be partially excused (he didn't mean it, it's not that big a deal, why are you being so sensitive, just get over it, etc.). This phenomenon is amply treated by Kristof and WuDunn in *Half the Sky*, in which women in certain communities who are raped are then shunned, injured, killed, or forced to marry their rapists—

all punishments that force the victims to share, and I would say actually shoulder, the blame of the shame on the community. This is a profound extrapolation of what happens daily in the sexual harassment paradigm. Individuals and organizations have begun to use more apt terminology (e.g. "survivor") in these cases, terminology that we as a nation and we as a legal community have not yet wholly embraced. We need to think creatively and together about a way to get away from the dangerous dichotomies of perp/victim, respondent/complainant, and defendant/plaintiff.

If more individuals in the academic workplace learn to "think Sus3an," or at least to understand that this may be how many others think, then the workplace will open up to a better understanding of the legal and social ramifications of Titles VII and IX, a fundamental factor for universities who aim to keep up with the rapidly changing demographics of this century. In their article on "Tempered Radicalism," Meyerson and Scully cite Chesler's ability to "break away from dominant professional symbols and myths to question their validity, and to undertake innovative theory building and research. Being free of existing professional paradigms has enabled him [Chesler] to develop new bodies of knowledge now recognized as important to the profession" (qtd. in Meyerson, 589). They also cite Stonequist, who says that those on the margins are "acute and able critics" (qtd. in Meyerson, 589). On the question of gender, calling it what it is and understanding the concerns and critiques "from the margins" will open up the conversation in revealing and solution-oriented ways.

Solutions

1. Think "Sus3an." That is, have individuals and groups do exercises in thinking about language more broadly, from a wider variety of perspectives.
2. Use examples of deconstruction to break taboos and make "rarer" images more a part of the visual (and audible) toolkit. The more we include diverse peoples and ideas throughout the workplace, the more natural these diverse peoples and ideas will be.
3. Publicize data about changing demographics in US colleges and universities.
4. Have Title VII and Title IX become household words on campus. This can be done through publicizing pertinent scholarship on the issues, holding legal workshops, having round table discussions, and culling stories from university students and employees.

5. Assign one Title IX officer and make sure the entire campus knows who he or she is. Invite the Title IX officer to key meetings, including of student affairs, capital projects, the Board of Trustees, academic affairs, and make clear that the Title IX officer is representing Title IX.

6. Reinforce the idea of challenging the status quo across the organization. Have it be a part of conversations between advisers and first-year students, among staff and faculty, and between employees and managers. Use the theme as part of a daring convocation or commencement speech or an employee training session. Reward those who actively and constructively challenge the status quo in real ways (research opportunities, endowments, publicity, networks).

7. Call gender shrapnel what it is. Define it, give examples of it, and ask for remedies to current problems and impediments to future potential problems. Take very much into consideration how gender shrapnel intersects with other types of shrapnel (racial, religious, etc.) and address the categories in an explicit way.

8. Attempt to get away from Manichean terminology that reinforces blame sharing. Move away from "victim" and toward "the individual who was harassed," or "the model survivor," or toward other, better terms generated in the specific organization.

9. Create a Standing Committee on Women in your workplace.

10. Develop a Gender Action Group with an online forum.

NOTE

1. Martin lists nine strategies for deconstructing organizational language. These include dismantling a dichotomy; examining silences; attending to disruptions and contradictions; focusing on the element that is most alien to a text or a context; interpreting metaphors as a rich source of multiple meanings; analyzing "double-entendres" that may point to an unconscious subtext, often sexual in content; separating group-specific and more general sources of bias by "reconstructing" the text with iterative substitution of phrases; exploring the unexpected ramifications and inherent limitations of minor policy changes; and using the limitations exposed by "reconstruction" to explain the persistence of the status quo and the need for more ambitious change programs (355). Martin suggests that it would be a useful exercise to perform deconstructions from a variety of ideological viewpoints

in order to have a grasp on how different employees interpret a variety of work situations. On a more general note, Sheryl Sandberg, in her final chapter of *Lean In*, states: "We need to be grateful for what we have but dissatisfied with the status quo. This dissatisfaction spurs the charge to change. We must keep going" (172).

CHAPTER 11

Common Denominators and Potential Modes of Communication

For the multitudes of us who are alumni of schools—high schools, community colleges, colleges, and universities—the institution whose halls we passed through serves as a marker of a time in our lives, the things we learned, the experiences we had, the friendships we forged; it basically becomes a small part of who we are. I have great affection for my undergraduate university, and I treasure the four years I had there for the many things that time has given me throughout my life—a profound and sincere love of learning and critical analysis, a *joie de vivre*, an amazing group of lifelong friends, and a sense of place and memory that stands out as different and unique. And so I really am an alumna of the place, and I really do view it as a community. It is easy for me to freeze the institution's image at the warm moment of the day and year of my graduation because I do not work there and am less invested in the day-to-day workings of the place than I was all those years ago.[1] I bring this awareness of and appreciation for the nostalgia evoked by an educational institution to my analysis of the day-to-day work environment of the academic workplace.

This chapter seeks to list and describe the common denominators of an organization, that is, the elements that naturally and/or deliberately draw constituencies together and send some type of unifying image to the world beyond. It also aims to look at many of the ways in which it is fine for an organization *not* to be unified or united, to be apart, but respectfully so. With each additional word I write of *Gender Shrapnel*, I am poignantly aware of the strong ties so many have to the institution

© The Editor(s) (if applicable) and The Author(s) 2016
E. Mayock, *Gender Shrapnel in the Academic Workplace*,
DOI 10.1057/978-1-137-50830-0_11

where I work, their nostalgia for its place in their lives, their loyalty to the idea of the institution's success, and their investment in maintaining the traditions they hold dear. I know full well that my words here, my mere daily existence in the workplace, and my critical observations about the present and future of the institution can seem like an affront to all of those who work assiduously for what they believe to be the common good of the institution. While in Chapter 12 I'll talk a lot about different groups defining "common good" in varying ways, here I'd like to focus on which elements of the work environment draw us together in effective ways, and which elements can and should allow us to stay respectfully apart.

Janet Morgan Riggs of Gettysburg College writes in "Working to Build a Cohesive Faculty Community" that, despite the relatively small number of employees at her institution, building a community requires work. She cogently describes the typical role of a faculty member and why, in many cases, this role demands so much and therefore might take time that, years ago, naturally lent itself to community building. Morgan Riggs suggests that Friday faculty lunches, Friday afternoon social hours, and creative teaching and learning programs can help to bring faculty together in formal, work-oriented ways, as well as in informal, purely social ways. These are excellent suggestions because they combine the formal with the informal, thus making the events open to everyone but not required of anyone. They allow for a "way in" through the work, rather than just through informal social networks. As an additional professional strategy to build community, organizations can and should offer a broad-based orientation session for all new employees that allows for shared breakfasts or lunches. When this group of new employees spends ample, early time together, they often start to lean on each other for professional mentoring across the organization's units, as well as for the development of their social lives in the new setting. In addition, this allows more veteran members of these individuals' departments to meet and get to know more of the newcomers, thus building connections and the potential for new friendships for everyone. New employee orientation should have required sessions and/ or events that are both beneficial for the attendees and useful for building an affinity for the workplace and its workers.

Human Resources staff and upper-level managers must keep in mind that it is absolutely acceptable for an individual not to engage completely or even much in the larger community. That person might well spend all of her or his time advising students on career, fellowship, study abroad, or co-curricular issues. While this heavy load of advising might remove the individual from the Friday lunch or happy hour circuit, we recognize, of course, that this type of advising is a huge benefit to the institution as a whole. Likewise, an individual might be a top-notch researcher most of whose moments away from teaching and advising must be spent on the work. This is fine and good, and there are many other ways to engage that person—by reading her or his research, making an occasional comment or asking a question about it, highlighting the excellent work through the institution's media, and so on. Not everyone needs to "belong" in the visible ways often emphasized, especially in smaller work environments.

The question of building community is intimately (if covertly) related to gender shrapnel, especially in the realms of gender diversity in hiring and promotion and the question of the "right fit" (treated in Chapter 8). In other words, how well do women employees (and students, in the case of the education workplace) fit in the environment of their institution, to what degree do they feel like they are a part of the place, and that their presence and opinions matter? The McKinsey Global Survey titled "Moving women to the top" points out that companies that prioritize gender diversity "also report a higher share of women in their senior ranks" (two of web PDF). The McKinsey staff queried respondents about the following measures to "recruit, retain, promote, and develop women": options for flexible working conditions/locations; support programs, facilities to help recon-cile work and family life; programs to encourage female networking, role models; encouragement or mandates for senior executives to mentor junior women; visible monitoring of gender-diversity programs by CEO, execu-tive team; assessing indicators of hiring, retaining, promoting, developing women; programs to smooth transitions before, during, and after parental leaves; performance evaluation systems that neutralize impact of parental leave, flexible work; skill-building programs aimed specifically at women; gender-specific hiring goals, programs; inclusion of gender-diversity indi-cators in performance reviews; requirement that each promotion pool include at least one female candidate; gender quotas in hiring, retaining, promoting, developing women (four of web PDF).

While generating an exhaustive list such as this one is extremely useful, it also has its pitfalls, some of which we can anticipate given what we've learned so far in *Gender Shrapnel*. I firmly believe it would be excellent to have managers and administrators keep this list and its goals on the front burner, but I also want them to treat the strategies in a nuanced way. For example, some women (and employees in general) might not want work–life balance to be considered a top priority. They might feel more private about their needs and less likely to share family information in the workplace, especially if they sense that a familial identification can cause them harm in the workplace. Skill-building programs aimed specifically at women might carry an inherent bias with them, as with the example of the women's investment workshop held at my institution. In addition, I like the idea of quota systems because they are proven to have had an impact in, for example, Scandinavian and some Western European and Northern African political systems. Nevertheless, managers considering this strategy must also have in mind the perception of or reaction to quota systems and the possible fallout for women chosen through this type of system.

In this age of advanced technologies, schools are becoming increasingly savvy about how to spread their marketing message. At this point, the large majority of colleges and universities use multiple platforms to increase the visibility (and audibility?) of their "brand." Websites, blogs, twitter and its tweets, strengthened connections to the traditional news media, alumni publications, e-mail communications, and even traditional letters sent by post are the commerce of everyday communications. They matter—a lot. They matter because they are public outlets through which the college or university declares itself one, unique, individual entity with a beautiful campus in a wonderful setting, with its accomplished students, dedicated staff and faculty who live and breathe the institution's mission, and devoted alumni. Of course, the core message of an institution can be discerned from consistent perusal and analysis of what is published in the institution's media. But the casual surfer should be aware because, oftentimes, what is portrayed on a website or sent out in an alumni magazine is not wholly consonant with the day-to-day realities of the campus or does not reveal deeper, more hypocritical underlying problems. For example, a website that shows student after accomplished student in a different foreign country would tend to tell us that the institution values study and work abroad, that it cherishes language, culture, and a deepening understanding of others. It is most likely completely true that the institution does indeed value these things, but the day-to-day realities of the campus might speak more to cuts in foreign language education, fewer resources for humanities majors, and less appreciation for the advising that encourages such student pursuits. Another example might be that the official university website has a statement about valuing diversity, but then the university-sanctioned student paper scorns all women for being "sluts" and all homosexuals for being less than valuable human beings. No doubt, it is nigh on impossible for an institution to have one, monolithically consistent message, nor should it want to. Nevertheless, a serving of daily hypocrisy by the university media can be avoided.

If an institution has appointed and consistently trained a competent Title IX officer, it can benefit from amplifying her or his role on campus. Although in the past it was not common practice for Title IX officers to evaluate institutions' websites, paper calendars, alumni magazines, and blog posts before they were released to the public, it might actually have become a best practice to do so. Having one person who knows both the institution and Title IX law and practice and whose eye is trained to catch images of gender shrapnel could eliminate direct and subliminal messages that employees might not have caught (and, really, might not be trained to catch). At my institution, it used to just be the Women's and Gender Studies faculty who would catch unintended messages of gender shrapnel, but I do believe that there is now enough consciousness on campus that we're starting to hear more calm protests from other constituencies on campus. This is a good sign that there has been some consciousness-raising on campus that has benefited everyone. At one colleague's campus, the media office produced an admissions video that was informative, colorful, and very "glossy." They proudly shared the video with current students, staff, and faculty, and only two people noticed that not one female faculty member was featured in the entire video and that, in fact, the male faculty members featured were among the newest (youngest) group. They brought this to the attention of the media office, who, to their credit, listened. These expensive mistakes are entirely avoidable, and the core institutional message can remain the same. The positive impact of these gender shrapnel "catches" is that they broaden the potential audience for campus media outlets.

At another institution, there is much conversation about who gets publicity on the website and in the alumni magazine and who doesn't. There have been several documented examples, including the one I previously cited of a woman professor having two books come out and getting no time on the website while at the same time a man professor went to a conference and was featured on the website. Many other such instances have occurred. It might well be that the men are getting out the word about their work more forcefully and that the media office is hearing them more clearly, but that's not a good enough excuse. Remember: men do not lose points when they self-promote, but women do. The media office has to seek stories actively and give fair time according to level and frequency of accomplishment.

It is quite possible that print media cause the most long-lasting damage because mistakes made after printing cannot just be whisked away with the click of a mouse. My institution has always published a print "Facebook" with photos of each member of the new incoming class. The Class of 2013 Facebook featured four sophomore men in coats and ties walking down the storied Colonnade. The men appear all to be White, and no woman appears in the photo. This is the ostensible representation of the Class of 2013—all male, all White, all coat and tie. It recalls the alleged opening line of one of our long-retired professors to his students on the first day of class, "Students are expected to wear a coat and tie to this class." This line appears to have remained unaltered even 20 years after co-education. Our print media should not in any way replicate these words that we allowed someone to say for too long.

There are several issues of my institution's alumni magazine that have caught the eye of those attuned to gender shrapnel. One celebrated the 100th anniversary of our business school. On the cover was a photo of all of the business school faculty (at that point, at least 75 % male), with images of well-known male figures from the history of the business school hovering above the group. Some of the faculty in the business school felt the image represented the appreciation for patriarchal control over the current group. In any case, just a photo of the current faculty might have sufficed. The Fall 2008 issue of the magazine features our president with one of our (male) biology professors touching tomato plants out in a field. The caption is "{Our University} Goes Green." I recognize that most of the world, highly conscious feminists included, would not see this as sexist in the least. It's good to go green, right? Good for everyone—women, men, children, animals, plants, and the planet. Yes, it is. Nevertheless, I have found that, on our campus, only one "lefty" platform can sustain attention and focus at any given time. That is, the culture seems able to put up with only so much lefty politics. If taking care of the planet, a most noble goal, indeed, reigns, then other areas of focus lose. As we dim lights on campus and in buildings to save energy, we neglect to ask the individuals who walk and work there if they still feel safe. In this sense, going green brushes directly up against public safety, which usually has much to do with women feeling safe in public spaces on campuses where sexual assault is an acute problem. It is great to go green, but also go equitable at the same time! Imagine an alumni magazine on whose cover it says, "{Our University} goes compliant!"

One final example that might have struck some as hypocritical or alienating was the Fall/Winter 2009 alumni magazine with a cover with the simple word "civility" and an image of orange-clad workers struggling to gather up the crumbling stone pieces of columns and supports of an ancient marquee that says just, "Civility." They are heroically trying to "rebuild" civility. This cover struck a very complex chord with me and still does. My institution prides itself on a 265-year-old student-run honor system that was conceived in pre-Revolutionary times and strengthened in Civil War times. The honor system calls upon students to find within themselves and the hallowed walls of the university the will not to lie, cheat, or steal. While I and many others have enjoyed the fruits of working with students who understand these actions to be wrong and who seem to take the moral imperative truly to heart, I have never been able to separate the words and spirit of the honor system from yet another male tradition that forgets how well women have fared when the words "honor" and "civility" are invoked. As I have said many times in forums on whether the honor system could sufficiently and coherently handle cases of sexual assault, age-old honor systems are about men understanding other men's behaviors in public, with women as the shrapnel. In the honor system of the Spanish Renaissance, for example, honor meant that women had to remain chaste or put on a charade that demonstrated chastity. It was all about women's purity and men's valor surrounding women's purity. Current-day honor killings have everything to do with this concept. These gender-shrapneled "ideals" do not suggest fair play, equal access, or anything approaching them, especially not in the twenty-first century, and especially not on the numerous US campuses that devote special attention to their honor codes and systems.

Once women and men are living with or under an honor system that throws students out for using (with permission) one another's meal cards but that calls sexual assault "conduct unbecoming to a gentleman" and traditionally has meted out light sentences to the wrongdoers, they are also subject to codes of civility that accompany honor. The article on civility in the alumni magazine does include blurbs by individuals from the institution who clearly state that civility should not limit disagreement or argument, and this is positive. Nevertheless, when we blanket the campus with civility, we sometimes ignore the severity with which we should respond to certain situations. In other words, when a student rapes another student, the civil language of "conduct unbecoming" is not sufficient and does, in fact, sugarcoat the issue and conceal that an actual felony has occurred. I am in favor of using strong language in strong circumstances so that institutional messages are sent and heard.

The 2011 case of Glover v. the NBA (*The New York Times*, 12-15-2011) highlights the ways in which an organization can ignore even the most oft-repeated and reported offenses and then have to pay a big price for the concealment and the soft-pedaling of its language and actions surrounding harassment. The case also brings one very interesting, very significant tangentially related gender shrapnel point: In this case, Warren J. Glover, former Director of Security for the National Basketball Association (NBA), reported cases of sexual harassment of women in the organization over a ten-year period. These reports were consistently ignored, Glover was overlooked for what would have been a natural promotion given his consistently strong performance evaluations, and, eventually, Glover was fired. Glover was not a direct victim of sexual harassment but he caught the shrapnel by continuing to express concern for public safety and continuing to report the illegal incidents he witnessed. In the end, the NBA appeared to retaliate against him for not getting on board with harassment. In 2014, the National Football League (NFL) clumsily navigated the Ray Rice domestic violence video. After several missteps, the League launched an anti-domestic violence campaign. This seems like a good idea, but, of course, the hypocrisy of the public service announcements that follow completely degradingly sexist advertisements can be a bit much. Many institutions inhabit this hypocrisy all too easily.

The careful, and not tokenized, inclusion of women and women's accomplishments in the ubiquitous media output of an organization allows women and men to see women as professionals in their work roles and as equal contributors in the workplace. I recently browsed through the Fall 2011 *Davidson Journal* (the college's alumni magazine) and found it to be a model of equity, at least from a faculty member's standpoint. The issue focuses on the inauguration of the college's 18th president, Carol Quillen, and features her inauguration speech. It includes as well numerous photos and short pieces on student work (men's and women's), alumni accomplishments, nostalgic, old school photos, and a long, thorough section on faculty accomplishments, in which female and male faculty seem to be equally represented. Academics, sports, and the arts also seem to be fairly evenly represented. My sense is that the magazine has been carefully vetted by several people who are well versed in equity issues and how they relate to media text and images. I just now visited my own institution's homepage, and the site as it stands now is well balanced and welcoming. It includes pieces on four students (two men, two women, two of Color, two White) and their travels, the accomplishments of women and men faculty, publications by one alumnus and one alumna. This is a good snapshot—one that could be replicated day-in and day-out. It is crucial to have people with different perspectives "vet" these media processes to begin to send out equitable messages and begin to diminish the perception of male as universal and female as other.

This vetting process can be relatively straightforward. Each media office should send out drafts of every major publication piece to the Title IX officer and four other people to get impressions and incorporate changes. The Title IX officer can be the consistent voice of the vet, while the four people can be rotated each time or every other time to ensure that fresh perspectives are sought and the publications reflect the diverse culture (or the aspirationally diverse culture) of the institution. Campus media serve the purpose of putting the institution's best foot forward—appealing to alumni and alumni donors, members of the Board of Trustees, prospective students, parents of prospective and current students, the surrounding community, and to the current staff, students, and faculty members themselves. I wonder if these "branding" tendencies, these desires to mark one institution as always different, more unique, better than others, haven't occluded another purpose of journalistic media outlets, which is to give to its public a certain truth about the events and circumstances on campus. Don't get me wrong—I'm not blaming my own institution for not doing this; no institution in its right mind in the current climate would have the courage to publish less than positive information about itself. But it would be both refreshing and constructive for campus media to share more of the truth. Then, when things are bad, people will know and can work together to improve them. When things are rosy, people will know and recognize them truly as rosy. This would really be refreshing.

Joanne Martin concludes her article on deconstructing organizational taboos by stating, "If feminist perspectives were fully incorporated, the usual emphases on rationality, hierarchy, competition, efficiency, and productivity would be exposed as only a very small piece of the organizational puzzle" (357). I believe that feminist perspectives that are related to authenticity and fearless critical thinking are essential to breaking traditional modes of organizational management. Two guest columnists to *The New York Times* in recent years have spoken to this desire for individuals and media outlets to think more critically and analytically. In 2007, Atul Gawande, a general surgeon at Harvard Medical School, wrote of the fatal oversights at the Walter Reed Army Medical Center. Gawande writes, "The real puzzle was how one institution could be responsible for helping to save the highest percentage of battle-wounded soldiers in history and for providing such disturbingly neglectful care afterward." He goes on to say that the records show that "in one part of the hospital good people succeeded, and in the other good people failed." I really like Gawande's emphasis on "good people." He is saying that success and failure are possibilities for all of us. We're not bad people because we fail. He asserts that "the primary difference was whether leaders accepted the value of negative thinking or not." This notion of "negative thinking" is key. Gawande says that leaders who collected data—both positive and negative—about the performance of personnel and equipment were able to address shortcomings and improve performance. These leaders were unafraid to find and signal publicly the shortcomings in order to seek long-term success, and this worked! As Gawande says:

> Negative thinking is unquestionably painful. It involves finding and exposing your inadequacies, which can be overwhelming. And not every problem can be solved. You live in a state of perpetual dissatisfaction. That's an unhealthy way to be in large parts of your life: you don't want to constantly seek out the inadequacies of your children, your looks, your abilities as you age. But in running schools or businesses, in planning war, in caring for the sick and injured? Negative thinking may be exactly what we need. (Web)

Steven C. Bahls, President of Augustana College, similarly encourages a form of negative thinking among employees:

> When institutions fail, it is often because they have strayed from their values. Think of the financial institutions that have failed recently because they strayed from their traditional role of sound stewardship to one of reckless speculation. What if AIG had had a few more contrarians in the governance process? Although academe may indeed have a few people who have a hard time taking "yes" for an answer, that is far better than too many. (Web)

Whether we call ourselves "negative thinkers" or "contrarians," the point is that we're thinking critically and carefully about a situation in order to make it better.

In a 2009 opinion piece in *The Chronicle of Higher Education*, philosophy professor Simon Critchley writes of "cynicism we can believe in," which I view as intimately connected to Gawande's "negative thinking." Writes Critchley, "Cynicism is basically a moral protest against hypocrisy and cant in politics and excess and thoughtless self-indulgence in the conduct of life. In a world like ours, which is slowly trying to rouse itself from the dogmatic slumbers of boundless self-interest, corruption, lazy crony- ism and greed, it is Diogenes' lamp that we need to light our path. Perhaps this recession will make cynics of us all" (Web). In this scheme, cynicism is simply a heightened awareness about what is wrong and a desire to make it right by means of generosity, truthfulness, open-mindedness, and hard work. Critchley's cynicism (via Diogenes) reiterates the principal points about "negative thinking" made by Gawande. Human beings will make mistakes, and that's fine. What is not fine is a refusal to learn from one's mistakes, especially when they can profoundly affect others' lives.

Solutions

1. Remember that rosy nostalgia about an institution can be very positive among certain constituencies, especially among alumni who are not involved in the day-to-day functioning of the institution.
2. Make sure all staff, faculty, and students on campus know who the Title IX officer is.
3. Ensure that one part of the Title IX officer's job is to "vet" print and electronic communications sent from the institution to its current students and their parents, alumni, Board members, and staff and faculty. The Title IX officer will be able to edit content so that it is fair, balanced, and broad-minded. Every single publication from an institution sends direct and indirect messages about the values of the institution, and a well-trained Title IX officer will help to make the publication message more consistent with the institution's mission statement.
4. If gender equity matters at an institution, then administrative lead- ers should consistently say that it does in both formal and informal settings and in both oral and written communications. Just as with "going green," gender equity will benefit from consistent, vocal leadership from the administration.
5. Administrations, staff, students, and faculty can all learn a lesson in critical thinking and inquiry by being unafraid to engage in "nega- tive thinking" or "cynicism." This means that it is fine and good to make mistakes, acknowledge them, learn from them, and then not make them again. Negative thinking is more apt to prevent further harm than is rosy thinking.

NOTE

1. My undergraduate alma mater, the University of Virginia, in 2014, experienced Title IX shock when *The Rolling Stone* reported on an alleged gang rape at one of the University's fraternities. While this article's content was found to be unreliable, the University of Virginia continues to address underlying issues of sexual violence. See also Jon Krakauer's *Missoula. Rape and the Justice System in a College Town* for an in-depth look at rape and the climate of sexual violence on this Montana campus.

REFERENCES

Critchley, Simon. 2009. Cynicism we can believe in. *The Chronicle of Higher Education*, 1 Apr 2009. Accessed 1 Apr 2009. Web.

Davidson Journal. Fall 2011. Print.

Gawande, A. 2007. The power of negative thinking. *The New York Times*, 1 May 2007. Accessed 1 May 2007. Web.

W&L Alumni Magazine. Fall 2008. Print.

W&L Alumni Magazine. Fall/Winter 2009. Print.

CHAPTER 12

"Tempered Radicalism" and Holding the Powerful Accountable

I first read Debra Meyerson's and Maureen Scully's 1995 article "Tempered Radicalism and the Politics of Ambivalence and Change" in 2007. The article helped me immeasurably to understand how institutions' politics, procedures, and decision-making processes can fundamentally change the stance or positions of their employees. It made me feel stronger, more clearly analytical about my institution and my relationship, more willing to speak out, happier in my own day-to-day work. Tempered radicalism is a process enacted by "the people who work within mainstream organizations and professions and want also to transform them" (586). Meyerson and Scully elucidate what led to the creation of this new term:

> These individuals can be called "radicals" because they challenge the status quo, both through their intentional acts and also just by being who they are, people who do not fit perfectly. We chose the word "tempered" because of its multiple meanings. [...] Temper can mean both "an outburst of rage" and "equanimity, composure," seemingly incongruous traits required by tempered radicals. (586)

This description seemed to fit to a tee several individuals who had already left my institution. Looking back, it also seems to fit me and more than dozens of colleagues of mine from dozens of organizations. I found relief in the notion of "tempered radicalism" for several reasons: it described a phenomenon, the "professional mystique," to which I had been trying to give voice as I experienced difficulties and struggles over

© The Editor(s) (if applicable) and The Author(s) 2016
E. Mayock, *Gender Shrapnel in the Academic Workplace*,
DOI 10.1057/978-1-137-50830-0_12

values in my institution; it described people whom I still liked, very much, in fact; it made me feel like I was not alone, despite my sense of alienation in the institution where I had worked for years; it suggested that all was not lost, that good relations were still possible, and that change can be effected; it meant that I could still be myself *and* continue to work at my institution. This was indeed revelatory, and something that I immediately shared with dozens of colleagues at other institutions who I knew were seeking similar relief. At the same time, I shared the article with an upper-level administrator who was someone I had known to reasonably advocate for reasonable change. I thought he would respond to the article in many of the same ways in which I had—that he would recall his days as a faculty member, that he would understand the conflicting desires of different, equally sincere university constituencies, and that he would recognize that I saw myself as a tempered radical, that is, a new colleague of his who would advocate for change while working for the good of the institution.

In the end, I never learned what the person thought of the concept of tempered radicalism. He never responded to the invitation to share this idea. If the lack of response had just been a result of lack of time, and not lack of interest, that would have been fine. But I suspect it was from a fear of engaging in the question of giving me too much credit or free rein, and of addressing difficult matters head-on. I really hadn't been laying down the gauntlet by sending that article. I was simply inspired by a theoretical and practical notion that seemed to me to be the key to establishing authentic work relationships with a lot of different people and groups. In retrospect, I think maybe the person viewed this invitation as a threat, which was very far from my tempered radical intentions. It was a lesson for me to realize that my good intentions could certainly be interpreted as anything but.

This chapter highlights a series of organizational concepts established by Meyerson and Scully in "Tempered Radicalism": the question of "fit"; the view of status quo and change; what it means to be a "team player"; "insider language"; workplace exchanges vis-à-vis emotion and reason; attrition. I examine each of these concepts because they offer broadened approaches to analyzing gender in the workplace and to vigilance surrounding gender in the workplace. In addition, I offer and define the term "radioactivity," especially as it relates to gaining or expending "capital" in the workplace. While Meyerson and Scully establish the concept of tempered radicalism as a deliberate way for individuals to negotiate identity (identities) and to navigate the workplace, I also emphasize (and Meyerson and Scully do mention) the importance of radicalism (non-tempered!) as an important driver for workplace change.

It is useful here to consider Mumby and Putnam's conceptualization of "work": "From this perspective, *work* refers to the process through which the individual maintains control over his or her own physical, mental, and emotional resources to perform task activities, while simultaneously recognizing the extent to which organizations are the sites of 'linked fates' (i.e. social collectives in which individuals coordinate their activities to maintain community and to achieve organizational goals)" (476). Of course, this idea of work as a way for an individual to maintain control in order to perform certain tasks *and* for individuals to understand their connection to the larger group gives a whole new, much more amplified meaning to the word "workplace." The workplace, then, is the physical location of the site of individuals performing tasks for greater organizational ends *as well as* the metaphor of "linked fates." The workplace is where we go to work and it's the place that requires our attention to the balance between self and collective. And this should hold true no matter the individual's location in the hierarchy. Keeping in mind that managers and administrators also must balance their identities with the fate of the organization allows us to limit the focus on hierarchy and reframe the gender conversation so that it includes each individual's relation to or with her or his organization.

The question of "fit," still so predominant in hiring and promotion conversations in the twenty-first-century workplace, speaks directly to the existence of what Meyerson and Scully call "the dominant culture" (586). The authors describe the hardship for women and underrepresented groups to fit into the dominant culture, citing separatism (separating from the organization) and surrender (silencing oneself and surrendering one's identity) as two principal solutions adopted by those from a marginal culture (586). Of course, the authors offer the paradigm of the tempered radical as a better solution than just quitting or just putting up and shutting up. The tempered radical adopts "the dual project of working within the organization and working to change the organization" (586), thereby understanding the status quo and recognizing the often glacial pace of change. As Meyerson and Scully have said, tempered radicals can advocate for the status quo in one situation and work toward change in a different one (589). An example of this from my workplace is that I fully support the tradition and culture of faculty and staff having strong connections to students by knowing them well, completing extensive advising, recommending opportunities to them, and maintaining connections after students have graduated. This is part of what our admissions office "sells" to prospective students and their parents and is a fundamental reason for my wanting to work at this institution. In this case, I very much support what is put forward as the status quo. At the same time, I do not support the tradition and culture of honor (also very prominent in the marketing and alumni materials) because of all the ways in which the concept and reality of "honor" silence women and overextend the idea of the masculine hero. Therefore, I have steadily contributed to conversations about honor and gender bias.

We often hear the term "team player" tossed around in and about the contemporary workplace. On a sports team, the goals are unequivocally clear: the team wants to have each of its members in the best shape possible in order to allow them to train together and, ultimately, to win contests. In organizations made up of paid employees, the overarching goals look a bit like those of sports teams, but "victories" and "losses" are not as clearly delineated. "Team player" therefore becomes a less concrete term in the workplace and may make more fraught the concepts of equity and justice that Title VII (and Title IX, for educational institutions) promotes. In other words, employees in a workplace might have utterly different ideas about how the work should be done and what constitutes an organizational loss or victory. I remember one colleague at another institution recounting a particularly poignant moment. The colleague was trying to do what was best for "the team" (in his mind, the entire organization) but was trying to rewrite a contractual agreement to the detriment of a long-time male employee. He really believed that he was just doing his job, that he was being true to a contract, that he was being a team player. The long-time employee viewed the entire situation completely differently. There had been a contractual understanding, and he thought his colleague was not honoring it. When the long-time department head of this particular employee went to the colleague to attempt to have him see the employee's side and remedy the situation, the department head heard himself saying that he knew they both held certain aspects of the institution dear, but that they weren't always the same cherished aspects. That didn't make the institution belong any less to any one person. In the end, this conversation made the department head and the long-term employee considered even less the "team players" that many wanted them to be.

An additional example of this in my own realm was the day I did not sit with the administrative team at a faculty meeting. I knew the administration was going to unveil to the faculty initiatives that were unpopular, unvetted among broad constituencies, and probably also unfeasible. I did not believe in the initiatives and could not pretend that I did. Several administrators and faculty members chided me after the meeting for not being a real "team player." In my mind, I couldn't have been more of a team player at that moment because I was unafraid to express that I believed the institution wasn't on the right course, and I was willing to help find that right course, whatever it was to be.

Meyerson and Scully make an additional significant point about what they call "insider language" (592). They state that we humans, by adopting and using language that at first shocks us in one way or another, learn to become less shocked by this insider language. Less shocked, and, perhaps, less critical and analytical. The authors state (in reference to Cohn's article about language use among defense intellectuals), "Thus, the power of language was not in the ability to communicate technically, but rather in its capacity to rule out other forms of talk, thought, and identity" (592). One of the examples cited by Meyerson and Scully is the use of the term "collateral damage" in place of "human death." At many institutions and, I would argue, in much media coverage, I find that when we discuss sexual assault, we avoid the use of the term "rape." I believe that the term rings harshly on the ears of many individuals, that the individuals are wholly uncomfortable with the term and the image it brings to mind, and that there is a soft-pedaling that takes place in order to mitigate harsh realities of the sexual assault climate. At the same time, I believe that the term "rape" is now used far too blithely, demonstrating an astonishing comfort with the concept and its harsh realities.

Meyerson and Scully also point out that a tempered radical attempts to balance the emotion and passion that give rise to a desire for change with the need to present herself or himself as a "reasonable feminist" (593). The risks of not expressing the "heat, passion, torment, and temper that characterize the experience of being a tempered radical" (593) range from experiencing unnecessary pent-up frustration to being inauthentic to oneself and to the workplace. At the same time, as Meyerson and Scully state (through Mumby and Putnam), "real, spontaneous, emotional expression is far from the norm in most organizational contexts" (593). The tempered radical, in the end, must learn to discern the moments at which the expression of raw emotion feels right from the moments at which silence and/or calm discourse suit the setting. This is no easy task; in fact, it is an onerous one that requires the constant balancing act that in part characterizes tempered radicalism. A while ago, I was invited to participate in my institution's women's leadership summit. The invitation sprang from participating students who had appreciated my mentorship over the years, not from the numerous administrators involved in the organization of the event, although they were, after years of "dealing with" my tempered radicalism, at least willing to extend the invitation. My way of balancing my passion for change and expertise in Women's and Gender Studies with the far-less-than-radical approach of the organizers of the event is to state clearly that, if I'm to participate in the summit, I will be there as myself. That is to say, I'll be the tempered radical who will not only balance emotion and reason but also *combine* the two to provide an authentic perspective on women's leadership and organizational management.[1] I can think of no better way to model leadership. Anne Kreamer writes:

> The goal of any person or organization should be to allow emotion at work, in all of its gendered nuances, its *due*—but not to excess. Again, as with most of life, it's a Goldilocks and the Three Bears calibration question— you want not too soft or too hard, not too cold or too hot, but the elusive "just right." After doing the research for this book, my strong sense is that very few workplaces have their emotional temperatures set anything close to just right—rather, that they are way too cold or way too hot or swing wildly from one extreme to the other. And that, I think, despite universal lip-service acknowledgement of "emotional intelligence," is because paying careful, systematic attention to emotion has been considered beyond the scope of managers and the managed, too personal, too intangible, implicitly sexist, essentially off-limits. (203)

While I believe Kreamer makes an excellent, nuanced point here, I also believe that the thermostat of the workplace is set by these authentically expressed extremes of the managers and the managed. That is, that there may be no real thermostat at all, but rather a need to understand and absorb the expression of the extreme emotions as a part of daily interactions. And this might be exactly where the not-yet-canonized concept of emotional intelligence comes into play.

Kreamer goes on to talk about the enduring interplay between the individual in the workplace and the collective and the need to balance the needs of both. This notion is clearly connected to what Mumby and Putnam call "linked fates" (476). Managers do need a certain level of emotional intelligence to understand their employees' emotions, needs, and productivity, while employees ("the managed," in Kreamer's words) who consider themselves tempered radicals, that is, who work for reasonable change at the same time that they value the organization and its work, must have ways to "hold the powerful accountable" (an expression used by Paul Krugman in a *New York Times* op-ed about Molly Ivins [web]). An understanding and acceptance of tempered radicalism in the workplace allows employees to incorporate a set of checks and balances for work practices put into play by managers and administrators. This certainly ties into the "linked fates" ideal.

Workplaces that have the benefit of only a few "out" tempered radicals run the risk of losing them. When only a few employees consistently encourage workplace change, they can become what I have termed "radioactive," borrowing from the group The Firm. The "I'm Radioactive" (1985) lyrics "Don't you stand, stand too close / You might catch it" have often run through my mind as I have been called upon by colleagues to help them navigate difficult work issues. I have worried that, if I visibly help and/or speak out on behalf of this colleague, then the co-worker's fate will be doomed because it is, in fact, linked to my fate. That makes me radioactive—those who stand too close might catch it. On the other hand, female and male students and co-workers have come to me for specific reasons and out of a real need for help. These reasons include sexual assault, sexual harassment, pay inequity, parental leave dates and time, timelines for tenure and promotion, exclusion, and isolation. And I have wanted to respond in concrete, timely ways to help them. I have worked behind the scenes to help students and colleagues, and sometimes that has meant that I have had to have others use my words so that they will be heard ("workplace ventriloquism," described in Chapter 7). At times, I have worked visibly on behalf of colleagues, who, in turn, have feared for their own status, amount of professional capital, and futures in the workplace as they have sensed a certain degree of radioactivity around me.

If there were more of us, more tempered radicals willing and able to work for change, then we would be less of an oddity in the workplace and would therefore be less radioactive. Our presence would be more reassuring to those around us because, in some very real ways, we might be managing institutional risk at the same time that we are tangibly helping individuals. Meyerson and Scully write of the importance of recognizing tempered radicals and guarding against their attrition—their leaving because change is too slow, or because they are devalued, or because they have lost the energy to "play the game" (598). I have witnessed these types of attrition at many colleges and universities, in law firms, medical practices, and certainly in politics. Young employees who fit the description of the tempered radical (whether they know it or not) may work for change for years before burning out. But, if change happens too slowly, or the price they pay for being tempered radicals is too high, then they will leave. This attrition is a component of gender shrapnel. Employees are hit with feeling or actually being marginal and marginalized, try to remedy the marginalization, and tire of the unsuccessful efforts. After an organization has made such an investment in such an active sector of the workforce, it loses in more ways than several.

Meyerson and Scully remark: "The labor of resistance may be divided among those who push for change from the inside, from the outside, and from the margin, each effort being essential to the others and to an overall movement of change" (598). I wholeheartedly agree with this statement, but I dislike that it's true. I want "real," not "tempered," radicalism to be able to work because it can propose the greatest justice in the workplace. There is something about working from the inside that seems overly complicit and hypocritical. Nevertheless, I have learned through many years in various workplaces that change seems to be effected most slowly from the outside and the margin and, while not leap years faster, somewhat faster from the inside. The unfair result of having change come from the inside is that the language of the outside is often co-opted, thus augmenting hypocrisy, and the insiders often serve as ventriloquists of those real radicals whose "capital" is overspent. Maybe the role of the tempered radical is also to accept that this degree of hypocrisy from the inside is necessary. Therefore, maybe the range of activism, from insider to tempered radical to radical, is necessary for effecting workplace change. We absolutely need the real radicals to motivate change among the tempered radicals and the insiders. Real radicals employed by a college or university who want to stay employed must still play by many of the rules of the game, although real radicals who have tenure might have the freedom to run greater risks of expression of desire for change. Tenured radicals in academic institutions can refrain from "drinking from the company Kool-Aid" and establish a critical distance from the institution in order to evaluate mission, decisions, and actions without too much fear of reprisal. In mental health language, tenured radicals can cultivate more of an independent, and not *co-dependent*, relationship with their employers. Anne Wilson Schaef connects co-dependence to the function of major cultural institutions:

Since they have no boundaries, co-dependents take on another's sadness, happiness, fear, or whatever people around them are feeling and/or thinking. I think we will see in Chapter 5 how three of our major institutions—the family, the school, and the church—actively train us not to form boundaries. They teach us to think what we are told to think, feel what we are told to feel, see what we are told to see, and know what we are told to know. This is cultural co-dependence training. We learn that the reference point for thinking, feeling, seeing, and knowing is external to the self, and this training produces people without boundaries. In order to have and experience boundaries, a person must start with an internal referent (knowing what one feels and thinks from the inside) and then relate with the world from that perspective. (50)

Nancy Johnston's 2011 work *Disentangle* is a useful guide for the employee who has experienced a form of harassment or discrimination and who needs to learn to establish greater separation from the institution. The role of the tempered radical is clearly linked to this concept of disentanglement. The tempered radical learns to understand her or his own perspective and to navigate through an often-differing institutional or organizational perspective while still being true to self and productive at work.

Solutions

1. Share Meyerson and Scully's "Tempered Radicalism" piece with others in the workplace and encourage its use in training sessions for new employees. This will establish that outspokenness for change is acceptable and will speak to a more democratic working environment.
2. Keep in mind the "linked fates" of the individual and the workplace. How can each benefit the other? Consider the danger of establishing overly linked fates. Allow and encourage employees to voice opinions counter to organizational mission and action.
3. Pose these questions: Which individuals are consistently working for change that could be beneficial for all members of the workplace? Can these individuals work together? Can they be helpful to others who find themselves in a position in which they believe they have less voice?
4. Ponder the possibility that all workers have the good of the organization in mind.

5. Be careful with the use of common business terms, such as "good fit" and "team player." These suggest the existence of an in-group and an out-group, which can give rise to plentiful gender shrapnel.
6. Understand that "holding the powerful accountable" allows an organization to be more transparent, decrease incidents of violations of Title VII and Title IX, and promote workplace justice.
7. Recognize that the best leaders are not afraid to admit when they have made a mistake, welcome opinions different from their own, and do not fear change.

NOTE

1. Ropers-Huilman and Shackelford (*Gendered Futures in Higher Education,* Chapter 7) provide significant data on how professed feminists in higher education have to balance their work lives with their work toward change. This discourse clearly relates to that of tempered radicalism.

REFERENCES

Johnston, Nancy L. 2011. *Disentangle. When you've lost your self in someone else.* Las Vegas, NV: Central Recovery Press. Print.
Meyerson, Debra E., and Maureen A. Scully. 1995. Tempered radicalism and the politics of ambivalence and change. *Organization Science* 6(5): 585–600. Print.

CHAPTER 13

"Small Wins": Establishing Dependable and Flexible Institutional Structures

This chapter aims to look at the much-touted organizational management strategy of "small wins" in the context of gender shrapnel. Karl Weick's (1984) article in *American Psychologist* advocated for a parsing of monumental societal issues into smaller pieces that would allow for more immediate solutions, termed "small wins." He believed that this approach was more psychologically beneficial for individuals and organizations and more effective for policymaking. Of course, in the ensuing three decades, many management experts have extolled the benefits of the "small wins" approach. These include Teresa Amabile and Steven Kramer, whose 2011 *The Progress Principle* has the "small wins" subtitle, "Using Small Wins to Ignite Joy, Engagement, and Creativity at Work." This Harvard Business Review Press publication has been widely cited, and for good reason. But I'll come back to that.

First, I want to do a little "negative thinking" with Meyerson and Scully about the potential danger of going whole hog on small wins. Meyerson and Scully affirm the benefits of a small wins approach: large problems can be reduced to a manageable size; small wins can be experiments; small wins encourage us to pick our battles carefully; small wins are driven by unexpected opportunities (595). They also astutely extol the virtues of "small losses" as "a source of discovery (Sitkin 1992)" (595), a point I greatly appreciate because it demonstrates how our acknowledged failures can lead to creative successes. Nevertheless, Meyerson and Scully also recognize that, "while a small wins approach can help a tempered radical push change while maintaining her identity, we should point to some risks

© The Editor(s) (if applicable) and The Author(s) 2016
E. Mayock, *Gender Shrapnel in the Academic Workplace*,
DOI 10.1057/978-1-137-50830-0_13

associated with the small wins approach" (596). The risks are that higher-level tempered radicals might not grasp the urgency of change for other employees and that small wins may be too reactive a way for tempered radicals to operate. This approach could train tempered radicals toward passivity and away from advocacy for change (596). The authors also make clear that a small wins approach keeps present the dichotomy between the insider and the dissenter (596), which has its benefits and drawbacks. While a clear pull of oppositional politics is predictable and therefore somewhat stable, it also produces a degree of stagnation in which the same dissenters are always dissenting, thus immobilizing their capacity for even the smallest of wins. Weick defines "small wins" thus:

> A small win is a concrete, complete, implemented outcome of moderate importance. By itself, one small win may seem unimportant. A series of wins at small but significant tasks, however, reveals a pattern that may attract allies, deter opponents, and lower resistance to subsequent proposals. Small wins are controllable opportunities that produce visible results. (43)

One additional risk for gender shrapnel that I see in this definition is its insistence on "deterring opponents." To undo patriarchal approaches and invite oppositional, critical discourse, we actually need to welcome opponents, as long as they are opponents who have studied the issues and bring a spirit of debate to the table. Despite these warnings of the potential shortcomings of small wins, a small wins approach certainly has many advantages in terms of keeping an organization moving forward and, at the same time (and intertwined with the notion of progress), inspiring creativity and productivity in individual employees, as deftly established by Amabile and Kramer.

Amabile's and Kramer's combination of the now-immortal "small wins" concept with an awareness that employees' work satisfaction is closely tied to organizational progress is in many ways unique. Their research very significantly finds the following:

> Conventional management wisdom is way off track about employee psychology. When we surveyed hundreds of managers around the world, ranging from CEOs to project leaders, about what motivates employees, we found startling results: 95 percent of these leaders fundamentally misunderstood the most important source of motivation. Our research inside companies revealed that the best way to motivate people, day in and day out, is by facilitating *progress*—even small wins. But the managers in our survey ranked "supporting progress" dead last as a work motivator. (5)

Amabile and Kramer thus emphasize the importance of the "inner work lives of *employees*, not managers" (5). The two authors take the measured "small wins" strategy and some of the testosterone-driven suggestions of the management guru Jim Collins (e.g. from *Good to Great*) and stir throughout a theoretical emotional intelligence, sometimes cast as the estrogen of the management world.

It is important to recognize that Collins' *Good to Great* (2001) became the management bible of the first decade of the new millennium because it shaped how contemporary managers approached the twenty-first-century workplace.[1] I became aware of the work during my time in the administrative post because so much of the catchy business/organizational lingo I heard came from the Collins work. Something about the lingo did not sit right on my gender-shrapneled ears. When I read the work, I uncovered the numerous worrisome patriarchal, hierarchical components of Collins' advice for managers of the world. Masculinist rhetoric prevails in the work. All epigraphs in the book are by and about men. Furthermore, Collins writes in Chapter 2, on "Level 5 Leadership": "It is very important to grasp that Level 5 leadership is not just about humility and modesty. It is equally about ferocious resolve, an almost stoic determination to do whatever needs to be done to make the company great" (30). Collins adds, "Level 5 leaders are fanatically driven, infected with an incurable need to produce *results*. They will sell the mills or fire their brother if that's what it takes to make the company great" (30). To parse these statements requires just a basic understanding of gendered language. Leaders who can express "humility and modesty" are de facto—*men*. Why is this? Because it is a given that they are excellent and, therefore, they are provided the luxury of presenting themselves as humble or modest. Women leaders and/or aspiring women leaders *do not have this luxury*, and I believe that the same is true for people of Color. They are presumed to be deficient and, therefore, any demonstration of humility or modesty weakens their stance. At the same time, Chapter 5 on language amply demonstrated that women also socially are not supposed to appear arrogant. And so, Collins' language here presumes an audience of male CEOs and presidents *only*. In addition, the testosterone-driven vocabulary of ferocity, stoicism (i.e. no apparent emotion!), selling the mills, firing the brother, and inexorably and unwaveringly working for the good of the company entrenches further the gendered roles of man as leader and woman as subordinate, and of both as wholly uncritical of workplace realities. Collins is not writing for a twenty-first-century workplace that welcomes and acknowledges the many strengths of a variety of women executives.

In addition, Collins overuses the term "blessing" (e.g. p. 34), which drips in privilege and hierarchy with a sense of muted Christian morality, while also referring to the importance of business leaders having strong religion and family support (61), thus reinforcing the gendered spheres notion (men in the public workplace, women at home).[2] Collins also refers to "workmanlike diligence" (39) (thus erasing women again from the picture of workplace leadership) and advocates for top leaders to have "councils" (217). These councils are not billed as either voted or representative, thus bringing with them the risk of simply replicating the leader's sex, race, religion, age, and viewpoints. Finally, Collins also emphasizes "the degree of *sheer rigor* needed in people making decisions in order to take a company from good to great" (44). "Sheer rigor" (italicized in the work itself) ignores the complexity of what individual employees bring to the workplace and the crucible of sex, age, race, religion, and so on, that a diverse workplace of the twenty-first century will likely engender.

While I am criticizing the drivingly masculinist rhetoric of Collins' work, I do believe the work contains useful suggestions for running effective organizations. Collins advocates for "a climate where the truth is heard" (73–80), thus encouraging broader input from all employees. He also praises companies that "hired self-disciplined people who didn't need to be managed, and then managed the system, not the people" (125). I like this idea that you can manage the system and not the people, but I prefer Amabile and Kramer's suggestion that managers and team leaders be more involved in motivating employees *through the work* and that they apply "nourishing" tools, such as "show[ing] that you respect people and the work they do," "recognize[ing] and reward[ing]the accomplishments of your people," "provide[ing] emotional support when needed," and "create[ing] opportunities for the development of friendship and camaraderie in the team" (146–47).

Earlier in this chapter, I referred to "theoretical" emotional intelligence in discussing Amabile and Kramer because the two authors do not talk as much about sensitivity toward individual employees as about a broad approach that tells managers to be cognizant of providing challenges, oversight, advice (when necessary), and encouragement. They also clearly emphasize that "negative events are more powerful than positive events, all else being equal" (7), which demonstrates to students of gender shrapnel the extreme power of each little piece of shrapnel that scatters. We can see how the small pieces of shrapnel, "small losses," so to speak, can overwhelm the work environment with negativity by lodging in different areas of the workplace and manifesting as *inhibitors*, the term used by Amabile and Kramer for "events that hinder project work" (7), and *toxins*, Amabile and Kramer's term for "interpersonal events that undermine the people doing the work" (7). These findings by the authors of *The Progress Principle* regarding the monumental effects of negative events in no uncertain terms underscore the absolute necessity for the US workplace to understand the concept and realities of gender shrapnel. Robin J. Ely and Debra E. Meyerson put forth the possibility of a "dual agenda" (594) of gender equity and increased productivity, which relates quite well to Amabile and Kramer's study of the influence of positive and negative work events on the progress made at work:

> We hypothesized, however, that it was the explicitly gendered organization of the plant—with masculine men maintaining control of women (and emasculated men)—that fostered an inequitable distribution of roles and responsibilities between men and women and, *at the same time*, increased absenteeism, created inefficiencies, and lowered morale. That is, it seemed clear to us that gender was a central axis along which power and control were exercised in the plant. [...] This link between the plant's business problems and its gender inequities made the dual agenda for change concrete. (Ely and Meyerson, 593–594)

From the dense data provided by Amabile and Kramer and by Ely and Meyerson, we know that work does not advance when negative events recur *and* when employees hit by shrapnel are severely undermined.

Amabile and Kramer advocate that managers "manage for progress" (10), and they link this progress closely to the "inner work life effect" (6) of the employees. The inner work life effect focuses on the possibilities for "creativity, productivity, work commitment, and collegiality" (6) in the lives of employees and employers. "Collegiality" tends to be a very charged term in the Academy because it is associated with congeniality and civility—codes of behavior that again retrench gender roles in that congenial women should just be nice and in that powerful men have the luxury of being civil (because things are already going their way). Nevertheless, I believe that the authors here are advocating for opportunities to build the friendship and camaraderie they establish as "nourishers."

In my own workplace, I have seen in action the really compelling small wins approach offered by Amabile and Kramer. I have observed supervisors who are extremely adept at establishing an environment of small wins that allows employees the success and energy to then dream bigger. These supervisors build consensus slowly by gathering many voices and views on strategic planning and having individual voices manifested in final planning documents. Each time small faculty groups appear again to do the laborious work of strategic planning is a small win. When an employee reported that she had experienced racial discrimination, I watched a supervisor call together the diversity committee to have them address the specific issue and then heard the supervisor call the employee to see if she would like to talk more in the employee's office. The supervisor was ready to drop everything in order to listen and to act, which set the tone for what would and would not be tolerated. These small actions translated into progressively bigger wins. Although this supervisor worked for a large unit of the university, the person knew it was not the best endowed unit and responded by working in small ways to improve the daily lives of the employees, which, in turn, allowed the supervisor to make progress in terms of the cache of the unit for the broader public.

One example of concrete small wins was the creation of a $10,000 budget to take care of faculty members with small needs (as small as clocks in classrooms, chalk, a new screen, an Americans with Disabilities Act (ADA)-approved office chair) to have them addressed right away, without fiddling through 17 different budgets for the right one to take care of the employee. Another example was that the supervisor asked each department to submit successes of administrative assistants and faculty in order to centralize them and forward them to the university's communications office. This permitted a broader view of all employees and an ability for the university community to recognize and admire a variety of successes. In effect, what the supervisor accomplished in a short time was the reality of individual employees' progress and inner work life satisfaction.

Meyerson and Scully tell the story of a female surgeon who changed her work environment by firmly and consistently treating members of her surgical team and their patients with respect and compassion (apparently unlike most of her peers) (596). This had the small wins effect of changing, at the very least, the local work environment of that surgical team.

My institution has encouraged several small wins in the gender arena. As mentioned previously, we have changed the term "freshman" to "first-year student," which communicates immediately to new students a consciousness about gendered terminology and then becomes a part of the permanent culture. Students and faculty have pushed for greater awareness and action surrounding the high incidence of sexual assault on campus. As a result, the administration has supported numerous speakers and round tables to address the topic and has hired additional mental health professionals to help students work through the shrapnel of assault. The administration has signaled the gaps in child care access in our small community and has worked locally with child care providers to address the gaps in tangible ways. These small wins are good for everyone. The one gigantic danger I see, however, is that small wins in the gender arena often brush up against the monumental culture of patriarchy, and so the small wins can come off as even smaller and, oftentimes, as insincere, half-assed efforts to put a band-aid on a big gaping wound. We often run the risk of too-great hypocrisy when we address *only* the smaller problems.

For the "Solutions" section of this chapter, I rely upon excellent "small wins" suggestions put forth by a variety of authors, business executives, politicians, and philosophers. First and foremost, I highly recommend the outstanding work of Amabile and Kramer on this issue. In addition, I use the following sources, in order: a variety of articles from *The Chronicle of Higher Education*, *Ms.*'s article on "Paycheck Feminism," the McKinsey Global Survey titled "Moving Women to the Top," and the National Council of Women's Organizations' book *50 Ways to Improve Women's Lives*.

Solutions
From Amabile and Kramer's *The Progress Principle*:

1. The entire work offers a rich array of potential small wins in the workplace. The focus should be on creativity, productivity, autonomy and guidance (as needed), and resources for establishing a happy and productive "inner work life" among individual employees and groups of employees. (Nobel, web)

From *The Chronicle of Higher Education*:

1. Organizations should have one and only one mission statement. This allows the organization to send a clear, consistent message to all of its constituencies about the organization's identity and values (Morphew and Taylor, online). If a variety of groups contribute to the crafting of the organization's mission statement, then the end product should reflect that variety of perspectives.
2. Administrators and managers should not speak ill of their employees as a group to the outside world. As employers, it is their job to see and cultivate the best in each employee and in the group as a whole.

Steven C. Bahls, President of Augustana College, takes this one step further by encouraging administrators to "facilitate understanding of the crucial role that professors play on a campus. Because of the corrosive and pervasive nature of those myths, I have begun working with new trustees to help clarify the helpful and important role that faculty governance can play" (web). This approach encourages administrators to educate newcomers and "outsiders" from the outset about the organization's mission, its opportunities, and its employees' engagement from start to finish in the organization's mission. It also establishes trust between employer and employees and, therefore, removes obstacles to getting the work done.

3. Gloria Gadsen, Associate Professor of Sociology at East Stroudsburg University of Pennsylvania, addresses the issue of diversity in hiring and retention: "Ultimately, if predominantly white institutions want to diversify their campuses, they will have to make greater efforts to retain the minority faculty members they hire. Those institutions understand that they must respond to the needs, concerns, and problems of their students from underrepresented groups. I look for the day when minority faculty members also receive serious and consistent attention" (web). Gadsen suggests the creation of official support groups within the university and, of course, a host of programs such as those offered by Student Affairs offices to underrepresented groups of students.

4. Sheila O'Rourke praises the University of California's ten-campus system for amending the instructions for faculty review committees in order to evaluate and give proper credit for faculty work that "promot[es] diversity and equal opportunity." This type of recognition can come in the areas of scholarship, teaching, mentoring of students and/or colleagues from underrepresented groups, career counseling, and organizing pertinent programs. Giving real credit where credit is due in these areas also recognizes the often underrecognized work of women and minorities who are often called upon for this type of extra advising or mentoring.

From "Paycheck Feminism" in *Ms.* (30–33):

5. Stop making unemployment, retirement, and other benefits contingent on steady, full-time work.
6. Don't make flexible hours a barrier to health insurance, and *do* stop charging women more for health insurance.

7. Guarantee workers paid family and medical leave.
8. Provide high-quality child care.
9. Stop taxing women's income unfairly/disproportionately.

From the McKinsey Global Survey (4–6):

10. Offer options for flexible working conditions.
11. Insist upon visible monitoring of gender-diversity programs by the CEO and executive team.
12. Create programs to ensure smooth transitions before, during, and after parental leaves.
13. Establish performance evaluation systems that neutralize the impact of parental leave and flexible work.
14. Have gender-specific hiring goals and programs.

From the National Council of Women's Organizations' *50 Ways to Improve Women's Lives*. Consult the book for specific recommendations for action in each area. These specific recommendations constitute the "small wins" component of these very big ideas.

15. Champion Women's Studies (Ellen Boneparth, 51–53).
16. Demand Pay Equity (Nancy L. Hurlbert, 54–56).
17. Advance Women in Business (Hedy M. Ratner, 65–67).
18. Nourish Women's Ambitions (Marie Wilson, 77–78).
19. Celebrate Women's Achievements (Molly Murphy MacGregor, 106–108).
20. Put a Stop to Sexual Harassment (Marty Langelan, 119–121). The specific actions mentioned in this piece are included in *Gender Shrapnel*'s Chapter 14, Training Principles.
21. Eradicate Racism (Mal Johnson and C. DeLores Tucker, 122–124).
22. Uphold Women's Rights as Human Rights (Sarah Albert, 138–140).

NOTES

1. As recently as 2014, Carl J. Strikwerda, President of Elizabethtown College, cites and lauds the Collins work as a means to manage colleges (*Chronicle*, 11-10-2014).
2. See Lesley DiMare's "Rhetoric and Women: The Private and the Public Spheres" for further analysis of the separate spheres notion.

REFERENCES

Collins, Jim. 2001. *Good to great. Why some companies make the leap…and others don't*. New York: HarperCollins. Print.

Strikwerda, Carl J. 2014. Risk managing or risk averse? Neither approach is fully suited for higher education. *The Chronicle of Higher Education*, 10 Nov 2014. Accessed 10 Nov 2014. Web.

Weick, Karl E. 1984. Small wins. Redefining the scale of social problems. *American Psychologist* 39(1): 40–49. Print.

CHAPTER 14

Training Principles: Checks and Balances, Sample Training Sessions, and Recommendations for Promoting an Equitable Work Environment

PROPOSAL FOR A SYSTEM OF GENDER CHECKS AND BALANCES IN ORGANIZATIONS

Any proposal to address and eliminate gender discrimination at a university must begin with a realistic assessment of the current situation, undertaken by a body both committed to change and empowered to re-examine potentially harmful policies and practices. University leadership must then continue the process by demonstrating their commitment to ongoing training, education, and routine evaluation.[1]

Recommendations on the elements of the proposal are set forth below, divided into the following segments:

- Assessment (data collection and analysis)
- Creation of a standing, permanent body to examine gender-based discrimination throughout all levels of university administration and faculty and to recommend reform when and as needed
- Follow-through via appropriate leadership, training, independent oversight, and routine evaluation

© The Editor(s) (if applicable) and The Author(s) 2016
E. Mayock, *Gender Shrapnel in the Academic Workplace*,
DOI 10.1057/978-1-137-50830-0_14

I. Assessment

Data Collection
1. Collect data on numbers of women in administrative, faculty, and staff posts during the past ten years.
2. Collect data on complaints made through the formal system during the past ten years.
3. Collect documents that have outlined women's concerns about climate, policies, and practices during the past ten years. These documents will come from a variety of sources, for example: yearly or semi-yearly reports of meetings with presidents; documents written by faculty members and submitted to officials in the administration; the proposal for a Committee on the Status of Women; documents generated to date by the "Committee on Women"; articles in the student press.
4. Meetings with individuals and groups on campus to gather and document current concerns regarding gender inequality.

Data Analysis
1. Examine progress made in hiring and retention of women in administrative, faculty, and staff posts during the past ten years.
2. Categorize formal complaints (e.g. quid pro quo versus hostile environment harassment). Analyze (a) the consistency of reporting structures and techniques over the years; (b) the rankings of most frequent versus least frequent type(s) of complaints; (c) the consistency of types of resolutions offered.
3. Analyze documents to discern common themes and issues.
4. Examine current documented concerns and compare to findings from nos. 1, 2, and 3, above.

II. Establishment of a Standing, Permanent Body on Gender Discrimination

A permanent Status of Women Committee must be created. Membership on this committee must be recognized as a serious and time-consuming administrative responsibility, with appropriate consideration given to membership in the context of merit pay, tenure consideration, and promotion. In the short term, the committee must be given primary responsibility for undertaking the assessments set forth above and developing a set of recommendations to be implemented by the university administration.

In particular, the committee should use the results of their assessments to consider revision of policies and procedures, with particular emphasis on the following:

1. Examine Faculty, Employee, and Student Handbooks for instances of discriminatory rhetoric. Discuss how the words "civility" and "honor" speak to an all-male tradition and how this rhetoric can be modified to communicate a more contemporary and egalitarian purpose.
2. Ensure that introductions and conclusions to each policy are conceptually in line with the outline of the policy itself.
3. Re-examine the complaint system to determine how it can best serve the community.
4. Establish a policy that prohibits fraternization between faculty members and students.
5. Create a safe place for whistle-blowers and a means by which their concerns can be brought before the committee and/or the independent oversight authority (see infra). The policy and practice surrounding whistle-blowing are unclear, and very few individuals feel secure making legitimate complaints.
6. Facilitate the independent oversight of gender initiatives by preparing for the independent oversight authority a periodic report on the committee's goals, progress, and issues of concern. The committee should also be empowered to invite the oversight authority to become involved in any particular situation/issue.

Furthermore, the committee must serve as an ongoing resource for individual employees or groups of employees with gender-based climate concerns. The committee will be able to hear the concerns, articulate them for the institutional leaders, and suggest remedies or specific changes. In particular, the committee should have responsibility for designing and maintaining a university-created website that provides abundant resources for climate issues for women.

III. Follow-Through via Leadership, Training, Independent Oversight, and Evaluation

The university's administration needs to be fully aware of best practices related to gender and diversity in higher education. Employees of the institution will not receive adequate training if it does not come from those who are adequately trained. Training needs to be both theoretical (examination of rationale for training, approaches, language use, behavior modification, etc.) and practical (focused on the institution, its strengths and weaknesses, the profound effect that individual administrators can have in certain situations). All administrators should satisfy a set of clear standards demonstrating that they are prepared to act consistently with the university's desire to achieve gender equity.

Leadership
The university must have leaders who insist upon the following:

1. Education and training, in particular for the Board and administration, then for all constituencies.
2. Avoidance of discriminatory rhetoric.
3. Zero-tolerance for discrimination in all environments and situations (in practice, be careful with the use of this term if the institution has not reached zero-tolerance).
4. Conscious modeling of language use and behavior.
5. Articulation of a university mission that emphasizes equality and equity and that goes beyond a perceived need to please a predominantly male alumni core.
6. Awareness of the effects of discrimination against employees on the students who witness it.
7. Improvement of oversight by Title IX officer and examination of links with Title VII issues.

Training
Training for all employees should be conducted by experts and take place on a semi-annual basis. An assessment system for training effectiveness should be in place before training begins. Sessions should be in small groups, and there should be ample opportunity for further interaction between trainers and employees. In particular, there must be a focus on the distinction between quid pro quo harassment and hostile environment harassment. The latter must be addressed more clearly and specifically, and both must not be tolerated.

Independent Oversight
The university's administration must commit to establishing an independent oversight authority with a mandate to eliminate gender discrimination at the university. The authority should be made up of one or more

persons not dependent on the university administration for financial support or position. The individual(s) who will fill this role should be selected by various stakeholders/constituents for limited terms, and should have broad powers to investigate both formal and informal complaints, assess the progress of the Status of Women Committee, and oversee the Complaint process.

Routine Evaluation
There must be an annual review of policies and practices that affect gender equity (e.g. hiring, retention, University Policy on Discrimination, Harassment, and Retaliation, performance review, salary determinations). This review should take place with the assistance of the permanent Status of Women Committee.

SAMPLE TRAINING SESSIONS

I am not a lawyer, but I sometimes play one in this book. Friends of mine and I joke that, with the state of play of gender shrapnel in the workplace, we can't really depend upon lawyers anymore. We just need to call our "feminist," whom we need to have on speed-dial. The feminist, suit on, game face ready, and briefcase in hand could accompany us to our difficult meetings and just tell everyone to put their issues on the table. "Okay, everyone," she would say, "now we're ready to talk. Let's have some straight-talk about gender and find our way out of this mess." It's a decent cartoon image, but the workplace doesn't afford such interactions or have the luxury of straight-talk in a professional world obsessed with managing risk. So, I am purposefully playing the lawyer in this chapter without being one. I *want* us to have in mind the legal frameworks that shape discussions on gender, but I also firmly believe that actual, real feminism and intersectionalism have to be on the table for real change to be effected. That is, without understanding the covert and overt operations of gender and race, among other categories, and without a true desire for equity in the workplace, everything is lost. There will be no real strides made to clear the shrapnel until we all agree that we actually want to.

How many among us have attended an employer-sponsored workshop on the prevention of sexual harassment? How many have attended more than one? Organizational managers and human resources officials who are aware (and should be aware) of Title VII and Title IX law and of the potential risks of violation in their own organizations usually require every employee to attend at least one sexual discrimination, harassment, and retaliation prevention workshop early in the employee's career. Oftentimes they leave the training course up to their in-house general counsel, although more and more frequently this training is being out-sourced, especially to companies that offer online workshops. In this chapter, I will briefly address the importance of consistent and ongoing training in sexual harassment prevention for each and every employer and employee, then underscore the common shortcomings of current training and workshops, and finally offer guidelines for sound training practices in organizations seeking both to establish an equitable working environment *and* to "manage risk."

Hart and Secunda's ardent defense of social framework evidence (information from experts, such as sociologists and organizational behaviorists, on sexual discrimination and harassment) supplies an excellent legal framework for the concept of gender shrapnel and displays the tensions in the legal profession about the validity of research on sexual discrimination. The two legal scholars write that: "As many legal scholars have noted, workplace discrimination today is more subtle—often involving structural and organizational norms that are less easy to identify as discriminatory—than the explicit exclusions that characterized early civil rights litigation" (41). Recall how in one gender shrapnel story Yolanda tried to make a university official understand that the use of the word "bitch" in reference to her was analogous to the use of the "N-word" in reference to an African-American employee. "Bitch" is so commonly used that people forget that its use stems from a gender binary that quite literally has women on the bottom (and casts women as non-humans). In Yolanda's case, she needed to help others develop more effective gender analyses, and she needed to signal that the university had established a pattern of unwitting gender discrimination. Hart and Secunda add: "*Contextual Evidence of Gender Discrimination* can only be fully understood as part of a body of work that includes criticism of the theory of implicit bias and challenges to legal theories that provide a remedy for the kinds of subtle discrimination that infect workplace decisions without conscious awareness on the part of the decision makers" (69). Of course, they are providing here a legal definition of gender shrapnel: "subtle discrimination that infect[s] workplace decisions without conscious awareness on the part of the decision makers." For successful training on sexual discrimination and harassment, organizational managers must be able to grasp the notion of gender shrapnel at the very beginning of the training sessions. I recall clearly when, after a single round of training on how to manage institutional complaints, a colleague of mine very sincerely asked, "Wow, am I part of the problem?" He had learned enough in that session to understand that he may have been spreading shrapnel unintentionally for years. This awareness from the outset is key.

I cannot overemphasize that sending employees to an online link to complete a sexual harassment prevention workshop *is not the right way to go.* While such an approach provides interaction between an individual employee and a computer screen, it provides absolutely no interaction between the individual employee and her or his group environment. It is just a superficial, check-the-box approach to risk management and contributes little toward preventing real cases of sexual discrimination and harassment in action. Employees take away from such a workshop exactly what they bring to it, and no more.

My employer contracted with a group called United Educators, which is an "insurance organization." From their name, I could not figure out if they worked in education or insurance, and I believed the distinction to be important. The screen-to-screen definitions of workplace harassment, protected groups, methods to deal with harassment, and academic freedom covered the bare minimum of what needs to be covered. A more significant, major shortcoming of the workshop, however, were the case studies and accompanying photographs. Chapter 10 of *Gender Shrapnel* focused on the need to have official documents and communiqués of an organization vetted by a variety of people before making them official. This online harassment prevention workshop very certainly needed some careful revisions before being launched to the hundreds of employees of our organization. Examples provided in sexual harassment prevention sessions must reflect real-life incidents in type and frequency. Documented cases of men harassing women are far more frequent than of women harassing men. Therefore, don't use an online workshop that flips the frequency. The very first example of hostile environment harassment in the online workshop we were assigned to do featured a woman in a low-cut jacket making sexual comments about a man in a wheelchair. This set the tone for the entire discussion of harassment. I couldn't figure out if it was supposed to apologize from the start, saying in a way, "Sorry we have to do this workshop. Sorry that men are going to be blamed for demanding sexual favors and for creating hostile work environments. We're so sorry, in fact, that we'll skew the images to make sure that you know that women can harass, too." This apologetic approach does not help anyone because it does not reflect real-world workplace dynamics.

The second example of hostile work environment harassment, which featured discrimination against a Latino male, again featured a male victim. The third example featured a 65-year-old male victim. In sum, in the first three case studies presented, three out of three showed men as the victims of hostile work environment harassment. This representation of 100 % of the sexual harassment victims being male very strongly misrepresents the real statistics, which show approximately 16 % of documented sexual harassment cases in the USA to be filed by men.

The workshop then reminds the employees that sexual jokes can contribute to a hostile work environment. This point is illustrated simply by a photograph of a woman's open mouth, which then turns into four copies of the photograph joined together. This graphic does nothing to illustrate the point; it serves only to fragment women's bodies and sexualize our mouths. *The very first example* that features a woman who believes herself to be harassed teaches us the "reasonable person" standard, and, you guessed it, this example shows the alleged victim as not reasonable. What?!! As Susan Estrich writes in *Sex and Power*, "Respected scholars have argued that the 'reasonable person' whose evaluations of what counts as 'severe' and 'pervasive' as a matter of law is an implausible fiction: There are no reasonable people of a gender-neutral sort when it comes to sexual relations" (193).[2]

I'm guessing that the large majority of our employees were less attuned to these visual demonstrations of women as harassers and women as unreasonable non-victims. This in and of itself is dangerous because the workshop then glosses over how real sexual harassment happens and reinforces preconceptions about women as sexual predators and women as easy liars about things like rape and sexual harassment.

When the workshop treated the issue of e-mail harassment, the final lesson was: "Remember: Don't write anything electronically that you wouldn't want your mother or your boss to see or wouldn't want to see on the front page of a newspaper." This caveat was accompanied by a photograph of a mother! This final lesson on workplace harassment reinforced sex-based stereotypes about the role of mothers. The workshop then did a very quick lesson on quid pro quo harassment with a one-line definition. Although I have always said that hostile work environment is a "sneakier" kind of harassment than quid pro quo because there is not usually a clear ass-grab or a series of sexist posters hung in the workplace, quid pro quo harassment still does require a full lesson, along with clear statements about how this form of harassment is closely related to hostile work environment harassment.

In the "Who is Protected?" section, one case shows a male coach's "touchy-feely" approach to a female athlete, whom the coach then invites alone to his hotel room. The lesson states that this is not necessarily harassing behavior and must be determined on a case-by-case basis. Instead of suggesting a hard line for professors and coaches to take, the workshop suggests the softest line possible. In this section, too, there is another example of a woman who is a senior-level scientist harassing a junior colleague. In the STEM areas in which women are the most underrepresented for a host of reasons related to gender shrapnel, this image was extremely hard to take. Finally, the workshop ended with an invitation to do a course evaluation, which I thought would allow me to critique the workshop as I have done here. Instead, the workshop *only* gathered demographic information on me, the employee, and gave me no opportunity at all to evaluate.

For an organization truly to get at the root causes and effects of sexual discrimination, harassment, and retaliation, it needs to engage in clear, honest, and ongoing discussions among its managers and employees, and these need to be based on clear, honest written policies. Dean W.H. Knight of the University of Washington School of Law uses "four letters [that] should be used to analyze and to propel gender success—V, P, L, P—Vision, Perspective, Leadership, and Persistence" (470). Dean Knight adds that, "Leadership demands that we help both to set and to drive an agenda that pushes gender opportunity" (475). Peirce, Rosen, and Bunn Hiller emphasize the importance of organizational leadership on transparent communication about policies and of providing choices for mechanisms of reporting and investigation (235–238). The following training principles are based in part on these concepts. I provide here a longer and more complex road map for organizations to increase awareness about gender shrapnel and to decrease incidents of sexual discrimination, harassment, and retaliation. Although this plan requires intensive work in the early going, sticking to the plan will slowly change the culture of the organization, will decrease unproductive work incidents, and will expand the inner work lives of employees and managers.

Training 1: Training the Trainers

Preparation
Gather together the individuals in the organization who will be in charge of training workshops (plural!) on sexual discrimination, harassment, and

retaliation. A good cohort to have in place includes the President/CEO, director of human resources, in-house counsel, and five at-large employees chosen from different areas of the institution. If the organization is a college or university, at least one member of the Women's and Gender Studies Program should be included for her or his scholarly expertise on gender issues. If the organization has a Committee on the Status of Women, then one representative from that committee should serve on the team of trainers. The more diverse this group, the better. This group should plan on four 90-minute meetings together, preferably spread over two to three weeks.

Four Training Sessions with the Trainers

Training Session 1 (90 Minutes)
Hold the first meeting of the "trainers." The first meeting should include a group discussion of the following questions: (Questions 1–8 come from Ely and Meyerson, p. 591.) Devote five to ten minutes to each question. Take notes and distribute the summary before the second meeting of the group. Assign one reading (from *Gender Shrapnel in the Workplace* and/or from Amabile and Kramer) for the second session with this group.

1. How does the organization do its work?
2. What is valued here?
3. What is ignored here?
4. What do we as employees of the institution take for granted?
5. How does taking these issues for granted affect women's prospects for advancement?
6. How does taking these issues for granted affect the organization's effectiveness?
7. How many women have secured positions of power in the organization?
8. How are women valued for their contributions to the organization?
9. What are the parallels between the obstacles for women here and the obstacles for underrepresented groups?

Training Session 2 (90 Minutes)
Hold the second meeting of the trainers. Briefly address the written summary from the first meeting. Have a broad, 45-minute discussion of a selection from *Gender Shrapnel*. Topics addressed might include:

1. What is "gender shrapnel," and what's the "accidental" part of it?
2. What are examples of gender shrapnel in my workplace, or in a friend's?
3. What made the gender shrapnel incident so volatile?
4. How can an employee recognize that she or he has been hit by gender shrapnel?
5. How can the manager recognize the occurrence of gender shrapnel? How can she or he work to clear some of the shrapnel before it hits others?
6. How can the employee and the manager work together to clear shrapnel?
7. What has to happen if they cannot work together to clear the shrapnel?

Take notes and distribute training summary before the third training session. Homework for all trainers: Create a list of at least ten elements of an equitable workplace. For the third session, distribute a brief reading from Marty Langelan, "Put a Stop to Sexual Harassment" (*50 Ways to Improve Women's Lives* [119–121]).

Training Session 3 (90 Minutes)
Hold the third meeting of the trainers. Briefly address the written summary from the second meeting and allow for comments and observations up to this point in the training.

1. Review Glossary of basic terms surrounding prevention of sexual discrimination, harassment, and retaliation. (See text below.)
2. Review Stages of Confronting Sexual Harassment. (See Chapter 3.)
3. Comment on short selection by Marty Langelan, "Put a Stop to Sexual Harassment."
4. Review two case studies, one focused on quid pro quo harassment and the other focused on hostile work environment harassment. (See case studies in Chapter 15.)
5. Introduce PowerPoint presentation on how to create a more equitable work environment. Consider editing according to cohort's suggestions. (See text below.)

Training Session 4 (90 Minutes)
Hold the fourth meeting of the trainers. Briefly address the written summary from the third meeting and allow for comments and observations up to this point in the training.

1. Complete together the Jonathan Segal Higher Ed Hero Workshop, titled "Pricelessness of Prevention." This has ample information for managers and employees. Make sure to discuss the presenter's emphasis on the inappropriateness of sexual discrimination, harassment, and retaliation, rather than the illegality of these actions. Does it serve employees well to focus on both inappropriateness and illegality? Consider adding to policy (1) language of the EEOC, (2) the text of Title VII and Title IX, and (3) links to other legal resources.
2. Discuss how this group will implement training sessions with the rest of the organization's employees. The eight trainers might choose to split into two or three groups to do training sessions with small groups of employees. The trainers will need to decide if they want to use the preceding training materials in three sessions for the rest of the employees and what they would like the schedule to look like.
3. Finally, put into place a plan for meeting with trainers three times a year. This will keep alive and current the discussion of sexual harassment prevention, will continue a spirit of camaraderie surrounding the work among this group, and have the training of all employees be ongoing. Consider having trainers present simple, non-required informational sessions (with Q&A) during staff and faculty development weeks. This no-pressure situation offers an excellent way both for the trainers to practice their presentation of these issues and to field questions and for the employees to attend sessions on a voluntary basis (in addition to those required by the college or university).

PREPARATION FOR TRAINING THE ORGANIZATION'S EMPLOYEES

1. See training principles outlined above.
2. Once the trainers have agreed upon their approach, they should practice the training sessions with each other.
3. Give ample notice of the time commitment for these training sessions.
4. Create a shared file site for recent research on the issues.

5. Update articles and case studies as appropriate.
6. Require employees to attend all training sessions (the number to be determined by the group of trainers), as outlined above, and then one workshop a year thereafter.
7. Consider creating an online workshop as a *complement to, not a replacement of,* the face-to-face training sessions.

GLOSSARY OF TERMS USED IN *GENDER SHRAPNEL IN THE ACADEMIC WORKPLACE* AND TO BE USED IN TRAINING SESSIONS

American Association of University Women (AAUW): AAUW advances equity for women and girls through advocacy, education, philanthropy, and research (http://www.aauw.org).

Academic Ventriloquism: (See "Workplace Ventriloquism")

Blind-Eye Phenomenon: An organization that ignores sexual harassment and discrimination is telling its female and male students and/or its employees that the prevailing attitudes and behaviors are acceptable and repeatable, thus contributing constantly to a cycle of cultural affirmation of patriarchy. The "blind eye" phenomenon actually *foments* the belief in masculine superiority and the acceptance of harassment and discrimination based on gender.

Concrete Wall: Buzzanell and Lucas' term for the "glass ceiling" in the context of minority women.

Discrimination: Judging an individual on the basis of a group or category to which that person belongs or is perceived to belong, instead of on the individual's merits.

Equal Employment Opportunity Commission (EEOC): The US EEOC is responsible for enforcing federal laws that make it illegal to discriminate against a job applicant or an employee because of the person's race, color, religion, sex (including pregnancy), national origin, age (40 or older), disability, or genetic information. It is also illegal to discriminate against a person because the person complained about discrimination, filed a charge of discrimination, or participated in an employment discrimination investigation or lawsuit. Most employers with at least 15 employees are covered by EEOC laws (20 employees in age discrimination cases). Most labor unions and employment agencies are also covered. The laws apply to all types of work situations, including hiring, firing, promotion, harassment, training, wages, and benefits. (http://www.eeoc.gov, "Overview")

Earnings Gap: The differential between the average amount men earn per year and the average amount women earn per year. Overall, women still earn only 79% of what men earn each year. Figures are consistently lower for women of color.

Feminist Activism: The creation of a platform for gender equity in all areas and the actions taken to promote the platform.

Feminine Mystique: Betty Friedan's term that gives name and shape to the phenomenon of the disillusionment that women of the 1950s and 1960s felt both in the home and in the nation in general.

Feminist Fuse: Related to the "Last Straw" phenomenon, the feminist fuse results from the repression of feelings and confrontation surround-ing harassment. This plays into the stereotype that feminists have no sense of humor. While some in the workplace are unaware of the jokes, comments, exclusions, and impediments that define the environment for certain women, the women in question tire of the repetition and the abuse and can no longer have even the mildest of sense of humor in harassing contexts. In welcoming work environments, the fuse is lengthened and the sense of humor can be restored.

Gender Shrapnel: A series of small workplace explosions that occur when no one person or organization is purposefully discriminating against women based on sex, but when the gender norms of our homes and of our public interactions that consistently follow a patriarchal flow are rep-licated in the workplace, entrenched in the workplace, and then become the fabric of a pattern of sexual discrimination. This pattern is normally not consonant with the organization's professed values and is often in direct opposition to Title VII and Title IX law. Hart and Secunda write of the same phenomenon, referring to: "Subtle discrimination that infect[s] workplace decisions without conscious awareness on the part of the decision makers" (60).

Gender Socialization: The process by which members of a society learn to behave as is "expected" of their gender (feminine or masculine).

Gendered Spheres: The notion that men occupy certain areas (usually in the public sphere) and that women occupy distinctly different areas (usually in the private sphere). *Also called "Separate Spheres."

Glass Ceiling: Coined in 1986 in the now famous *Wall Street Journal* article by Carol Hymowitz and Timothy Schellhardt and subsequently the object of study in governmental (The Glass Ceiling Commission of 1991) and numerous university research projects, the "glass ceiling" refers to the significant barriers women face in acceding to higher-level jobs (e.g. beyond minimum wage, hourly jobs) and advancing in the organizations in which they work.

Hostile Work Environment (HWE) Harassment: The situation in which the harassing behavior of anyone in the workplace—not only a boss or supervisor—causes the workplace to become hostile, intimidating, or offensive and unreasonably interferes with an employee's work. (Chamberlain, 2–3)

Intersectionality: In the case of gender, the ways in which other "protected categories," such as race, religion, sexual orientation, age, and ability, crisscross with gender and reinforce and complicate notions of White, male privilege.

Last Straw: Those who have been harassed generally do not speak of specific harassing events, but the distress surrounding those events accumulates. Eventually, a harassing incident occurs that the individual simply cannot abide. The individual, who has ignored, "let go," or repressed a series of harassing moments in the past, reacts and attempts to confront the "last straw" event. At that moment, the onlookers view the individual as overly sensitive, since they likely have been unaware or not critically thinking about the environment and the incidents that it has allowed in the past. The collision between the onlookers' view of "something minor" with the victim's knowledge of a whole heap of events exacerbates the feeling of alienation of the victim, the inability to confront the specific event and, especially, the overall, generalized patterns of harassing behavior(s). In addition, individuals can arrive at the "last straw" through a combination of others' harassing experiences and their own.

Maternal Wall: When women encounter severe bias once they have children. Maternal Wall is the most open form of gender bias. It stems from stereotypes that link motherhood with lack of competence and commitment. The leading study on maternal wall stereotypes found that, compared to women with identical resumes but no children, mothers were: 79% less likely to be hired, 100% less likely to be promoted, offered $11,000 less in salary for the same position, held to higher performance and punctuality standards. Bias against mothers stems not only from assumptions about what mothers are like but also from assumptions about how mothers should behave. Even today, women often encounter statements indicating that mothers don't belong in the workplace. Such statements can either be hostile ("Mothers belong at home") or benevolent ("I assumed she didn't want the fellowship because she just had a baby"). (Taken from The Gender Bias Learning Project website, http://www.genderbiasbingo.com/index.html.)

Office of Civil Rights (OCR):   Federal civil rights laws and the Health Insurance Portability and Accountability Act (HIPAA) Privacy Rule, together protect your fundamental rights of non-discrimination and health information privacy. Civil Rights help to protect you from unfair treatment or discrimination, because of your race, color, national origin, disability, age, sex (gender), or religion.

Paycheck Feminism: Kornbluh and Homer's term for activism surrounding increased pay equity. Government labor policies devised many decades ago, when there were far fewer women in the workplace need to be revised in order to find ways "to better value women's work."

Professional Mystique: Based on Betty Friedan's notion of the "feminine mystique," the professional mystique updates the term by acknowledging that women and men both can experience gender-based disillusionment in the workplace.

Pyramid Problem: A term coined by Mary Ann Mason, who relies on data on men's and women's representation in organizations, pay, and family formation as a measurement of gender equity at a given institution in order to draw attention to the high number of women in the lowest strata of the pyramid, with women with children found at the very bottom.

Quid Pro Quo Harassment: A supervisors' use of sexual demands in exchange for job security or perquisites.

Retaliation: When an individual employee calls attention to sexual discrimination or harassment and the employer responds with punitive measures. Retaliation in these cases is prohibited by law.

Rhetorical Anorexia: The situation in which a person who has experienced gender shrapnel allows her or his voice to have less and less volume, to take up less and less space, to shrink in size and importance, almost to disappear. It is a decision (or reaction) to occupy as little space as possible so as not to draw attention and not to attract unwanted shrapnel.

Rubbernecking: Seeing and gawking at cases of gender shrapnel, but not listening to or responding to them.

Separate Spheres: See "Gendered Spheres."

Sexual Harassment: Impeding a person's work on the basis of her or his sex. The two types of sexual harassment are Hostile Work Environment and Quid Pro Quo harassment. *See above.

Talk-as-Action: Krolokke and Sorensen cite feminist conversation analysts who study the concept of "talk-as-action" (158–59). "Talk-as-action" is increasingly important in the contemporary workplace, where "talk" is largely how the work gets done, whether it is oral talk—face-to-face conferences, meetings, dispensing of instructions—or written talk—memos, e-mails, reports. This means that the ways in which we talk *and don't talk* increasingly affect how we operate in the workplace and how efficiently the work gets done. Krolokke and Sorensen cite Judith Butler on this point, saying that it is she who elucidates the notion of "agency in speech" and how this agency is related to "performativity as a conceptualization of the constant tension between performances and the underlying conventions and the ways words and bodies are involved in both" (161).

Title VII: Also known as the Civil Rights Act of 1964, Title VII prohibits employment discrimination based on race, color, religion, sex, or national origin.

Title IX: Title IX (1972) prohibits discrimination based on sex in a federally funded educational program or activity.

Workplace Ventriloquism (Professional Ventriloquism): The shrapnel of silencing the dangerous voices, hearing the safe ones, and tacitly encouraging the safe voices to take credit for the ideas of those who can no longer speak out. In its written form, "workplace ventriloquism" has been called "bureaucratic plagiarism" (coined by Gavin Moodie and cited by Carl Elliott).

RECOMMENDATIONS FOR CREATING A MORE EQUITABLE WORK ENVIRONMENT

Consider the following questions:

- Which environments in your lives are the most female-friendly? (Think: friends, family, classroom, department, theater, music, sports, roommates, sorority, counseling, etc.)
- What are the elements of those environments that are welcoming to women and to traditionally underrepresented groups?
- Which environments in your lives seem particularly unfriendly for women and for traditionally underrepresented groups?
- What are the elements of those environments that are least welcoming to women and to traditionally underrepresented groups?

Recommendations for moving the work environment toward equity:

- Hire women and members of traditionally underrepresented groups at all levels and in all areas; be attuned to retention issues and address problems as soon as they arise
- Ensure that physical surroundings support women and men equally (e.g. cubicles, locker rooms)
- Encourage women and members of traditionally underrepresented groups to apply for posts that enhance their careers; encourage them to negotiate for better salary and benefits packages in these positions ("Nourish women's ambitions" [Marie C. Wilson])
- Ensure equity in the allocation of types and amounts of work assigned
- Recognize difference and value it at all levels; seek out ways to encourage all individuals to participate in workplace discussions; be particularly attentive to sex, race, class, sexual orientation; be vigilant about the "silencing" phenomenon
- Encourage all to speak; encourage dissent; encourage working together toward articulating problems and finding solutions ("Negative Thinking" [Atul Gawande])
- Support a community (or communities) of women and people of Color
- Conduct surveys and gather pertinent data in order to analyze women's experiences and those of members of traditionally underrepresented groups empirically
- Examine committee composition to ensure that women's voices are being heard throughout the workplace
- Recognize women's successes and those of members of traditionally underrepresented groups (e.g. Communications Office)
- Support internal and external programming related to women's issues and those of members of traditionally underrepresented groups
- Examine core values and their cultural import vis-à-vis gender
- Write clear, fair policies that establish workplace equity (healthcare; leaves; hiring, training, promotion; salary; discrimination, harassment, and retaliation)
- Train employers and employees with clear, "local" examples of policy violations; relevant case studies / Ensure ongoing and increasingly sophisticated training
- Adhere to policy; zero-tolerance on discrimination, harassment, retaliation / Do not allow scapegoating. Do not use "zero-tolerance" terminology unless it truly reflects the practices of your workplace.

NOTES

1. The author extends profound thanks to Professor Sarah (Sally) Burns of the New York University Law School for collaboration on the original document created to encourage a system of checks and balances at institutions of higher learning.
2. I couldn't agree more with Estrich on this point. Nevertheless, my sense of reasonableness on the Clinton-Lewinsky case differs vastly from that of Estrich, one of Bill Clinton's defense lawyers. While Estrich views the case as consensual, and therefore not harassing, I view it as harassing principally because it took place in the most iconic workplace of the USA, thus setting a standard for our threshold of hierarchical sexual activity in the workplace. Had it only taken place in a hotel room or private residence, then I would not necessarily call it sexual harassment.

REFERENCE

Hymowitz, Carol, and Timothy Schellhardt. 1986. Breaking the glass ceiling. *Wall Street Journal*, 24 Mar 1986. Print.

PART IV

Case Studies in Gender Shrapnel

CHAPTER 15

Gender Shrapnel Case Studies

Gender Shrapnel in the Workplace is, in and of itself, a series of case studies. Each chapter tells stories that illustrate the specific components of gender shrapnel outlined in that chapter. This chapter offers eight additional brief case studies in order to show how gender shrapnel concepts can be applied in the contexts of law, business, medicine, higher education in a military context, and secondary education. These brief case studies can be used in conjunction with the Training Principles outlined in Chapter 14.[1]

For each of the case studies, consider the following questions:

1. Has something inappropriate happened? If so, what is it? Is this inappropriate action also illegal under Title VII and/or Title IX law?
2. What are the gender components in the case? Consider the sex of the individuals involved, the degree of power tied to their professional positions, the overall work environment and the visual and audio messages it sends about gender, and the vocabulary used in the interactions among the individuals involved in the case.
3. Has gender shrapnel hit in this case? If so, how?
4. List the problems in this case.
5. Discuss potential solutions for all involved.
6. What other questions surrounding these cases need to be asked?

1. Making Partner A female law associate in a large Boston firm is working toward making partner. She attended Yale Law School, has a master's in public health policy, and has gained recognition at her firm for working

© The Editor(s) (if applicable) and The Author(s) 2016   205
E. Mayock, *Gender Shrapnel in the Academic Workplace*,
DOI 10.1057/978-1-137-50830-0_15

long hours on big cases. While working toward making partner, she has two children who are under three years. After the associate has had her two children, two of the law associate's performance evaluations state that the associate seems "frazzled" and "frenetic." Three years later, the law associate is denied partner and moves to another firm.

2. Business Model A large, well-known, and long-standing Washington, DC, business sells commercial real estate. Charisma and "face-time" really matter in order to attract and maintain steady clients. The headquarters of the company boasts ample office space, a room to play billiards, posters on the walls, of young, scantily clad women and a small basketball court out back. The company's president regularly smokes cigars, plays basketball, and goes fishing with his employees. A total of 25 of the company's 28 employees are men. Two of the three women are administrative assistants, and the third is a commercial real estate agent who likes to play basketball and shoot pool. The company hires a fourth female employee to join the ranks of the agents. This employee issues a formal complaint about the posters and the jokes that are made about them. Nothing is done about the complaint, and the employee leaves the company within one year.

3. Meds A large pharmaceutical company in Charlotte offers a women's leadership program to a handpicked group of up-and-coming women managers. The program includes in-house workshops on women and leadership, funds for program participants to travel to pertinent conferences on the topic, an assigned mentor, and regular social gatherings for program participants. The participants "graduate" from the program and take on higher-level managerial positions in the company. One of the participants becomes one of the company vice presidents. She discovers that the other company vice presidents, all male, have a long-standing Wednesday night poker game, at which some of the business conversations of the week take place. She is not invited to join the game, nor does she feel comfortable inviting herself. She attends a business dinner with colleagues and clients, and her supervisor asks her if she was a "party girl" in college. The new VP soon finds that not as much work is coming her way and that her male subordinate is being consulted on matters meant for her. She stays with the company and never complains about the incidents.

4. Military College A public military college in Texas is required to co-educate in the 1990s, and the institution's president responds by saying publicly that he is extremely dissatisfied with the decision. The institution co-educates and, within 15 years, 10% of its student population is female.

The chair of the computer science department repeatedly makes sexual comments to female colleagues in the biology department. He asks them "to sit on his lap" and "to warm him up," and he comments on various parts of their bodies. The female professors issue a formal complaint. The institution denies wrongdoing, but states that the female professors are allowed to avoid the male employee by not attending formal events, such as faculty meetings, convocations, and graduation. The female employees file a formal case with the EEOC.

5. High School Discipline A female high school administrator in Alabama with two years' experience as a classroom teacher and two years' experience as an assistant principal takes over as principal of a medium-sized high school. After two years with the new principal in charge, teachers, parents, and students complain that the principal does not state clear goals, runs over in meetings, is unaware of curricular changes, and disregards disciplinary needs. After four years, the principal is dismissed. Several parents speak vociferously about the need to hire a man in order to get the discipline question in order. A man is hired and is perceived by the parents to be stating clear goals, running meetings well, and instituting a degree of discipline.

6. Member of the Clergy A female minister in Nevada is called to visit an elderly, ailing patient at the local hospital. She arrives soon thereafter at the information desk of the hospital and states her business. She is told that the patient will wait for her (the female minister's) husband. "But I'm the minister. I have been called to visit with the ailing patient," states the minister. "Please just wait a moment and we'll see if we can clear this up," says the woman at the front desk. Fifteen minutes later, the receptionist returns with a manager, who then asks the business of the minister. The minister patiently restates her business, but also relays that she is concerned that time is passing and the patient is awaiting her visit. She is finally allowed back to the patient's room. The next day, she is called back to the same patient and confronts the very same situation with a different front-desk receptionist. It takes her 25 minutes on the second day to get to the patient's room for the visit.

7. Radioactivity A wife and husband work at the same carpet factory in North Carolina in different departments. The wife works on the factory floor, where there are 42 male employees and 18 female employees. The husband started out on the factory floor, but now works as the assistant director of public relations for the company. Over a period of six months,

the floor manager tells the wife and four of her female co-workers that he wants to take them out for drinks. He loudly "grades" their physical features and occasionally pats them on the buttocks and massages their shoulders. After six months of putting up with the manager's behavior, the wife and one other woman report the manager's behavior to the director of human resources. The director tells them that she will look into the matter. The floor manager is removed from the floor for one week's time and then returns. The floor workers are not given a reason for his absence. The two women who reported the sexual harassment receive no feedback on their case. A week later, the assistant director of public relations is demoted.

8. Mommies and Daddies A female surgical resident at a large, urban hospital in Los Angeles gives birth in January and returns to work eight weeks later. A male surgical resident's partner gives birth in March of that same year, and the male surgical resident returns to work four weeks later. All residents in the program receive their annual evaluations in mid-June, just before the end of the fiscal year. The performance evaluation for the female resident states that, "she has exceeded expectations, despite the time off for parental leave." The performance evaluation for the male resident states that "he has far exceeded expectations."

NOTE

1. For an instructor's guide with possible responses to questions for each case study, see Appendix.

PART V

Clearing the Shrapnel

CHAPTER 16

Final Remarks

I recently watched the 2005 film *North Country*, directed by Niki Carlo and starring Charlize Theron and Frances McDormand. I bought the DVD years ago, but it took me all this time to have the stomach to watch it. The film, which brilliantly maps and crisscrosses the issues of quid pro quo harassment, hostile work environment harassment, and sexual violence, is based on the true story of the women and men of the mines in the northernmost part of Minnesota. As women started to work in the mines, many of the men reacted to them with scorn (what makes you think you can do this job?), envy (why are you taking men's jobs?), and round after round of humiliation. The work environment becomes defined by the penchant for both quid pro quo and hostile work environment harassment. One woman, named Josey, newer to the mine than her co-workers, decides to take a stand and suffers further retaliation. Despite the long road, the many hardships, and profound hesitation on the part of female and male workers, Josey and her lawyer succeed in filing and winning a class-action lawsuit. In real life, the suit was won in 1988, but in the film version, the Anita Hill–Clarence Thomas hearings serve as a national backdrop to the regional Minnesota story. The members of the class won a small settlement and the great satisfaction of contributing to the drafting of sexual harassment legislation and its enforcement.

Josey's story differs in many of the details from many of the stories I have recounted in *Gender Shrapnel*. Nevertheless, the story drives home some of the common denominators of sexual discrimination, harassment, and retaliation (in a predominantly white environment). The harassing men

© The Editor(s) (if applicable) and The Author(s) 2016
E. Mayock, *Gender Shrapnel in the Academic Workplace*,
DOI 10.1057/978-1-137-50830-0_16

211

at the mines have the advantages of hierarchy, both in management and in the union, and of numbers. Women miners are the rarity, and, therefore, women are "the odd men out." The film portrays some of the male miners as non-harassing and as attempting at times to help the women miners who have been pushed, grabbed, and raped, whose work surroundings have been covered with excrement graffiti, and whose belongings have been covered in semen. The director draws a line of careful tension between signaling that these individuals help out ex post facto but play no role in preventing the abuse and sympathizing with the fact that everybody is living in fear of speaking out and losing their jobs. This highlights that the more people conceal and protect the wrongdoers, the more wrongdoing there is. The whole environment becomes toxic for all involved. The film also demonstrates well how one individual who refuses to submit to the toxic environment becomes a pariah, someone to avoid and to make the subject of damaging gossip and someone against whom further retaliation may seem "warranted" in the environment. While the film lasts slightly over two hours, the actual lawsuit lasted 14 years. Yes, 14 years. The law works slowly, and victories are few and far between, which points to the fundamental importance of advocating for profound cultural change both in the workplace itself and in the courtroom.

It is still difficult to read and watch accounts of sexual discrimination, harassment, and retaliation and, especially, of sexual violence because the stories do have these common denominators of scorn and humiliation, of converting one group of human beings into less than a group of human beings. But without the oral and written stories, many people will never understand the severity of sexual discrimination and harassment nor be capable of following their path of gender shrapnel.

Writing *Gender Shrapnel in the Academic Workplace* has been a long journey. The hybrid approach of recounting stories and then gleaning from them the common problems surrounding gender in the workplace has baffled individuals at academic presses and in the popular market. The academic folks wonder, Why tell stories? What do they matter? We need data, data, and more data. The trade folks insist: Tell your stories, make them count, and don't get bogged down with the academic framework. Doing both—telling the stories and supporting them with research—gives needed texture to the gender story and much-needed solutions for the gender-aggrieved workplace.

Gender Shrapnel has been, in part, a process of clearing my own shrapnel in order to help others clear theirs. For now, clearing the shrapnel is a repetitive exercise, more like a weekly house-cleaning. Just as the dust bunnies keep regenerating, so gender shrapnel keeps pinging and zigzagging through the workplace. As I wrote an early draft of this work, the national press was focusing on the Secret Service agents who chose to rent or buy female human beings as they prepared security for President Obama's visit.[1] Right now many social media outlets are rightfully focused on the Black Lives Matter campaign and are still mentioning the #YesAll Women campaign. These types of discrimination, many of which have led to extreme violence, whether among famous, infamous, or everyday ordinary people, never seem to stop. Our national and international leaders rise to stardom despite their gender and race inequities and inadequacies. After all, the international community knew about Silvio Berlusconi's penchant for statutory rape for years before his fall from power. The gender shrapnel they have spread is publicly cleared for a time, leaving in its wake a trail of nameless, faceless, disempowered women and men who must learn again to navigate the workforce, to gain enough power to be effective in it, and to move erratically through its minefields.

When more women and men workers can capably evaluate their work environments, find the strength to speak out consistently against injustice, become CEOs and presidents who vociferously do not tolerate workplace injustice, and find support in other like-minded individuals, then we will have cleared much of the gender and intersectional shrapnel that continues to cause too many "Ow, it got me" moments and to capture too much of our attention that could be placed more productively on the work itself.

Note

1. *The Washington Post* reporters Carol D. Leonnig and David Nakamura reported not only on the Secret Service scandal but also on the actions of "new Secret Service boss for the South American region," Paula Reid. Reid, a 46-year-old African-American woman in an organization with few African-Americans and few women, is reported to have been hired "to ride herd on a rowdy group of male colleagues." (April 21, 2012)

References

Leonnig, Carol D., and David Nakamura. 2012. Secret service scandal: Rising supervisor set uncovering of misconduct in motion. *The Washington Post*, 21 Apr 2012. Accessed 23 Apr 2012. Web.

North Country. 2005. Dir. Niki Carlo, Perf. Charlize Theron. Warner Brothers, DVD.

Appendix: Instructor's Guide. Case Studies in Gender Shrapnel

Gender Shrapnel Case Studies (from Chapter 15)

Gender Shrapnel in the Workplace is, in and of itself, a series of case studies. Each chapter tells stories that illustrate the specific components of gender shrapnel outlined in that chapter. This appendix offers possible responses to the questions posed about the eight additional case studies—from the academic realm and beyond—from Chapter 15. These brief case studies can be used in conjunction with the Training Principles outlined in Chapter 14.

Here is the set of questions for each of the case studies:

1. Has something inappropriate happened? If so, what is it? Is this inappropriate action also illegal under Title VII and/or Title IX law?
2. What are the gender components in the case? Consider the sex of the individuals involved, the degree of power tied to their professional positions, the overall work environment and the visual and audio messages it sends about gender, and the vocabulary used in the interactions among the individuals involved in the case.
3. Has gender shrapnel hit in this case? If so, how?
4. List the problems in this case.
5. Discuss potential solutions for all involved.
6. What other questions surrounding these cases need to be asked?

© The Editor(s) (if applicable) and The Author(s) 2016
E. Mayock, *Gender Shrapnel in the Academic Workplace*,
DOI 10.1057/978-1-137-50830-0

1. Making Partner A female law associate in a large Boston firm is working toward making partner. She attended Yale Law School, has a master's in public health policy and has gained recognition at her firm for working long hours on big cases. While working toward partner, she had two children who were under three years. After the associate has had her two children, two of the law associate's performance evaluations state that the associate seems "frazzled" and "frenetic." Three years later, the law associate is denied partner and moves to another firm.

1. Has something inappropriate happened? If so, what is it? Is this inappropriate action also illegal under Title VII and/or Title IX law?
   There is definitely a gendered aspect to this case, and the law firm would do right to review its approach to the performance evaluations and the dismissal. From a legal perspective, it is possible but might be difficult to prove sex-based discrimination (based on pregnancy bias, maternal bias, gendered language included in performance evaluation, and denial of partnership). There is no clear evidence of sexual harassment or retaliation, based on the contours of this case.
2. What are the gender components in the case? Consider the sex of the individuals involved, the degree of power tied to their professional positions, the overall work environment and the visual and audio messages it sends about gender, and the vocabulary used in the interactions among the individuals involved in the case.
   We only know that the law associate is a woman, but that's enough, given the abysmal statistics for the promotion of women associates to partner. There may indeed be increased stress in the employee's life, but the use of the adjectives "frazzled" and "frenetic" is somewhat fraught, especially if men associates who are new fathers do not face the same scrutiny nor the same descriptive language on their evaluations. The work environment is not described in enough detail to determine whether there are other signs or symbols that indicate that the environment is sending messages about gender-based perceptions of competence.
3. Has gender shrapnel hit in this case? If so, how?
   Yes. This is a case for which the term "gender shrapnel" is particularly useful because something doesn't feel right, and the something seems gendered, but the events described have not accumulated enough to determine that there has been outright discrimination or harassment.

4. List the problems in this case.

- Overall chilly environment for lawyers who are mothers
- Possible perceptions on the part of senior partners that working mothers are necessarily not handling new stressors
- Use of gendered language on written performance reviews might indicate that worse language is used in more informal work settings
- The employee seems not to have had a chance to respond to the evaluations (and, if she did, she might suffer retaliation for signaling the gendered language)
- The lack of promotion for the employee reinforces for all employees at the firm the stereotype that lawyer-mothers seem to show their stress too readily
- The movement of the employee to another firm might indicate that the firm from which she is departing does not embrace a balanced environment for all.

5. Discuss potential solutions for all involved.

- Have senior partners evaluate their assessments of all employees across the board; have them ask pointed questions about potential (intended or unintended) biases regarding gender, race, parental status, religion, class, age, national origin, and so on, that might manifest in the performance evaluations.
- Have a frank conversation with the employee about her response to the evaluations and lack of promotion. See if this case links to any others in the firm.
- Establish a mentoring system and network of support for junior associates.
- Research work–life policies and encourage their application in all cases.

6. What other questions surrounding this case need to be asked?
   It would be helpful to know more about the physical environment/layout of the workspace, the parental leave policies in place, the history of the evaluators on other reviews, and the possibility of the "rarity" of women in upper-level positions at the firm.

2. Business Model A large, well-known, and long-standing Washington, DC, business sells commercial real estate. Charisma and "face-time" really

matter in order to attract and maintain steady clients. The headquarters of the company boasts ample office space, a room to play billiards, posters on the walls, of young, scantily clad women and a small basketball court out back. The company's president regularly smokes cigars, plays basketball, and goes fishing with his employees. A total of 25 of the company's 28 employees are men. Two of the three women are administrative assistants, and the third is a commercial real estate agent who likes to play basketball and shoot pool. The company hires a fourth female employee to join the ranks of the agents. This employee issues a formal complaint about the posters and the jokes that are made about them. Nothing is done about the complaint, and the employee leaves the company within one year.

1. Has something inappropriate happened? If so, what is it? Is this inappropriate action also illegal under Title VII and/or Title IX law?

   Yes, several inappropriate events have taken place, and there are implications for Title VII and Title IX. The work environment itself is potentially harassing in its sexed depiction only of women and the jokes surrounding these depictions. Upper management has created an exclusive, gendered environment that, on the face, will both exclude women from equal opportunity and impose on men a certain gender-based behavior that might be required for their own survival and promotion. The lack of response to a formal work complaint constitutes further discrimination and harassment, and the employee's departure and potential loss of wages and benefits represent harm done.

2. What are the gender components in the case? Consider the sex of the individuals involved, the degree of power tied to their professional positions, the overall work environment and the visual and audio messages it sends about gender, and the vocabulary used in the interactions among the individuals involved in the case.

   • The numbers here are explicit. There are 25 male agents and two female agents.
   • Visual messages abound—the posters, the billiard table, basketball court, and cigars.
   • We have no specific information about language used in the environment, but we know there were jokes surrounding the posters of scantily clad women.
   • Women are most heavily represented at the lowest levels of the company, with still very few present there.

- There seems to be a demand of gender-role performance for survival and/or success in the company.

3. Has gender shrapnel hit in this case? If so, how?

Yes, very much so, and in more explicit ways than in Case 1. There are explicit legal implications due to the repeated nature of the sex-based discrimination and harassment.

4. List the problems in this case.

- The environment exudes a classic "boys-will-be-boys" approach to doing business—including the physical set-up and the types of group outings—and is therefore at the very least unwelcoming to nonconforming women (and possibly men) and most likely harassing.
- The posters
- The lack of response to a formal complaint
- The departure of one of the two female sales agents

5. Discuss potential solutions for all involved.

- Remove the posters.
- Provide consistent and frequent training for all—and first for the business's leaders—on creating equitable work environments.
- Discuss and implement ways to include everyone in the work— both in the work itself and in the group outings. Limit or eliminate the "gentlemen's club" feel to the work environment.
- Review the employee's complaint objectively and work toward explicit change based on the issues raised.
- Offer the possibility of real change and promotion to the employee who has departed and to other women and men interested in working at the business.

6. What other questions surrounding this case need to be asked?

- What is the culture at other businesses like this one?
- What are the ways to maintain the parts of the business environment that are effective while promoting equity in all visible and non-visible areas?
- How can the business protect itself from a lawsuit and at the same time respond responsibly and effectively to the concerns raised in the employee's complaint? In what ways can the business rectify the mistakes it has made?

3. Meds A large pharmaceutical company in Charlotte offers a women's leadership program to a handpicked group of up-and-coming women managers. The program includes in-house workshops on women and leadership, funds for program participants to travel to pertinent conferences on the topic, an assigned mentor, and regular social gatherings for program participants. The participants "graduate" from the program and take on higher-level managerial positions in the company. One of the participants becomes one of the company vice presidents. She discovers that the other company vice presidents, all male, have a long-standing Wednesday night poker game, at which some of the business conversations of the week take place. She is not invited to join the game, nor does she feel comfortable inviting herself. She attends a business dinner with colleagues and clients, and her supervisor asks her if she was a "party girl" in college. The new VP soon finds that not as much work is coming her way and that her male subordinate is being consulted on matters meant for her. She stays with the company and never complains about the incidents.

1. Has something inappropriate happened? If so, what is it? Is this inappropriate action also illegal under Title VII and/or Title IX law?
   Yes, something inappropriate has happened, but the legal impact of the events is difficult to discern because of the lack of fixed pattern of discrimination. The most convincing element of the case is the lack of work flow toward the woman VP and the deference given to one of the men who works for her. The company has much it could do to increase equity in the work environment.

2. What are the gender components in the case? Consider the sex of the individuals involved, the degree of power tied to their professional positions, the overall work environment and the visual and audio messages it sends about gender, and the vocabulary used in the interactions among the individuals involved in the case.

   • On the one hand, the company is addressing probable "pipeline" issues by creating programs and leadership opportunities for the women it employs. On the other hand, specific branches of the company seem unprepared to welcome new women leaders to their ranks.
   • "Rarity" is a problem here, given that only one of the VPs at this branch is a woman.
   • As in Case 2, the culture of the work environment is overtly masculine (tradition of male business leaders; all-male Wednesday

night poker game; inappropriate questions for the only female business leader) and therefore excludes women.

- Whether through the social network or through a lack of adaptation to women in the upper ranks, the men leaders are not working equitably with their female colleague. They are excluding her from the work flow and at the same time are effectively promoting her junior male colleague by diverting upper-level work to him.
- The "party girl" question seemed to happen only once and therefore doesn't create its own pattern. Nevertheless, the question is rife with gender problems—the question itself, the use of the word "girl," and the implication of some kind of party or sexual favors behind the question.

3. Has gender shrapnel hit in this case? If so, how?

Yes, most definitely. This employee has done everything she can to be prepared for breaking the glass ceiling, but the old networks reveal themselves to be still quite powerful.

4. List the problems in this case.

- The company has prepared women for promotion in the workplace, but has not prepared men for women's promotion.
- The high-level leaders are unwilling to incorporate fully a new high-level leader based on her sex and perceived gender.
- The high-level leaders demonstrate that they would always still rather consult with a man, even if his title and experience don't show that he is the most expert employee for this type of consultation.
- The poker game
- The "party girl" question
- The hiring of only one woman VP.

5. Discuss potential solutions for all involved.

- Have the men attend some of the sessions of the women's training program and/or develop training for all employees that elucidates gender shrapnel problems.
- The new female employee can go back to her mentors from the training program for advice on navigating the environment, complaints, legal actions, and future work opportunities.
- Eliminate the poker game or open it up, depending on the circumstances.

- Hire more women in the upper ranks and enhance leadership opportunities for them.
- Assess work flow for fairness.
- Assess work flow for potential for promotion—in all employees' cases.

6. What other questions surrounding this case need to be asked?

   - How does company culture influence equity in the work environment?
   - Who is in charge of making overt changes in the company culture?
   - How can "pipeline" programs make a difference beyond the face-to-face programming?
   - How can the company leaders be attuned to the silence of their new employee?
   - What training principles should be instituted for company leaders?

4. Military College A public military college in Texas is required to co-educate in the 1990s, and the institution's president responds by saying publicly that he is extremely dissatisfied with the decision. The institution co-educates and, within 15 years, 10% of its student population is female. The chair of the computer science department repeatedly makes sexual comments to female colleagues in the biology department. He asks them "to sit on his lap" and "to warm him up," and he comments on various parts of their bodies. The female professors issue a formal complaint. The institution denies wrongdoing, but states that the female professors are allowed to avoid the male employee by not attending formal events, such as faculty meetings, convocations, and graduation. The female employees file a formal case with the EEOC.

1. Has something inappropriate happened? If so, what is it? Is this inappropriate action also illegal under Title VII and/or Title IX law?

   Yes, this is a potential violation of both Title VII and Title IX law. The sexual nature of the chair's comments and the repetition of them imply problems of both quid pro quo and hostile work environment harassment. The EEOC would certainly need to address this case.

2. What are the gender components in the case? Consider the sex of the individuals involved, the degree of power tied to their professional positions, the overall work environment and the visual and

APPENDIX: INSTRUCTOR'S GUIDE. CASE STUDIES IN GENDER SHRAPNEL 223

audio messages it sends about gender, and the vocabulary used in the interactions among the individuals involved in the case.

- The institution is still mostly male. It's likely that the traditional military culture based on hierarchy influences the molding of the work environment.
- The institution's leader has publicly expressed disappointment about the move to co-education.
- The chair of a department—relatively high in institutional hierarchy—is making quid pro quo demands and creating a harassing environment based on sex.
- The chair's behavior is repeated and unwelcomed. In addition, it affects several people directly.
- Students and employees of the institution might learn from the handling of the case that the chair's behavior is acceptable and maybe even rewarded.
- The institution corrects none of the wrongdoing in its response to the formal complaint.
- Complainants are treated as "thin-skinned plaintiffs" and are encouraged to remove themselves from the routine tasks and events of their jobs.
- The EEOC has gotten involved.

3. Has gender shrapnel hit in this case? If so, how?

   Yes, very much so, and in legally actionable ways. Title VII and Title IX appear to have been violated due to the sexual discrimination and harassment permitted by the institution and the institution's own retaliatory response to the complainants.

4. List the problems in this case.

   - Co-educational objectives are not fulfilled, and the culture has not changed to send a message of equity to its employees.
   - The department chair does not understand the damage caused by his sex-based remarks.
   - The institution becomes aware of the issues and does nothing to correct the actions of the department chair, to issue an apology, or to rectify the overall situation.
   - The complainants clearly are not heard, and they are then the ones who have to do the additional work of the EEOC complaint to try to get the institution to comply with the law.

- The women are viewed as the problem, the ones who need to be shunted around.

5. Discuss potential solutions for all involved.

- Improve the Title VII and Title IX training for all individuals at the institution.
- When an individual harasses others, investigate immediately. If wrongdoing is confirmed, remove the person from the position and, if possible, explain why he is being removed. This is an important educational move for the community.
- Review the complaint intake system and system of adjudication for these cases.
- Be pro-active in the EEOC process. This is an opportunity to let go of cover-up and to embrace change.

6. What other questions surrounding this case need to be asked?

- Are there other, related incidents at the institution that require the same type of assessment and resolution for change?
- What are the history and relationship of the institution with Title VII, Title IX, and the EEOC?
- How can the institution change culturally ingrained behaviors?
- How can the institution repair the damage done to the biology professors?

5. High School Discipline A female high school administrator in Alabama with two years' experience as a classroom teacher and two years' experience as an assistant principal takes over as principal of a medium-sized high school. After two years with the new principal in charge, teachers, parents, and students complain that the principal does not state clear goals, runs over in meetings, is unaware of curricular changes, and disregards disciplinary needs. After four years, the principal is dismissed. Several parents speak vociferously about the need to hire a man in order to get the discipline question in order. A man is hired and is perceived by the parents to be stating clear goals, running meetings well, and instituting a degree of discipline.

1. Has something inappropriate happened? If so, what is it? Is this inappropriate action also illegal under Title VII and/or Title IX law?
   There appears to be no clear violation of the law, although there appear to be some vague gender issues at stake.

2. What are the gender components in the case? Consider the sex of the individuals involved, the degree of power tied to their professional positions, the overall work environment and the visual and audio messages it sends about gender, and the vocabulary used in the interactions among the individuals involved in the case.

   • The female principal is dismissed and is replaced by a man. This is not necessarily gendered because the only comments or rationale we have heard came from the parents.
   • The position of principal is highly visible and can influence young people's formulation of who is "fit" or "natural" to occupy the position. The removal of the woman and the hiring of the man might require an examination of the presence of other visible role models on campus.
   • The case revolves simply around some parents' perception of the motives for removal and hire. It may be that they saw discipline as the core issue, and that they saw it in a gendered way (the woman was "weak" on discipline; the man who replaced her would have the advantage of appearing immediately "tougher" on discipline).

3. Has gender shrapnel hit in this case? If so, how?
   It appears so, but it is difficult to pin it down, apart from the responses given in Question 2.

4. List the problems in this case.

   • The school system has fired a woman principal and hired a man principal. This is not necessarily a problem, but the reasons for such a change need to be made clear.

5. Discuss potential solutions for all involved.

   • The school system needs to make clear its expectations and timeline for its goals.
   • The school system needs to support all of its administrators as they carry out the system's mandates and set their own agendas.
   • The school system needs to establish an environment that allows boys and girls to see that men and women can and do accede to high-level positions.

6. What other questions surrounding this case need to be asked?

   • What other circumstances influenced the firing and subsequent hiring?
   • What is the experience of students and other staff at the school?
   • Are any cultural changes needed, and what are the best methods to encourage these changes?

6. Member of the Clergy A female minister in Nevada is called to visit an elderly, ailing patient at the local hospital. She arrives soon, thereafter at the information desk of the hospital and states her business. She is told that the patient will wait for her (the female minister's) husband. "But I'm the minister. I have been called to visit with the ailing patient," states the minister. "Please just wait a moment and we'll see if we can clear this up," says the woman at the front desk. Fifteen minutes later, the receptionist returns with a manager, who then asks the business of the minister. The minister patiently restates her business, but also relays that she is concerned that time is passing and the patient is awaiting her visit. She is finally allowed back to the patient's room. The next day, she is called back to the same patient and confronts the very same situation with a different front-desk receptionist. It takes her 25 minutes on the second day to get to the patient's room for the visit.

1. Has something inappropriate happened? If so, what is it? Is this inappropriate action also illegal under Title VII and/or Title IX law?
   The minister faces this sex-based discrimination two times at the same location. This is probably not legally actionable, but it could develop into something worse.

2. What are the gender components in the case? Consider the sex of the individuals involved, the degree of power tied to their professional positions, the overall work environment and the visual and audio messages it sends about gender, and the vocabulary used in the interactions among the individuals involved in the case.

   • The two different receptionists are operating from the assumption that ministers are men. They are trying to protect the patient from someone they believe could not have been called in.
   • The minister has to work harder just to do her job.
   • The lesson is not learned after the first day. The minister has to keep teaching the same lesson, to the detriment of her job and her parishioners.

3. Has gender shrapnel hit in this case? If so, how?
   Yes, it has. The female minister is viewed as being "out of place," is prohibited from entering a space to which she has been asked to work, and the actions are repeated.

4. List the problems in this case.

- The receptionists are not trained well enough to understand who can work and should be able to do work on-site.
- The patient is in ill-health and needs to talk right away. As gender shrapnel plays itself out, there is a significant delay, two days in a row.
- The minister has to do the extra work of legitimizing herself as a professional and training others—on the job.

5. Discuss potential solutions for all involved.

- Our media could certainly do their part in expanding roles for women, and thus making the average person not view a female minister as an oddity.
- Train employees to seek credentials that are based only on the credential, not on the sex, gender, skin color, religion, age, or national origin of the individual with the credential.

6. What other questions surrounding this case need to be asked?

- How can mistakes made on one shift not be repeated by the next shift of workers?
- How can managers work to change perceptions on a microcosmic level?
- How can managers change the workplace environment overall?

7. Radioactivity A wife and husband work at the same carpet factory in North Carolina in different departments. The wife works on the factory floor, where there are 42 male employees and 18 female employees. The husband started out on the factory floor, but now works as the assistant director of public relations for the company. Over a period of six months, the floor manager tells the wife and four of her female co-workers that he wants to take them out for drinks. He loudly "grades" their physical features and occasionally pats them on the buttocks and massages their shoulders. After six months of putting up with the manager's behavior, the wife and one other woman report the manager's behavior to the director of human resources. The director tells them that she will look into the matter. The floor manager is removed from the floor for one week's time and then returns. The floor workers are not given a reason for his absence. The two women who reported the sexual harassment receive no feedback on their case. A week later, the assistant director of public relations is demoted.

1. Has something inappropriate happened? If so, what is it? Is this inappropriate action also illegal under Title VII and/or Title IX law?

    Yes, the factory is engaging in both quid pro quo and hostile work environment harassment. The management also seems to have retaliated against the husband of one of the complainants.

2. What are the gender components in the case? Consider the sex of the individuals involved, the degree of power tied to their professional positions, the overall work environment and the visual and audio messages it sends about gender, and the vocabulary used in the interactions among the individuals involved in the case.

    - There are significantly more male than female workers.
    - There may be a glass ceiling problem, given the husband's fast ascent in the company.
    - The floor manager, who manages the floor workers, is clearly initiating quid pro quo harassment and treating women workers differently from men workers. His rhetoric and actions are blatantly sexist.
    - The director of human resources is a woman. She appears to be another cog in a poorly functioning machine.

3. Has gender shrapnel hit in this case? If so, how?

    Yes, it has. There are clear legal violations (sexual discrimination, harassment, and retaliation) with other gendered implications (glass ceiling, in particular).

4. List the problems in this case.

    - The abuse of power
    - Women as "rarity" as floor workers
    - A lack of formal process for the two complainants
    - A lack of communication surrounding the one-week absence of the floor manager
    - The demotion of the complainant's husband

5. Discuss potential solutions for all involved.

    - Improved training from the top down, *including* for the office of human resources
    - Creation of clear internal complaint processes
    - Clear communication surrounding results of complaints

- Removal or vigilant monitoring of individuals found not in compliance
- Check the solutions and make sure they are as fair as possible for all involved.

6. What other questions surrounding these cases need to be asked?

- Beyond just Title VII and EEOC/OCR compliance, how can this workplace become more equitable for all?
- What is the role of the human resources office? What is their relationship to the general counsel of the company?
- How are men also victims of gender shrapnel that seems visited upon women?

8. Mommies and Daddies A female surgical resident at a large, urban hospital in Los Angeles gives birth in January and returns to work eight weeks later. A male surgical resident's partner gives birth in March of that same year, and the male surgical resident returns to work four weeks later. All residents in the program receive their annual evaluations in mid-June, just before the end of the fiscal year. The performance evaluation for the female resident states that, "she has exceeded expectations, despite the time off for parental leave." The performance evaluation for the male resident states that "he has far exceeded expectations."

1. Has something inappropriate happened? If so, what is it? Is this inappropriate action also illegal under Title VII and/or Title IX law?

The main impropriety is the mention of parental leave in the performance evaluation of the female surgical resident (compared to the lack of mention of this in the evaluation of the male resident). The surgical residents should be evaluated on actual performance, not on time legitimately spent away.

2. What are the gender components in the case? Consider the sex of the individuals involved, the degree of power tied to their professional positions, the overall work environment and the visual and audio messages it sends about gender, and the vocabulary used in the interactions among the individuals involved in the case.

The principal gender comparison available from the details of the case is the presence of one female and one male surgical resident who each is using parental leave in the same fiscal year. The good news is that both residents felt at liberty to use parental leave. The bad news (although more details of the case would help this analysis) is that the woman seems to have been penalized for parental leave, while the man was not, and he might even have been rewarded for taking leave.

3. Has gender shrapnel hit in this case? If so, how?

Yes, primarily in the mention of parental leave in one person's evaluation and its lack of mention in the other person's.

4. List the problems in this case.

- The performance evaluators have too much in mind the recent pregnancy and childbirth of the female surgical resident.
- The female surgical resident may have been penalized for being on parental leave. Even if there was no intention of penalty, the words in the evaluation give the perception of penalty, which is damaging enough.

5. Discuss potential solutions for all involved.

- Enhanced training for the individuals who carry out performance evaluation
- Consideration of the language of the workplace—what you can and cannot say and what you can and cannot write—in order to be fair to all employees.
- Reconsideration of the two letters and revision of the one that mentions the parental leave.

6. What other questions surrounding these cases need to be asked?

- The big question that remains is whether or not the female surgical resident was actually penalized in the evaluation ("has exceeded expectations"), especially in comparison to her male colleague ("has far exceeded expectations").

BIBLIOGRAPHY

Amabile, Teresa M., and Steven J. Kramer. 2011. *The progress principle: Using small wins to ignite joy, engagement, and creativity at work.* Cambridge, MA: Harvard Business Review Press. Print.

American Association of University Professors Policy Documents & Reports. 9th ed. 2001. Washington, DC: AAUP. Print (also available online).

American Association of University Women website. http://www.aauw.org. Web.

American Association of University Women. *Crossing the line. Sexual harassment at school.* Executive summary. Accessed 19 Dec 2011. Web.

Anderson, Jenny. 2011. National study finds widespread sexual harassment of students in grades 7 to 12. *The Chronicle of Higher Education,* 7 Nov 2011. Accessed 7 Nov 2011. Web.

Ashburn, Elyse. 2008. New data predict major shifts in student populations, requiring colleges to change strategies. *The Chronicle of Higher Education,* 20 Mar 2008. Accessed 21 Mar 2008. Web.

Asma, Stephen T. 2011. Gauging gender. *The Chronicle of Higher Education,* 30 Oct 2011. Accessed 1 Nov 2011. Web.

Bahls, Steven C. 2010. Administrators must dispel the derogatory myths about professors. *The Chronicle of Higher Education,* 10 Jan 2010. Accessed 12 Jan 2010. Web.

Baker, Kelly J. 2014. Writing about sexism in academia hurts. *The Chronicle of Higher Education,* 9 Oct 2014. Accessed 10 Oct 2014. Web.

Bassham, David J. 2008. *Developing & maintaining a sexual harassment free workplace. A guide for managers.* Published by author. Print.

Beck, Howard. 2011. Former NBA employee says sexual harassment concerns were ignored. *The New York Times,* 16 Dec 2011. Accessed 16 Dec 2011. Web.

© The Editor(s) (if applicable) and The Author(s) 2016
E. Mayock, *Gender Shrapnel in the Academic Workplace,*
DOI 10.1057/978-1-137-50830-0

Birken, Sarah A., and Jessica L. Borelli. 2015. Coming out as academic mothers. *The Chronicle of Higher Education*, 14 Jan 2015. Accessed 15 Jan 2015. Web.

Brown, Brené. TED talk on vulnerability. http://www.ted.com/talks/brene_brown_on_vulnerability.html. Accessed 9 Apr 2012. Web.

Buzzanell, Patrice M., and Kristen Lucas. 2006. Gendered stories of career. Unfolding discourses of time, space, and identity. In *The Sage handbook of gender and communication*, ed. Bonnie J. Dow and Julia T. Wood, 161–178. London: Sage. Print.

Cain Miller, Claire. 2015. Is the professor bossy or brilliant? Much depends on gender. *The New York Times*, 6 Feb 2015. Accessed 9 Feb 2015. Web.

Cameron, Deborah. 2007. *The myth of mars and venus. Do men and women really speak different languages?* Oxford: Oxford University Press. Print.

Chamallas, Martha. 1996. Feminist constructions of objectivity: Multiple perspectives on sexual and racial harassment litigation. In *Applications of feminist legal theory to women's lives. Sex, violence, work, and reproduction*, ed. D. Kelly Weisberg, 808–825. Philadelphia, PA: Temple University Press. Print.

Chamberlain, Elizabeth M. 1997. Courtroom to classroom: There is more to sexual harassment. *NWSA Journal* 9(2): 135–155. Accessed 31 Jan 2007. Web.

Choosing the Right College. 2006. Intercollegiate Studies Institute. Web.

Clair, Robin Patric. 1998. *Organizing silence. A world of possibilities*. Albany, NY: State University of New York Press. Print.

Cleveland, Jeanette N., and Kathleen McNamara. 1996. Understanding sexual harassment: Contributions from research on domestic violence and organizational change. In *Sexual harassment in the workplace. Perspectives, frontiers, and response strategies*, ed. Margaret S. Stockdale, 217–240. Thousand Oaks, CA: Sage. Print.

Crenshaw, Kimberlé. 1991. Mapping the margins: Intersectionality, identity politics, and violence against women of color. *Stanford Law Review* 43: 1241–1299. Print.

_____. 1996. Whose story is it, anyway? Feminist and antiracist appropriations of Anita Hill. *Applications of feminist legal theory to women's lives. Sex, violence, work, and reproduction*, 826–844. Philadelphia, PA: Temple University Press. Print.

Crenshaw, Kimberlé W., and Walter R. Allen. 2014. Don't let the gender gap overshadow racial and economic disparities. *The Chronicle of Higher Education*, 27 Oct 2014. Accessed 6 Jan 2015. Web.

Cronin, Lynn, and Howard Fine. 2010. *Damned if she does, damned if she doesn't. Rethinking the rules of the game that keep women from succeeding in business*. New York: Prometheus. Print.

Crouch, Margaret A. 2011. *Thinking about sexual harassment. A guide for the perplexed*. Oxford: Oxford University Press. Print.

De Welde, Kristine, and Andi Stepnick (eds.). 2015. *Disrupting the culture of silence. Confronting gender inequality and making change in higher education.* Sterling, VA: Stylus. Print.

DiMare, Lesley. 1992. Rhetoric and women: The private and the public spheres. In *Constructing and reconstructing gender. The links among communication, language, and gender*, ed. Linda A.M. Perry, Lynn H. Turner, and Helen M. Sterk, 45–50. Albany, NY: State University of New York Press. Print.

Dziech, Billie Wright, and Michael W. Hawkins. 1998. *Sexual harassment in higher education. Reflections and new perspectives.* New York: Garland. Print.

Edelman, Lauren B. 2004. The legal lives of private organizations. In *The Blackwell companion to law and society*, ed. Austin Sarat, 231–252. Oxford: Blackwell. Print.

Edelman, Lauren B., and Shauhin A. Talesh. 2011. To comply or not to comply—That isn't the question: How organizations construct the meaning of compliance. In *Explaining compliance. Business responses to regulation*, ed. Christine Parker and Vibeke Lehmann Nielsen, 103–122. Cheltenham, UK: Edward Elgar. Print.

EEOC. http://archive.eeoc.gov/stats/harass.html. Accessed 11 Oct 2011. Web.

EEOC. http://archive.eeoc.gov/types/sexual_harassment.html. Accessed 11 Oct 2011. Web.

EEOC. Prohibitions on discrimination against workers with caregiving responsibilities. http://www.eeoc.gov/policy/docs/caregiving.html. Accessed 19 Oct 2011. Web.

Elliott, Carl. 2012. Faking it for the dean. *The Chronicle of Higher Education*, 7 Feb 2012. Accessed 8 Feb 2012. Web.

Equal Employment Opportunity Commission (United States) website. http://www.eeoc.gov. Web.

Estrich, Susan. 2000. *Sex and power.* New York: Riverhead. Print.

Feminist Majority Foundation Education Equity Program. http://feminist.org/education/FMFprogram.asp. Accessed 18 Jan 2015.

Flores Niemann, Yolanda. 2012. The making of a token: A case study of stereotype threat, stigma, racism, and tokenism in academe. In *Presumed incompetent. The intersections of race and class for women in academia*, ed. Gabriella Gutiérrez y Muhs, Yolanda Flores Niemann, Carmen G. González, and Angela P. Harris, 336–355. Boulder, CO: Utah State University Press. Print.

Fortune Chernik, Abra. 2001. *Issues in feminism. An introduction to women's studies*, 289–293. Mountain View, CA: Mayfield. Print.

Friedman, Jaclyn. 2007. Because things are worse, people are paying attention. Interview with Katha Pollitt. *Women's Review of Books* 24(2): 14–15. Print.

Gadsen, Gloria Y. 2008. Minority report. *The Chronicle of Higher Education*, 24 Oct 2008. Accessed 27 Oct 2008. Web.

Gender Action Group (GAG) Blog. http://gag.academic.wlu.edu. Web.

Glenn, Cheryl. 2004. *Unspoken: A rhetoric of silence*. Carbondale, IL: Southern Illinois University Press.

Glick, Peter, and Susan T. Fiske. 1996. The ambivalent sexism inventory: Differentiating hostile and benevolent sexism. *Journal of Personality and Social Psychology* 70(1996): 491–512. Print.

Glick, Peter, and Susan T. Fiske. 1999. Sexism and other 'isms': Interdependence, status, and the ambivalent content of stereotypes. In *Sexism and stereotypes in modern society*, ed. William B. Swann Jr., Judith H. Langlois, and Lucia Albino Gilbert. Washington, DC: APA. Print.

———. 2001. An ambivalent attitude: Hostile and benevolent sexism as complementary justifications for gender inequality. *American Psychologist* 56(2):109–118. Print.

Goldin, Claudia. 2014. A grand gender convergence: Its last chapter. *American Economic Review* 104(4): 1091–1119. Print.

Grant, Adam, and Sheryl Sandberg. 2014. When talking about bias backfires. *The New York Times*, 6 Dec 2014. Accessed 17 Feb 2015. Web.

———. 2015a. Madam C.E.O., get me a coffee. *The New York Times*, 6 Feb 2015. Accessed 9 Feb 2015. Web.

———. 2015b. Speaking while female. *The New York Times*, 6 Feb 2015. Accessed 9 Feb 2015. Web.

Gray, John. 1993. *Men are from mars and women are from venus. A practical guide for improving communication and getting what you want from your relationships*. New York: HarperCollins. Print.

Gray, Garry C., and Susan S. Silbey. 2011. The other side of the compliance relationship. In *Explaining compliance. Business responses to regulation*, ed. Christine Parker and Vibeke Lehmann Nielsen, 123–138. Cheltenham, UK: Edward Elgar. Print.

Hart, Melissa, and Paul M. Secunda. 2009. A matter of context: Social framework evidence in employment discrimination class actions. *Fordham Law Review* 78: 37–70. Print.

Hemmings, Clare. 2011. *Why stories matter. The political grammar of feminist theory*. Durham, NC: Duke University Press. Print.

Hill, Anita. 1995. Thomas versus Clinton. In *Debating sexual correctness. Pornography, sexual harassment, date rape, and the politics of sexual equality*, ed. Adele M. Stan, 122–125. New York: Delta. Print.

Hirshman, Linda. 2008. Where are the new jobs for women? *The Chronicle of Higher Education*, 9 Dec 2008. Accessed 9 Dec 2008. Web.

Hochschild, Arlie Russell. 2001. *The time bind: When work becomes home and home becomes work*. New York: Holt. Print.

Hotelling, Kathy. 1991. Sexual harassment: A problem shielded by silence. *Journal of Counseling & Development* 69: 497–501. Print.

In context. Campus sexual assault. Reader's guide. *The Chronicle of Higher Education*, Fall 2014. Web (PDF). Accessed 8 Jan 2015.

Jasinski, Jana L. 2001. Theoretical explanations for violence against women. In *Sourcebook on violence against women*, ed. Claire M. Renzetti, Jeffrey L. Edleson, and Raquel Kennedy Bergen, 5–21. Thousand Oaks, CA: Sage. Print.

Julie & Julia. 2009. Dir. Nora Ephron, Perf. Amy Adams, Meryl Streep, Stanley Tucci, Chris Messina, Linda Emond. Sony, DVD.

June, Audrey Williams. 2013. Fixing the gender pay gap can lead to faculty discord. *The Chronicle of Higher Education*, 31 Oct 2013. Accessed 6 Jan 2015. Web.

Klinkenborg, Verlyn. 2007. Politeness and authority at a Hilltop College in Minnesota. *The Chronicle of Higher Education*, 15 Oct 2007. Accessed 15 Oct 2007. Web.

Know your IX. Empowering students to stop sexual violence. http://knowyourix. org/. Accessed 4 Jan 2015. Web.

Kornbluh, Karen, and Rachel Homer. 2009. Paycheck feminism. *Ms*, Fall:28–33. Print.

Krakauer, Jon. 2015. *Missoula. Rape and the justice system in a college town*. New York: Doubleday.

Kreamer, Anne. 2011. *It's always personal. Emotion in the new workplace*. New York: Random House.

Kristof, Nicholas D., and Sheryl WuDunn. 2010. *Half the sky. Turning oppression into opportunity for women worldwide*. New York: Vintage. Print.

Krolokke, Charlotte, and Anne Scott Sorensen. 2006. *Gender communication theories and analyses. Silence and performance*. Thousand Oaks, CA: Sage.

Krugman, Paul. 2007. Missing Molly Ivins. *The New York Times*, 2 Feb 2007. Accessed 18 Jan 2012. Web.

Langelan, Marty. 2005. Put a stop to sexual harassment. In *50 ways to improve women's lives. The essential women's guide to achieving equality, health, and success*, 119–121. National Council of Women's Organizations. Maui, HI: Inner Ocean Publishing. Print.

LeBlanc, Robin M. 2010. Teaching to spite your body. In *Feminist activism in academia. Essays on personal, political and professional change*, ed. Ellen C. Mayock and Domnica Radulescu, 45–60. Jefferson, NC: McFarland. Print.

LeMoncheck, Linda, and Mane Hajdin. 1997. *Sexual harassment: A debate*. Lanham, MD: Rowman & Littlefield. Print.

Levine, Judith A. 2013. *Ain't no trust. How bosses, boyfriends, and bureaucrats fail low income mothers and why it matters*. Berkeley, CA: University of California Press. Print.

Lewin, Tamar. 2014. Handling of sexual harassment case poses larger questions at Yale, 1 Nov 2014. Accessed 3 Nov 2014. Web.

Lewis, W. Scott, Saundra K. Schuster, and Brett A. Sokolow. Gamechangers: Reshaping campus sexual misconduct through litigation. In *The NCHERM 10th anniversary whitepaper, 2000-2010*. http://www.ncherm.org. Accessed 5 Sept 2011. Web.

Lipman, Joanne. 2015. Let's expose the gender pay gap. *The New York Times*, 13 Aug 2015. Accessed 13 Aug 2015. Web.

Litosseliti, Lia. 2006. *Gender & language. Theory and practice*. London: Hodder. Print.

Lorde, Audre. 2001. The transformation of silence into language and action. In *Issues in feminism. An introduction to women's studies*, 5th ed, ed. Sheila Ruth, 188–190. Mountain View, CA: Mayfield. Print.

Lukes, Robin, and Joann Bangs. 2014. A critical analysis of anti-discrimination law and microaggressions in academia. *Research in Higher Education Journal* 24 (August). http://www.aabri.com/manuscripts/141824.pdf. Accessed 11 Aug 2015. Web.

MacKinnon, Catherine. 1979. *Sexual harassment of working women. A case of sex discrimination*. New Haven, CT: Yale University Press. Print.

Macklem, Timothy. 2003. *Beyond comparison. Sex and discrimination*. Cambridge: Cambridge University Press. Print.

MacLean, Nancy. 2006. *Freedom is not enough. The opening of the American workplace*. New York: Russell Sage. Print.

Maher, Frances, and Mary Kay Thompson Tetreault. 2007. *Privilege and diversity in the academy*. New York: Routledge. Print.

Mahoney, John. Workplace fairness. It's everybody's job. http://www.workplace-fairness.org/. Accessed 5 Jan 2015. Web.

Martin, Joanne. 1990. Deconstructing organizational taboos: The suppression of gender conflict in organizations. *Organization Science* 1(4): 339–359. Print.

Mason, Mary Ann. 2009a. How the 'snow-woman' effect slows women's progress. *The Chronicle of Higher Education*, 16 Sept 2009. Accessed 17 Sept 2009. Web.

____. 2009b. Title IX includes maternal discrimination. *The Chronicle of Higher Education*, 19 Nov 2009. Accessed 28 Nov 2009. Web.

____. 2011. The pyramid problem. *The Chronicle of Higher Education*, 9 Mar 2011. Accessed 10 Mar 2011. Web.

Mayock, Ellen. 2010a. Gender shrapnel and institutional language in the academic workplace. In *Estudios de Mujeres. Volumen VII. Diferencia, (des)igualdad y justicia*, ed. Ana Antón Pachecho Bravo, Isabel Durán Giménez-Rico, Carmen Méndez García, Joanne Neff Van Aertselaer, and Ana Laura Rodríguez Redondo, 149–159. Madrid: Fundamentos. Print.

____. 2010b. 'Mothering language' in the academic workplace. In *Feminist activism in academia. Essays on personal, political and professional change*, eds. Ellen C. Mayock and Domnica Radulescu, 126–141. Jefferson, NC: McFarland. Print.

Mayock, Ellen C., and Domnica Radulescu (eds.). 2010. *Feminist activism in academia. Essays on personal, political, and professional change*. Jefferson, NC: McFarland. Print.

Mentor, Ms. 2009. I'm ok, he's sleazy. *The Chronicle of Higher Education*, 11 June 2009. Accessed 11 June 2009. Web.

Meritor Savings Bank v. Vinson. 1996. *Applications of feminist legal theory to women's lives. Sex violence, work, and reproduction*, ed. D. Kelly Weisberg. Philadelphia, PA: Temple University Press. Print.

Meyerson, Debra E., and Deborah M. Kolb. 2000. Moving out of the 'armchair': Developing a framework to bridge the gap between feminist theory and practice. *Organization. The Interdisciplinary Journal of Organization, Theory, and Society* 7(4): 553–571. Print.

Moffitt, Kimberly R., Heather E. Harris, and Diane A. Forbes Berthoud. 2012. Present and unequal: A third-wave approach to voice parallel experiences in managing oppression and bias in the academy. In *Presumed incompetent. The intersections of race and class for women in academia*, ed. Gabriella Gutiérrez y Muhs, Yolanda Flores Niemann, Carmen G. González, and Angela P. Harris, 78–92. Boulder, CO: Utah State University Press. Print.

Montell, Gabriela. 2010. Damning with praise. *The Chronicle of Higher Education*, 18 Nov 2010. Accessed 19 Nov 2010. Web.

Morgan, Phoebe. 2001. Sexual harassment: Violence against women at work. In *Sourcebook on violence against women*, ed. Claire M. Renzetti, Jeffrey L. Edleson, and Raquel Kennedy Bergen, 209–222. Thousand Oaks, CA: Sage. Print.

Morgan Riggs, Janet. 2010. Working to build a cohesive faculty community. *The Chronicle of Higher Education*, 10 Nov 2010. Accessed 11 Nov 2011. Web.

Morphew, Christopher C., and Barrett J. Taylor. 2009. College rankings and dueling mission statements. *The Chronicle of Higher Education*, 19 Aug 2009. Accessed 20 Aug 2009. Web.

Mumby, Dennis K., and Linda L. Putnam. 1992. The politics of emotion: A feminist reading of bounded rationality. *The Academy of Management Review* 17(3): 465–486. Print.

Murrell, Audrey J. 1996. Sexual harassment and women of color: Issues, challenges, and future directions. In *Sexual harassment in the workplace. Perspectives, frontiers, and response strategies*, ed. Margaret S. Stockdale, 51–66. Thousand Oaks, CA: Sage. Print.

National Council of Women's Organizations (NCWO). 2005. *50 ways to improve women's lives. The essential women's guide for achieving equality, health, and success*. Maui, HI: Inner Ocean. Print.

National Geographic Channel. 2012. America's port: Port of Los Angeles. Television.

Nobel, Carmen. 2011. How small wins unleash creativity. *Harvard Business School Working Knowledge*, 6 Sept 2011. Accessed 18 Jan 2012. Web.

North, Anna. 2015. Black women want top jobs (but they aren't getting them). *The New York Times*, The Opinion Pages, 23 Apr 2015. Accessed 28 Apr 2015. Web.

Nosek, Brian A., Mahzarin R. Banaji, and John T. Jost. 2009. The politics of intergroup attitudes. In *The social and psychological bases of ideology and system justification*, ed. J.T. Jost, A.C. Kay, and H. Thorisdottir, 480–506. Oxford: Oxford University Press. Print.

O'Donohue, William (ed.). 1997. *Sexual harassment. Theory, research, and treatment.* Boston, MA: Allyn and Bacon. Print.

O'Rourke, Sheila. 2008. Diversity and merit: How one university rewards faculty work that promotes equity. *The Chronicle of Higher Education*, 26 Sept 2008. Accessed 26 Sept 2008. Web.

Office for Civil Rights, U.S. Government Department of Education. http://www.hhs.gov/ocr/. Web.

Orenstein, Peggy. 1994. *Schoolgirls. Young women, self-esteem, and the confidence gap.* New York: Doubleday/Anchor. Print.

Peirce, Ellen R., Benson Rosen, and Tammy Bunn Hiller. 1997. Breaking the silence: Creating user-friendly sexual harassment policies. *Employee Responsibilities and Rights Journal* 10(3): 225–242. Print.

Perry, Linda A.M., Lynn H. Turner, and Helen M. Sterk (eds.). 1992. *Constructing and reconstructing gender. The links among communication, language, and gender.* Albany, NY: State University of New York Press. Print.

Phillips, Dave. 2015. Marine commander's firing stirs debate on integration of women in corps. *The New York Times*, 12 July 2015. Accessed 13 July 2015. Web.

Poole, Dennis L. 1998. Politically correct or culturally competent? *Health and Social Work* 23(3). No pagination. Web.

Ranganath, Kate A., and Brian A. Nosek. 2008. Implicit attitude generalization occurs immediately; explicit attitude generalization takes time. *Psychological Science* 19(3): 249–254. Print.

Renzetti, Claire M., Jeffrey L. Edleson, and Raquel Kennedy Bergen (eds.). 2001. *Sourcebook on violence against women.* Thousand Oaks, CA: Sage. Print.

Romaine, Suzanne. 1999. *Communicating gender.* Mahwah, NJ: Lawrence Erlbaum. Print.

Ropers Huilman, Becky (ed.). 2003. *Gendered futures in higher education. Critical perspectives for change.* Albany, NY: State University of New York Press. Print.

Ropers-Huilman, Becky, and Monisa Shackelford. 2003. Negotiating identities and making change. Feminist faculty in higher education. In *Gendered futures in higher education. Critical perspectives for change*, ed. Becky Ropers-Huilman, 135–147. Albany, NY: State University of New York Press. Print.

Rosser, Sue V. 2012. More gender diversity will mean better science. *The Chronicle of Higher Education*, 29 Oct 2012. Accessed 6 Jan 15. Web.

Rubin, Edward, W.H. Knight, and Katherine Bartlett. 2006. A conversation among deans from "results: Legal education, institutional change, and a decade of gender studies". *Harvard Journal of Law & Gender* 29: 465–484. Print.

Rudman, Laurie A., Eugen Borgina, and Barbara A. Robertson. 1995. Suffering in silence: Procedural justice versus gender socialization issues in university sexual harassment grievance procedures. *Basic and Applied Social Psychology* 17(4): 519–541. Print.

Ruiz, Michelle. 2015. "He said *WHAT* at work?" *Cosmopolitan* special report on sexual harassment at work. *Cosmopolitan* (March):136–143.

Ruth, Sheila. 2001. *Issues in feminism. An introduction to women's studies*, 5th ed. Mount View, CA: Mayfield. Print.

Sandberg, Sheryl. 2013. *Lean in: Women, work, and the will to lead*. New York: Knopf. Print.

Schaef, Anne Wilson. 1986. *Co-dependence. Misunderstood-mistreated*. New York: HarperSanFrancisco. Print.

Segal, Jonathan A. 2009. Pricelessness of prevention for higher ed hero conferences. In *Interactive workshop*, 8 September.

Seligson, Hannah. 2008. Girl power at school, but not at the office. *The Chronicle of Higher Education*, 31 Aug 2008. Accessed 31 Aug 2008. Web.

Speaking freely. http://home.wlu.edu/~mayocke/SpeakingFreely/index.htm. Accessed 21 Oct 2011. Web.

Stan, Adele M. (ed.). 1995. *Debating sexual correctness. Pornography, sexual harassment, date rape, and the politics of sexual equality*. New York: Delta. Print.

Stein, Nan. 1998. Sexual harassment in school: The public performance of gendered violence. In *Minding women: Reshaping the educational realm*, ed. Christine A. Woyshner and Holly S. Gelfond, 227–245. Cambridge, MA: Harvard Educational Review. Print.

Stewart, Jeanine Silveira. 2010. Mothering out of place. In *Feminist activism in academia. Essays on personal, political and professional change*, ed. Ellen C. Mayock and Domnica Radulescu, 98–111. Jefferson, NC: McFarland. Print.

Stockdale, Margaret S. (ed.). 1996. *Sexual harassment in the workplace. Perspectives, frontiers, and response strategies*. Thousand Oaks, CA: Sage. Print.

Sue, Derald Wing. 2010. *Microaggressions in everyday life. Race, gender, and sexual orientation*. Hoboken, NJ: Wiley. Print.

The Gender Bias Learning Project. http://www.genderbiasbingo.com/index.html. Web.

The gender divide in academe. Insights on retaining more academic women. *The Chronicle of Education*, PDF collection of articles. Accessed 13 Mar 2015.

The glass ceiling. *The Economist*, 5 May 2009. http://www.economist.com/node/13604240. Accessed 12 Oct 2011. Web.

Title IX: http://www.usdoj.gov/crt/cor/coord/titleix.htm. Accessed 9 July 2008. Web.

Title VII: http://www.eeoc.gov/policy/vii.html. Accessed 9 July 2008. Web.

Toossi, Mitra. A century of change: The U.S. Labor Force, 1950-2050. Bureau of Labor Statistics. http://www.bls.gov/opub/mlr/2002/05/art2full.pdf. Accessed 27 Mar 2012. Web.

U.S. Bureau of Labor Statistics. 2011. *Spotlight on statistics. Women at work*, 1–16. March 2011. http://www.bls.gov/spotlight/2011/women/pdf/women_bls_spotlight.pdf. Accessed 26 Sept 2011 (PDF). Web.

U.S. Department of Education. 2015. Title IX Coordinators, 24 Apr 2015. http://www2.ed.gov/policy/rights/guid/ocr/title-ix-coordinators.html. Accessed 28 Apr 2015.

Un alcalde del PP llama 'puta barata' a una dirigente socialista. *El País*, 20 July 2015, p. 24. Print (no author indicated).

Werner, Charlotte, Sandrine Devillard, and Sandra Sancier-Sultan. 2010. McKinsey Global Survey Results. Moving women to the top. Web PDF.

Williams, Joan C. UC Hastings College of the Law, WorkLife Law. Gender Bias Bingo. http://www.genderbiasbingo.com. Accessed 29 Oct 2009. Web.

Williams, Joan C., and Rachel Dempsey. 2014. *What works for women at work. Four patterns working women need to know*. New York: New York University Press. Print.

Wilson, Marie C. 2006. *Closing the leadership gap. Why women can and must help run the world*. New York: Penguin. Print.

____. 2007. *Closing the leadership gap. Add women, change everything*. New York: Penguin. Print.

Wilson, Robin. 2009. New game plays on women's experiences of gender bias in academe. *The Chronicle of Higher Education*, 28 Oct 2009. Accessed 29 Oct 2009. Web.

Wooley, Susan C. 1992. Anita Hill, Clarence Thomas and the enforcement of female silence. *Women & Therapy* 12(4): 3–23. Print.

Yoshino, Kenji. 2006. The pressure to cover. *The New York Times Magazine*, 15 Jan 2006, 32–37. Print.

INDEX

© The Editor(s) (if applicable) and The Author(s) 2016
E. Mayock, *Gender Shrapnel in the Academic Workplace*,
DOI 10.1057/978-1-137-50830-0

CPSIA information can be obtained
at www.ICGtesting.com
Printed in the USA
LVOW13*2322301117
558172LV00017B/409/P

9 781137 514622